At the Sign of Midnight

Capitana de Comunidades Martha Stone (behind child) at the Basilica

At the Sign of Midnight

The Concheros Dance Cult of Mexico

Martha Stone

Illustrated by Laurie Cook

The University of Arizona Press

Tucson, Arizona

About the Author

MARTHA STONE refers to her experiences with the Concheros as "twenty-five years learning and unlearning in the dance cult." Resident of Mexico and longtime serious observer of religious dance ceremonies, Mrs. Stone was gradually instructed in the dance and formally elected to a "Mesa" or section of the dance organization, thereafter attending as a dancer the most esoteric and exclusive of the Concheros' ritual observances. After a decade, she was named *Capitana de Comunidades,* member of a board including the priest in charge and the chiefs of the various dance groups comprising the Association of Religious Dancers Pertaining to the Church of Tlaltelolco. Mrs. Stone's desire for greater understanding of Conchero origins took her into intensive reading of sixteenth-century Catholic Church history and caused her to acquire also considerable acquaintance with Nahuatl dictionaries derived from the codices or picture writings of the Prehispanic Aztec people.

THE UNIVERSITY OF ARIZONA PRESS

I. S. B. N.-0-8165-0337-0 cloth
I. S. B. N.-0-8165-0507-1 paper
L. C. No. 73-76303

Acknowledgments

I GRATEFULLY ACKNOWLEDGE MY INDEBTEDNESS to National University of Mexico Professors Ramón Beteta, Alfonso Caso, Rubén Campos, Wigberto Jiménez Moreno, Eduardo Noguero, Edmundo O'Gorman, Ernestina Salinas, and to Señorita Grovas and Rosita Stephenson Guizar for quickening my interest in their country, particularly in the mingling of the past with the present. This is also true of my friends in the National Museum, Amelia Martínez del Río de Caza, Salvador Mateos, Roberto J. Weitlaner, and Ignacio Bernal.

I am grateful to Helen Anderson, Olga and Yancy Edwards, Paul Friggens, Frances Gillmor (who has godmothered this project since the mid-thirties), and Edward Trueblood for their encouragement, suggestions, and valuable criticism of the manuscript; to my friend and teacher Cecil C. James for Nahuatl translations, to Enriqueta Artola for translations of danzante documents, and to Luisa María A. de Jaubert for translations in general; to James Dunlop, Juliette and Guillermo Echaniz (our neighbors who also taught me about Mexico), Neil Judd of the Smithsonian Institution, Isabel Kelly, Mary Myers, and Antonio Quiroz for giving me or helping me to obtain rare books that form a part of my sources.

I am also grateful to Sallie Aguirre, Clarence Benschoter, Claude Butlin, Hugh Edgerton, Lee Heidrich, Charles Pineo, Evelyn Plummer, and Mervin Smith for their generosity as to photographs, and to the friends who accompanied me to fiestas in distant places, or where I was a stranger; to Father Ángel Garribay K. for a letter of introduction that opened many doors to me; and to Father Domingo Guadalupe Díaz for cooperation, assistance, and friendship.

I deeply appreciate the aid of my friends who from time to time typed the manuscript — Helen Anderson, her daughter Nancy Thornblom, Phyllis Kirkpatrick, and our daughter Martita Boyle. Thanks are also due to the University of Arizona Press for effecting publication, and especially to my editor, Elizabeth Shaw.

I am also indebted to José Celis and to Francisco Arteaga for giving me my first opportunity to observe the Concheros at close range, and I owe even more to Don Manuel Luna and the Concheros under his orders who invited me to walk the trails with them, shared the dance circle with me and patiently explained their customs to me, finally accepting me into the inner circle of their organization, and making me one of them.

I owe María Nieves Sanchez Landeros de Marín more than there is space to set down here. For a quarter of a century she was always at hand to care for my comfort and manage my life. She accompanied me to most of the fiestas and played the part of judge, diplomat, or policeman with equal facility.

Of course I owe more to my husband Bill than to anyone. He always accompanied me to fiestas when business permitted and was so interested in the danzantes and their affairs that he immediately inspired their trust and friendship. It was a joy to watch their faces light with pleasure when the cry ran through the crowd, "The señor! The señor! Here comes the señor!"

MARTHA STONE

Contents

ILLUSTRATIONS

Foreword

THE CIRCLES OF FEATHER-CROWNED CONCHEROS dancing in the church-
yards of central Mexico attract the attention of passersby perhaps more
than any other religious dance group of the area. The visitor to Mexico
is caught by the insistent rhythm, the bright feather headdresses, the
armadillo shell stringed instruments. The fellow countryman of the
dancers also watches for awhile. But Mexican and tourist alike go by,
knowing little of the dance itself or the participants, the men and women
who, when the fiesta is over, go back to their daily work: the waitress,
the pushcart vendor, the day laborer. Those dancers live a life outside
their dedication, their military ranks, their pilgrimages, outside the public
fiestas and the private dancing before the altar of the little oratory in
their General's house.

Martha Stone did not pass by. For more than twenty-five years,
while her entomologist husband carried on his research in the combined
program of the Mexican and American departments of agriculture, she
has participated in the danzantes' ceremonial life and their daily human
problems. She has risen through the ranks, gaining new knowledge and
perspectives at each stage. She has been a "hanger-on," as she says,
observing, "walking with the dancers"; a Malinche; a Capitana de Mesa;
a Capitana de Comunidades in a Capitanía. With each step upward, she
once told me, she had to unlearn and relearn.

Now she has written a book about the Concheros which is more
inward than any yet written on the religious dancers of Mexico. It has
been written with the cooperation of the danzantes themselves so that
it would be true from their viewpoint.

Sometimes I have had the privilege of accompanying her. I was
present in the little oratory in one of the poorer barrios of Mexico City
for a *disciplina* when, in penitence, a danzante, about to withdraw from
the group after behavior violating their rules at a fiesta, knelt before

the altar and received the lashes across his shoulders which would discharge his sin and his obligation before he left. I was there for a strange reason. The Concheros had suggested that she invite an American friend because without an outside witness her readers would not believe that such an act of abasement had taken place. Martha Stone herself, of course, was not an outsider.

On another occasion I walked with her in the procession when the different *Mesas* of this great dance, interorganized through central Mexico, carried their banners up and down the aisles of the colonial church of Santiago Tlaltelolco. I stayed afterwards in the parish hall where she and the priest of the parish had both been invited to sit as counselors in formulating decisions and policies of the organization. The all-night deliberations seemed a dramatic continuation of the relation between European and Indian that had gone on in this place in the historic sixteenth century monastery and school of La Santa Cruz de Tlaltelolco ever since the great Franciscan chronicler, Fray Bernardino de Sahagún, had lived and worked there.

I am happy to have been on the fringes of some of the occasions which Martha Stone describes in this book. The danzantes themselves will be happy that by means of the book those outside the Concheros' dedication may now watch more understandingly their dance of devotion in the Mexican fiestas.

FRANCES GILLMOR

Concheros and Fiestas

WE STEPPED THROUGH THE GATES of a sixteenth-century churchyard just outside Mexico City and there they were: circle after circle of dancing Indians! Costumes of vivid yellows, purples, reds, blues, and greens flashed in the brilliant sunlight of a Mexican autumn. With little difference between the dress of men and women, the dancers swished skirts, tunics, togas, and capes. They whirled and dipped and rose on their toes. Feather headdresses billowed and waved. Beads and sequins spangled and sparkled on silks and satins. The crunch and thud of dancing feet blended with the *concha's* measured strumming, rolling, and surging, until everything pounded together in shimmering color and pulsating rhythm.[1]

When I could consider each group separately, the rapt concentration of the dancers forming the circle and the fervid intensity of the leaders in the center fascinated me. A dedicated few, set apart from and misunderstood by their own I thought, for the Mexican public watched them as curiously as the foreigner, then smiled archly and moved away, insensible to the flamboyant beauty of colors and fabrics without harmony, and steps of rhythm with awkward grace. The more I watched the dancers, the more I wanted to know what lay behind that remoteness and fervor — why they danced, and what the dance meant to them.

We had come to Mexico because my husband who was with the United States Department of Agriculture had been transferred from Florida to Mexico City. We arrived in June and the following October went to the fiesta at Los Remedios where we saw the Concheros. For years afterward I went from fiesta to fiesta trying to learn more about them. Bill was unable to leave his work, but after the first few years I often took our little daughter Martita along.

I had never seen anything like a Mexican village fiesta. A whole town turning out for a religious celebration was something new in my experience, and the fairs at the larger fiestas particularly delighted us.

~ 1 ~

Martita collected straw dolls, gaily painted pig banks and the like, while I loaded the car with carved trays, pottery vases, seed rosaries, and other handmade or homegrown Indian products.

Then there were the smells. The odor of meats frying on portable charcoal stoves mingled with the delicate aroma of fresh green corn boiling in the husk, and the sulphurous tang of the fireworks that went off at intervals. These combined with the church smells — the copal, the burning candle wax, and the flowers — to produce the fiesta smell that is like no other smell on earth.[2]

The people intrigued me even more — the quietly serious bent on worship, the gay chatterers, notwithstanding their devout intentions, frankly enjoying their friends; the dour, the philosophical, and the shrewd with merchandise to sell at the fair — coming and going, laughing, arguing, and jostling all day long. Those who interested me most were the Concheros, short, darkskinned, and Indian, with only a sprinkling of the lighter mestizo, forming pools of rippling color and movement at most of the fiestas.

At first I played up to the women dancers with friendly glances, and sometimes they would nod or smile at me. More often they acted as if I were not there. Once at Amecameca while trying to go around one dance circle in the crowded churchyard, we inadvertently backed into another. The dancers were furious! The masked devil rushed at us and lashed out with vicious swipes of his whip, just missing us several times. Martita screamed with terror! I lifted her in my arms and hurried out of the circle. The devil and another dancer followed, snatching at my camera and demanding to see my documents. They became so abusive and threatening that we made our way to the car and left the fiesta. Such experiences were rare, but more than once we found the dancers definitely hostile.

As I stood outside the circles, bowing and smiling and jotting down notes in a notebook, I saw that many of the headdresses were formed of bunches of tiny feathers stuck like feather dusters around a headband;[3] that only the better dressed wore the flowing ostrich plumes; that the brilliant costumes were more often of sateen or cheap rayon than of silk; and that many of them, even those with the gathered skirt drawn in at the waist with a drawstring, were Aztec in line and decoration, with an occasional touch of the sixteenth-century knight. Usually there were a few who danced in print dresses or in pastel-colored shirts with blue jeans or *calzones*.[4] The Concheros were obviously far from wealthy, or even well-to-do. Only in the dance did they rise to pomp and magnificence.

The music was twangy and monotonous, with rhythms that were probably of European origin, but the feeling of the dance was Indian. The steps were leaps, crosses, crosses in the air, stamps, bounces on toes, crouches, kicks, and half-kicks that were almost a shuffle, with the heel often playing an important part. Those in the center usually danced with swiftness and precision. Some held the upper part of the body perfectly straight with the head up, never glancing downward, while the hips and legs were limber and relaxed as they danced the tricky rhythms. Others hunched their shoulders and cradled their instruments and, fixing their eyes on the ground, danced into the earth as if they would become a part of it. Sometimes a few in a circle danced lackadaisically, barely lifting their feet from the ground and jumping flat-footedly instead of bouncing to their toes. Nearly always the children of a dance circle danced well.

The dance seemed full of ceremony and ritual whose meaning escaped me. For example, when a dancer left the circle even for a short time, he presented his headdress or his musical instrument to the four world directions, censed it, and kissed the banner. There was so much of this sort of thing that I began to search the libraries of Mexico City but found little about the Concheros. The sources I did find were not concerned with ritual, or why they danced, or what the dance meant to them.

When I noted that the dance chiefs commanded, granted permission, and gave information, I concentrated on them. Martita was older now and imitated all that she saw. I would ask them permission for her to dance behind a dancer to learn the steps, but that was as far as I could go until the fiesta in Acapilco. There I met a danzante, a serious, round-faced, small man, and in casual conversation with him I stumbled onto the path that I would follow for twenty years. It would take me by Pullman, automobile, and muleback from the lowliest slums of the nation's capital to isolated villages and distant mountaintops. Bit by bit, it would lead me from the obvious aspects of Concheros dancing in a churchyard to strange and secret ritual far from the eyes of the public.

San Lorenzo de Acapilco is a mountain village near La Venta on the highway to Toluca. The sixteenth-century church sits on the highest point, with a street up one side of the mountain to the west gate of the churchyard. Directly across from it, another street leads from the east gate down the other side. I had gone there to see the dance-drama of of the *arrieros* (muleteers), based on the mule trains that plied between the City of New Spain (colonial Mexico City) and Acapulco on the Pacific coast, but as usual my attention wandered to the circle of Con-

A *danzante* in full costume

cheros just inside the west gate. I bought a concha from a woman dancer, and had asked her to show me how to play it, when a haughty captain ordered her into the dance circle. After that she refused to look in my direction.

Finally I took refuge from a cold wind in a sheltered court between two parts of the old church, where I found a small circle of Concheros. While I stood watching them, I fell to discussing the dance with a quiet man standing near, who turned out to be José Celis.

"It appears that you have much respect for this custom left us by our ancestors," he observed. "You do not laugh."

"Why should I laugh? It is not funny. It is serious. Also, it is a beautiful custom."

"Why is it that you, a foreigner, are interested in it, señora?"

"Because I like ancient things and I think that your custom of this dance is ancient. You see, I have read the old books and. . . ."

"What old books are those?" he interrupted with sudden suspicion.

"The books of the history of Mexico before the Spaniards came. I read them before I saw the danzantes, señor. And when I saw the Concheros, I said, 'This is ancient! If I could understand this dance, I would know the history of Mexico!'"

"Sí, señora, it is the truth," he beamed.

"I want to write a book about the Concheros, so that all the world may know them. Then no one will laugh at them, señor, for it is only the ignorant who laugh."

"You are right, señora! It is the ignorant who laugh."

"But unless I myself understand the danza, I cannot write the book! And what am I to do? I go to fiestas and ask questions, and the public knows nothing except what anybody can see in the churchyard."

"Absolutely nothing, señora. The public knows absolutely nothing!"

"Unless some danzante is willing to explain the dance to me, I shall not be able to explain it in the book."

He made no reply to this, seeming to concentrate on the dancing.

"I hate lies!" I continued. "If I cannot learn the truth, I shall not write the book."

At that moment a *malinche* danced to the edge of the circle, stopped in front of him, bowed ceremoniously, and asked his permission to leave the circle for five minutes.[5] He gravely returned her bow and granted her request.

"Why, you are a danzante!" I exclaimed.

"Sí señora, I am. I have the grippe and cannot dance today, but I had the obligation to come here and so, señora, I came. That is why they are dancing in this shut-in place — because I have the grippe. This is my personnel. I am their capitán."

"Then perhaps you can send somebody to my house to teach me to play this concha."

"Sí señora, I know a person who will teach you."

I gave him my name and address. His name, he said, was Genaro García. We arranged the date on which he would send the person, and I wrote it down in my notebook.

The following Wednesday, at the hour he was to send someone, he himself appeared at our house.

"Señora," he explained, "I could not tell you at the fiesta where all the world could hear, but I am the only one of our mesa with the authority to teach you to play the concha. It is prohibited for anyone else. But I, I am a jefe, a capitán, I will teach you."

I ushered him into the living room where there was ample space for dancing, and brought a notebook and pencil from the adjoining library. He seated himself on the rosewood sofa and set about tuning his concha, glancing at himself from time to time in the mirror above the fireplace. Then he tuned my concha, talking all the while about the places he had been and the dance chiefs he had known. Did I know General This of the Bajío or Captain That of Toluca?

"No, señor," I replied to his questions. "I know only you."

Finally he showed me how to place my fingers on the strings of the concha for the easiest chord, and the first lesson had begun.

After about an hour of strumming, he suddenly burst out, "Señora, I, too, hate lies! If you wish, I will explain the dance to you."

And I had one foot inside the door of the dance cult.

Fiesta at Ameyalco

For nearly a year the capitán came, twice a week to our house to teach me Conchero music and dance lore. At first he was shy and suspicious, but gradually he became more at ease. One morning as we finished, I told him that I was not sure I could have my next lesson at the regular time.

"If you will give me your phone number," I said, "I will let you know when to come again."

He readily gave me the phone number of the bottling plant where he worked.

"And when they answer," I remarked, as I wrote in my notebook, "I shall ask for Señor Genaro García."

"*Pues* . . . señora . . . !"[1]

I looked up to find him squirming in his chair. "Yes, señor?"

"*Pues* . . . I am not really . . . Genaro García. *De veras,*[2] my real name is José Celis. It is just that sometimes . . . I say that I am Genaro García because . . . pues, . . . because I like that name."

According to José, the Concheros are not shell-people,[3] as they are sometimes called, but concha-people because they dance to the music of the concha, a ten- or twelve-string instrument of reedy tone with a concave back of armadillo shell or gourd. They are like a religious army marching to fiestas to make a sacrifice, or an offering, of their dance. Each group, or mesa, of about forty dancers is presided over by a captain (*capitán*), who is assisted by a second captain, two women captains (*capitanas*) to tend the altar and supervise the women, two sergeants (*sargentos*) to tend the altar and supervise the trips (*marchas*), two standard-bearers *(alféreces),* and lesser officers. Women dancers are *malinches* and men dancers are soldiers (*soldados*). The word *mesa* with the name of the dance "oratory" forms the name of the group, as Mesa del Señor de Llanito, the name of José's group. All of this has to do with their ancestors, for the *danzantes* (religious dancers) are "walking in the steps of their ancestors." What ancestors José did not say, but

I gathered that he meant their ancestors back to and including the ancient Mexicans before the Spanish Conquest. At any rate, "It is a custom left us by our ancestors," was his explanation of most danzante activities.

In September José invited Bill and me to a fiesta at San Miguel de Ameyalco. By that time we had learned that a religious fiesta could mean an eight-hour wait for a five-minute ceremony, or one that failed to take place at all, but this one held great promise. The Concheros were belligerently camera shy and José, a leader among them, had asked Bill to photograph him! Furthermore, it would be the first fiesta we attended by invitation of a danzante and, though we did not realize it then, our status among the Concheros had changed. José, by placing us under his tutelage for almost a year and by inviting us to attend this fiesta as one of them, had acknowledged us as "friends of confidence" before the danzante world.

The next Sunday we drove along the Toluca highway in the early morning light and turned right through miles and miles of muddy hinterland with no telegraph or telephone poles, no houses, and no other cars along the way. José had said that we would be the only outsiders there besides the hill-people from beyond the village and the danzantes from the capital. Four mesas were going to merge. The four top officers of the new group would be the former captains of the four mesas. A man from Ameyalco would be the godfather of the flag, for each mesa has a Mexican flag and each flag has a godfather. If the dancers defile their flag by unseemly behavior (like having a big *disgusto,* or quarrel, at fiesta-time), the godfather takes it from them and stows it in the church where it was first unfurled, thereby dissolving the group. The danzantes were going to honor the godfather by unfurling the flag for the first time at Ameyalco, his home town.

Ameyalco proved to be a tiny village nestled among the hills, an enormous pink church forming the high point of architecture with small whitewashed buildings clustered about it. The atrio [4] was deserted except for the men who were putting the finishing touches to the erection of four *castillos* (castles), as all Indian-made fireworks, except *cohetes* (rockets and firecrackers), are called.

"Where are the danzantes?" we asked.

"In the church," one of them answered.

Bill remained outside while I went in to pay my respects to the saint and to look for José and his dancers. The long, narrow, pewless nave was a tunnel of candlelight, smoke, and humanity. When my eyes became accustomed to the dimness, I could see that the danzantes were singing in front of the altar. Their banners waved back and forth and clouds of incense rose from the urns that the capitanas carried. I was just sinking to my knees in a space by the aisle when they began to leave. Three abreast they slowly backed down the aisle, playing their conchas and singing all the while. La Negra,[5] whose real name was María, caught sight of me and stepped out of line to greet me, embracing me in Mexican fashion. Natalia Hidalgo, a capitana and a person of importance, was less effusive. She took my hand, drew me into the aisle, and backed me out with them.

Outside José was talking to Bill. "Will you do me a little favor, señor? When the padre is in the center, will you take a picture? ¡Ay, qué bueno![6] I have obtained the permission for you to take the picture from the roof. Come, señor!"

He led the way to the door under the tower that flanked the church and opened it to reveal the stairs.

"Pues . . . que pues . . ." he began uneasily, looking at me, but I was too excited to listen to his "pues," which is so elastic that it may mean almost anything. When Bill started up the steps, I followed.

The narrow, spiral stairs curved steeply upward around a massive central support. Because of the continuous curve, the light from below grew dim until we were in complete darkness. Then light began to creep down from above, increasing to full daylight as we reached the top and found ourselves in the tower underneath the huge copper bells. Surrounding them was a network of thick wooden beams, and since there was no floor, we crawled across one of them to reach the arched roof of the church.

"An excellent view of the fiesta," was Bill's comment as he looked over the rim of the facade into the now crowded atrio. The black heads of the men as they removed their hats in front of the door formed a pattern with the dark *rebozos*, or stoles, drawn over the heads of the women. Pastel shirts above immaculate *calzones*, and dresses of subdued cotton prints, livened by a few of brightly colored rayon, contrasted with the black of the women in mourning.

Beyond the crowd in front of the door the castillos looked like small red and gray ferris wheels. Perhaps the first ones were made in the form of a castle, but now almost any figure might burst into flame at the firing. We could trace the outlines of faces on top of some and birds on the others.

"Probably angels and doves," said Bill.

"Doves! José told me about a dove with a gold bell hanging from its neck. He said a sixteenth-century friar killed it on a mountain near here and now the people of Ameyalco have a fiesta there every year. You don't suppose . . . ?"

"No, I don't. These doves probably symbolize the Holy Spirit."

He was right. More than ten years were to pass before I would attend ceremonies for the dove with the gold bell hanging from its neck.

The Concheros, playing a quick, catchy tune, danced in three colorful lines from behind the church to the corner of the atrio where they formed two concentric circles.

"There! Do you see?" I asked. "Just like the diagram in Clavijero's history: two concentric circles with the important people in the center.[7] Can you see anybody important in the center?"

"Yes, the priest is there, but I can't get a shot of him because of the crowd around him."

"See the devil dressed in red? Get a shot of him if you can."

"I'll get shots but they won't mean pictures, not in this light."

We could see tall, lighted candles on the ground near the priest, and the damp breeze brought whiffs of burning candle wax and copal. A lustrous green, white, and red Mexican flag rose in the center and, while the capitanas rang their bells and formed smoke crosses with their incense burners, all the banners in the circles dipped in the direction of the flag. Then the danzantes began to kneel.

"There goes the ceremony!" Bill clicked his camera.

At a timid touch of my sleeve, I turned to find a man with a blue shirt and a black hat standing behind me.

"You will have to descend, señora," he courteously informed me. "It is forbidden, the women on the roof."

I gathered up my paraphernalia and, telling Bill to stay there and take pictures, crawled across the beam again. The man bounced ahead and disappeared down the black shaft of the stairway. Slowly, I followed. When I reached the dark stretch I heard someone coming up. Then I smelled *pulque*.[8] I squeezed close to the central support to make room. There were two of them, reeking of pulque, and as soon as they had passed me they turned around and started down behind me, talking in loud, sibilant whispers that were neither Spanish nor English. I finished the stairs crab-fashion, my left elbow thrust out behind me and my head turned over my left shoulder. As light filtered up, I saw two Indians in calzones, one behind the other, their drink-fired eyes glaring from bushy, tousled heads.

"Just two drunks wandering around," I told myself.

When I reached the bottom and faced the door, I nearly fell off the step! Just outside, erect and grim, stood another white-clad Indian with a sword drawn across the opening.

"This can't have anything to do with me," I thought. "It must be part of the fiesta."

I sidled out the door to the right, keeping my back to the wall and a wary eye on the sword. That is how I happened to collide with the man with the gun. He was standing with his back against the wall beside the door. I took a quick step forward and the two of them "fell in" with military precision, the short, cocky man with the sword on my left and the tall one with the gun on my right. The latter grabbed my arm.

"You are going to the jail," he said in a grinding undertone. "To the jail! Understand?"

To my American mind jail meant iron door-gratings, barred windows, and jailers with heavy keys. I gave way to panic and tried to jerk my arm free, but he tightened his hold and the man on my left flourished the sword. Near its point was a blob of rust. "If he hits me with that," I thought, "I'll die of infection."

Rough, hostile bystanders crowded around us. "The other outsiders!" I thought, for when José had mentioned the hill-people from beyond the village, I had sensed something derogatory to them in his manner. Where were the nice, dignified people we had admired from the roof? And the women? In all that mob there was not a woman or a child. I remembered what an old-timer who had lived in Mexico for forty years once told me: "When the women and the children leave, it's time to be scared."

I was scared!

The man with the blue shirt and the black hat suddenly appeared and an expectant hush fell on the crowd. He now spoke with loud arrogance.

"You have no right to come here and break our laws. I have told you: it is prohibited — the women on the roof."

I thought of the stories I had heard about foreigners who had incurred the wrath of Indian villagers — the torture, the sadism, the hairbreadth escapes. Then I thought of Bill. If he should hear the uproar and rush down to rescue me, they would turn on him.

"I did not know it was prohibited, the women on the roof," I said in muted tones. "It was my ignorance. Did I not come down as soon as you told me? And I shall not go up again. Pardon me and many thanks for having told me." I smiled and inched backward.

The man with the gun jerked me in line. "Oh, no!" he gloated, squeezing my arm. "You are going to the jail, nothing less. Nothing less!"

Thunder crashed over the hills and a drop of rain fell here and there. Other Indians joined those around me and an angry muttering began. A sparsely bearded man in dingy white took a step toward me and, twisting his face in a gargoyle of hate, spat at me. As I swerved aside, I glanced over my shoulder at the gateway and our car. Then my eyes met those of the man with the gun — black disks of menace less than a foot away. Tension flicked over his face and tightened his mouth. His hand near the trigger twitched and I knew that if I moved he would shoot. Abrupt silence surrounded us. Raindrops pelted my face, but I held my gaze steady and tried to match his stare.

Suddenly, a cheerful voice rang out, "Have no care, señora. I have come, have no care!" and José came running along the side of the church, the skirts of his costume flapping as he ran.

"What happened?" he demanded as he reached us.

This was a signal for everybody to talk at once. The man with the blue shirt disappeared in the confusion and the Indians began to mill about, except the man with the sword and his comrade with the gun. They stood with weapons ready and attention fixed on me.

"We will talk to the one with the authority," said José.

He strode toward a long, rectangular building behind the church and I followed, the two weapon bearers on either side. A middle-aged man with torn calzones ran along behind us, great tears rolling down his face.

"The poor little bells!" he sobbed. "Ay, the poor little bells! They are going to break themselves to pieces!"

I risked a half-turn and spoke to him, "You are mistaken. I did not touch the bells."

The man with the gun whisked me back.

"Probably a drunken crying jag," I thought.

By this time rain was falling fast and the Concheros were crowding through the door at one end of the building. José veered toward them. "Here, take my crown and give me my hat," passing his feather headdress inside.

I tried to follow him, but the man with the gun jerked me back.

"Do not touch the señora," shouted José. "Do not dare to touch her!"

The man with the sword yanked me in the opposite direction.

"Is the one with the authority in there?" José pointed to the door at the other end of the building.

"Sí, sí," chorused the crowd.

We marched to the other door where my escort halted and José and I went inside. We found ourselves in a tiny cubbyhole, the one opening of which was a wooden door that was propped back against the adobe wall with a stick. A man with a blue shirt and black hat faced us. He looked like the man who had told me to come down from the roof, but apparently he knew nothing about the affair.

"It was not I who had her brought here," he told José. "It was the other official. You will have to wait for him."

He walked around us and stood between us and the door.

"The señora is a foreigner in our country," José spoke to his back. "She does not know our customs. If you were in her country and broke a law through ignorance, would you want to be thrown in jail?"

The man gazed out the door and chewed a straw.

"The señora is our patrona," continued José. "She gives us forty pesos a month which pays the expenses of an orphan girl among us. This girl made a vow to be a danzante when she was very young. Last year both her parents died and left her too poor for the marches that we of the danza must make. This unfortunate one would have to break her vow were it not for that forty pesos. As you can see, this makes the señora our patrona and whatever you do to her, you will have to do to all of us."

Silence.

"And, señor," emphatically, "we are forty-five of us from the Federal District here today!"

The man stiffened and stared outside. Then he stepped aside, swept off his hat, bowed to me and said, *"Pase, señorita!"*

"To where?" I demanded, remembering the promise of jail.

"Outside. It is finished." He smiled pleasantly.

I stalked over to the door. The forty-five Concheros were in close formation just outside in the downpour! When they saw me, they separated to form a passage to the door at the end of the other building. I lost no time taking advantage of it. As I passed them, my friends closed in behind me and together we scurried out of the rain.

As soon as we were inside the other room, José presented the chiefs, telling them that the foreign señora had studied their history and was interested in the customs left them by their ancestors. "She is now walking with me in the dance," he finished, meaning that I was one of his dance group. General Manuel Luna thanked me for my interest in their customs and offered his services whenever I should need them. Within a few years the small, wiry general was to become our best friend among the danzantes. Francisco Luciano, tall and handsome, drew laughter from the others by a facetious reference to my experience in the churchyard, while elderly Manuel Cortés bowed and murmured that it was a pleasure to have me there.

Then General Manuel Luna made a speech and asked a question, "*¿Estáis conformes, compadritos?*"

The danzantes answered in unison, "*¡El es Dios!*"

Compadritos means those who are godparents of the same person or thing, and I understood that he had asked them if they agreed to something, but I wondered why they answered, "He is God!" Later I learned that "*¡El es Dios!*" was their affirmative vote.

"Señora," remarked José, "it is due to the kindness of the chiefs that you are no longer in jail. They gave the order to get you out."

"In jail!" I gasped. "Was that the jail?"

"It was the jail."

"But it had no bars."

"Many jails in my country have no bars, señora."

José's short, elderly wife gave me a delicious chicken taco, and then the danzantes began to sing *alabanzas*, or songs of praise. José handed me my concha, for he had taught me the first they sang.

Santo, Santo, Santo,	Saint, Saint, Saint,
Señor San Miguel,	Lord Saint Michael,
Pesando las almas	Weighing souls
En el puro fiel.	In exact balance.

The leaders sang the first verse, or *planta*, which the others repeated after each subsequent verse. I sang with both groups, which was incorrect but I did not know it then.

The rain soon stopped and the women of the village huddled outside the door, smiling and bobbing their heads as we sang. I always try to make friends with the women of a strange place, but these had deserted me when the going was rough. I stared over their heads.

Then I saw Bill and the muggy afternoon took on a warm, comforting glow. Evidently the hill-people's ire had not included him, for in spite of the fact his blond hair was awry from the dampness, he looked as untroubled and untouched as he had when I had seen him last. He had found shelter from the rain under the flying buttress at the side of the church, and as I watched him he gathered up his cameras and strolled across the atrio, smoking his pipe, at peace with the world. He spoke to a small boy and when the child pointed in our direction, he quickened his steps to join us. José greeted him at the door and introduced him to the others as the husband of the señora and a *muy fina persona*.

"You owe these gentlemen many thanks," I told him, indicating the chiefs. "They saved me from jail and other worries."

He thanked them for any favors they had done me, but he was puzzled. I forestalled his questions by calling attention to the dark sky. Then it began to rain and we hurriedly said good-bye and drove away. Just outside the capital he stopped the car and turned to me, "Now tell me what's the matter."

I told him everything that happened from the time I left him taking pictures on the roof until he entered the danzantes' room after the rain. This book almost ended there.

       ✿   ✿   ✿

When José came for my next lesson, he dismissed the affair at Ameyalco briefly: "Ay, those people! Always they make the troubles."

Later we told a social worker who lived among the Otomies about the Ameyalco experience.

"I went on top of the church and they put me in jail," I said, "but I don't think that's really why they put me there."

"Is it an Otomí village?" he asked.

"I think so," Bill replied.

"Then I can tell you why."

"Why?" we both asked at once.

"Well, I'd say they put you in jail not because you went on top of the church, but because you crawled under the bells to get there."

"You're joking," said Bill.

"I'm not," the social worker assured him. "To an Otomí a woman is an inferior creature, but his church bells are holy. He believes that if a woman comes near them, they'll crumble away."

I remembered the man with the torn calzones and the tears streaming down his face.

"The poor little bells!" he had sobbed. "They are going to break themselves to pieces!"

I had thought he was drunk. Now I understood.

José Celis,
Instructor

USUALLY WHEN JOSÉ ARRIVED AT OUR HOUSE to teach me about the Concheros and the dance, he would sit on the sofa in the living room and tune the conchas. Then we would dance until I was exhausted. While I rested we would play and sing. Then we would dance another step. I soon learned that a step was more than a step as I knew it.

"What is a step, José?"

"A step is what a danzante dances when he marks the step in the center of the circle. This danzante goes to the center and makes the *firma*, the others making it also. The firma is as I have shown you: the forming of the cross with dance steps which ends with two vigorous stamps. After the firma, the danzante strums his concha until the others can follow him. Then he plays more loudly and calls out, '*¡El es — !*' or '¡El es Dios!' and starts his step."

"Why do the danzantes sometimes say, '*¡El es — !*' and not finish with the word 'Dios'?"

"Because, señora, we have to guard against those who stand around to see what they can see and to hear what they can hear."

"The public?"

"The public!"

"Is it true, José, that the danzantes must have the permission of the government before they can dance?"

"Sí, señora, we apply to the church and the priest obtains the license from the precinct headquarters."

"And are the priests friendly toward the danzantes?"

"Sometimes yes, sometimes no. There was the priest at San Juan, he did not like the danzantes. He always left when we arrived, usually slamming a door. On the other side there was the priest at San Pedro, he was the danzantes' friend. He gave us advice and helped us. He even put his hand on my shoulder and called me 'son'! He was a muy fina persona, señora."

José always danced with fervor, even in our living room. He strummed his concha all the while. My fingers and feet, however, refused to synchronize. The best I was ever able to do was to shake a painted gourd while I danced, but that was later. We leapt and swooped and stamped, while the living room quivered and the furniture rattled to the rhythm of our efforts. When my throat became dry and my breathing difficult, I would fall into an armchair and rest. Sometimes I would try to prolong the rest period by asking questions.

"José, about that song, 'Alabado,'[1] that you taught me the other day, did you say that the danzantes sang it during the *Disciplina?*"

"*Sí*, señora."

"They sing during the Disciplina," writing in my notebook.

"And in the *Recibimiento*, but not in the *Retiramiento*."

"What are the Reception and the Retirement, Don José?"

"The Reception is when a new member is received into the dance. He must present himself with wax candles and flowers, on his knees at the altar of his oratory.[2] It is serious, señora, but it is beautiful too."

"And the Retirement?"

"When a danzante refuses to accept the Disciplina, señora, he may retire himself from his mesa — and this is really sad."

"With no singing?"

"To the contrary. The danzantes loosen some of the strings of their conchas and tighten others so that they are out of tune. Then they play only to make a bad noise. It is very ugly, señora, but it signifies the discord that is going out of the mesa."

We always came back to the leaping and the stamping. José wanted me to dance at a fiesta soon. Twice a week for months the schedule continued without interruption. When the chandelier in the living room fell in the early hours one morning, Bill found that something had loosened the screw that had held it to the beam above the ceiling.

"Termites!" he decided.

I said nothing.

José enjoyed dictating to me, looking over my shoulder as I wrote as if he could understand English, and proceeding in schoolmaster fashion the minute my pencil paused. I noted that a costume was a "uniform," and a headdress, a "crown"; and that when the people of a village arranged to have danzantes at a fiesta, they agreed to take tacos and water to the churchyard for the number of danzantes invited that day.[3] Also, that while there was only one step for the firma, there were several *pasos de camino*.

"What is a *paso de camino*, Don José?"

"It is the tune we play when we dance away from the place where we have met to put on our uniforms and to prepare for the sacrifice.

We form three lines, then we dance to the church to sing the "Mañani-tas" to the Santo we are honoring and to ask his permission to dance.[4] After we back out of the church, the two outer columns dance in oppo-site directions, curving out, then in, until they meet to form a circle. Like this, señora. . . . ."

He took my pencil and made a sketch in my notebook

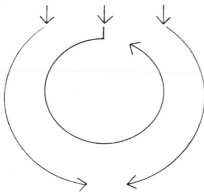

"Do the Concheros always dance in a circle?"

"They dance in many figures, señora. Sometimes they dance in a square, called 'forming the cross' or the 'general movement,' and in this they bow to the Four Winds. Often they do dance in a circle, but it should be a double or a triple circle with the important people in the center."

"Tell me, José, what are the Four Winds?"

"The frontiers, señora."

I did not understand this, but let it go for the moment. I had learned that some things were so taken for granted that questions about them only pointed the difference between the danzante and me. A question too many could result in a retreat behind a blank countenance and an alien silence filled with swift, surreptitious glances at me.

"And how does a village invite the danzantes to dance at a fiesta?" I went on quickly.

"They send an invitation to the captain of a mesa inviting a certain number of danzantes for a certain date, señora."

"Who decides who will go?"

"The *Jefe de Marcha*. Like this: 'Señor So-and-so, we will await you in the Plaza of San Bartolo to depart for Los Remedios at midnight of October the eighth!' "

"And the danzante has to go?"

"The danzante must report there in full uniform with his concha."

"Who pays his transportation?"

"He pays it. That is part of the sacrifice."

"Then the sacrifice is more than dancing in the circle?"

"The sacrifice is many things. For example, the danzantes do not take pulque while they are within the obligation, and on these marches, when they eat there is a sergeant at each door so that none can go outside."

"Why?"

"Because they are still making the sacrifice and, if they went outside and mingled with the public, someone might give them a drink, or encourage some other breach of rules."

"How strict the danzantes are!"

"We have to be. That is the only way we can preserve this custom left us by our ancestors. On the march anything that could in any way *llamar atención* — that is, call the attention of the public to the danzante — is punishable at the *cuartel general*."[5]

"In my opinion, just to see them in their beautiful uniforms would be to pay attention to them."

"And a danzante in uniform must not walk in the marketplace or play a concha out of tune. And now shall we dance, señora?"

I paid him ten pesos a week and in return I learned dance steps, dance tunes, songs, prayers, and rules. He was a stickler for rules.

We have stern rules, señora. When we go on marches like that to Chalma the field sergeant must carry a hammer, nails, and wire to mend any part of a uniform that may become damaged.[6] And the *malinche abanderada* carries thread, needles, and cloth to mend the banner if so much as a ribbon is loosened or torn.[7] We used to have One-in-Charge-of-First-Aid who carried herbs and other remedies to relieve any danzante who became ill. Now the danzantes prefer the remedies they buy at the drugstores, and the *encargado del botiquín* is no longer included on the march.

Sí, señora, these things are in our rules. No, not from the Bajío.[8] My rules come from Morelia. No, señora, I was not born in Morelia. I was born on a ranch in Guanajuato. When I was three years old, my father joined the Revolution and we never saw him again. That was when I went to live with relatives in Morelia. When I was five I began to *andar con los danzantes* [to walk with the dancers] and when I was eight I was received into the dance. My general was a great dance general, señora — as great as Lima Dulce of San Miguel or Cecilio Morales of Guanajuato — the great General Felipe Aranda!

He died six years ago, señora. The rules he had inherited from his ancestors he did not hand down to the next generation of his family. No, señora. As he had no son, in a formal, legal will, he left them to me. Imagine!

And they are good rules, señora. So many danzante rules of today are just prohibitions. They go like this:

Number One — It is prohibited to do this.
Number Two — It is prohibited to do that.

But it is what a man should do, not what he should not do, that makes the happiness of his life. Is it not so?

The dance has changed, señora. In the old days the Disciplina was expected and submitted to without a murmur. Now the young people are different. Would you believe it, not long ago a young man asked permission to leave the circle for five minutes and he stayed away for two hours "seeing the town." The field sergeant informed the general and the general ordered the young man to report at general headquarters — the oratory of the general, that is.

He came, señora, but he came late. He told the sergeant, "I am not your son and, therefore, I will not permit you to flog me. I do not have to be a danzante. I shall withdraw from this mesa!"

And he went away. Imagine! We never saw him again.

Sí, señora, we have the Disciplina in our mesa. The last one I executed was the little boy whose dancing you admired at Acapilco. I know he is only five years old, but he must learn. He asked permission to leave the circle for a drink of water and he hid behind a tree with some other little ones and played marbles! He had to be executed, as we call it, señora. I know you think he is cute. That is true. But it is also true that without the Disciplina we cannot preserve the dance. I sentenced him to a quarter of an *arroba*, which is an old term, señora, for a dozen lashes with a whip. I conducted him to a clean, new *petate* [mat] in front of the altar. There before the eyes of everybody, the sergeant carried out the sentence while the danzantes sang *Alabado*.

The Disciplina is harder for captains and generals than for malinches and soldiers. Not long ago, we had to execute a captain. It was within the hour of the sacrifice. We were in the circle. We had just finished one step and were about to begin another when I looked across and saw him taking a drink of pulque.

Later, I said to him, "Señor, you were drinking while you were in the circle."

"No, señor!"

"I saw you, señor."

"I did not know it was not permitted," he said, changing his argument.

"Have you not memorized Rule Thus-and-so of the regulations?" — and I unrolled my documents to show him.

"I did not know it," he insisted.

"Then you shall be executed," I told him, "for not making yourself familiar with the rules."

And we gave him one arroba and made him write that rule many times.

You have seen the elegant whip that is carried in the dance, señora? That is only for show. The whip that is called the disciplina is made of jute, the fiber of the maguey, señora, that stretches with every lash and is very painful.[9] The Disciplina is hard, eh, señora? But in no other way can we carry on the tradition of the dance. We call ourselves soldiers; soldiers do not scatter themselves in places of pleasure while on duty. If a man cannot discipline himself, he should be disciplined by his jefes. But in my opinion, if the discipline of his jefes does not teach him to discipline himself, he is no good and should be expelled from the mesa.

José was forty years old and was captain of a mesa, a group of about forty danzantes who had their oratory in Tacubaya. Their banner carried the motto "Union and Conformity to the Conquest of the Great Tenoxtitlan." José had worked at a bottling plant where the bottling was done by hand for seventeen years and was now earning about sixty cents a day.

Bill and I realized that to understand the dance I should attend both fiestas and *velaciones*. I had read that "only Indians exclusively" were admitted to the latter, and José's manner bore this out when he invited us "to visit" the Velación (Vigil) of the Dead.

"Don José, is a velación something you always have before you dance at a fiesta?"

"*Sí*, señora.*"

"And is it usually on Saturday night?"

"*Sí*, señora. The Saturday night before an ordinary fiesta we have a velación in the oratory. Sometimes several chiefs join together in an association, or capitanía, and once a year the capitanía has a velación that is called Velacíon General, but the one next Saturday night will be an ordinary velación. Only danzantes will be there."

"Tell me about it, José. I want to understand what I see."

"Write this down, señora: There are two regular velaciones in the year, one for the dead and the other at Easter. We will dress the *Xuchil....*"

"What is the Xuchil?" I interrupted.

"You will see it Saturday night. The order will be like this: The table sergeant will invite Capitán General Manuel Luna to raise the word; the standard-bearers will present the banners to the Four Winds; the capitanas and malinches will dress the altar; the danzantes will sing songs; they will dress the Xuchil; General Manuel Luna will offer the Santo Xuchil to the Four Winds; they will throw the flowers; they will give thanks, and that is all señora. We do this in honor of our *tatitos*."

"Tatitos? And what is that?"

"Tatas. You know what tata is, do you not?"

For one thing, it is how some of the Preconquest peoples addressed a god. In some Indian languages it means "father." More than that, I did not know. I waited.

"It is in honor of those jefes who have gone before us, señora; those who have died, the old chiefs, or ancestors — our tatitos!"

Two other words that puzzled me cropped up in conversation with José: *atropellar*[10] and *ánima*.[11] I found them easily enough in the dictionary, but it was years before I understood their danzante meanings.

The following Saturday night Bill had a cold, but he insisted on our going to the velación. We loaded the car with blankets and thermos bottles and set out for Colonia Simón with the crude map José had drawn for us. We were lost only twice before we stopped in front of a two-room house on an unpaved, sidewalkless, silent street. Not a light anywhere. Then a concha tinkled in the stillness.

"This must be the place," said Bill.

As I opened the car door José stepped out of the shadows by the house. "¡Ay, señor! You are ill. ¡Qué lástima![12] Do not remain in the car. That is not necessary. I shall arrange a bed for you in the other room. Other sick people are in there, too. Bring your blankets, señor, so that you can be comfortable."

But Bill declined, saying that he could not leave the car due to the night air, which satisfied José, for like many Mexicans he considered *el aire,* particularly at night, a serious hazard to health.

The tiny, windowless oratory was packed with danzantes in blue jeans and serapes, or dark cotton dresses and rebozos. José squirmed through the crowd, leading me to a seat on a backless bench along one side of the room. Then he called to La Negra.

"Remain at the side of the señora and explain our exercises to her," he ordered.

The room was a lean-to with the ceiling so low on our side that we could hardly stand without touching it. From the thin wooden shingles between us and the night sky dangled little strips of black cotton material.

"What are they?" I whispered to La Negra.

"Mourning," she replied. "For those of us who died this year."

The altar extended across one end of the room and held so many things that it was impossible to distinguish them all immediately: saints, both as images and paintings; crosses of several sizes and materials; flowers galore interspersed with lighted candles and fruit; and an alarm clock that was set for midnight.

"Why?" I asked La Negra.

"Because that is when we shall start to dress the Xuchil."

I thought of the *Codex Borbonicus,* the picture-writing manuscript of the ancient Mexicans, where the sign of midnight appeared on the sheet of the dance god.

"Do the danzantes often start things at midnight?"

"Always," La Negra assured me. "Always the important thing starts at midnight."

As José had said, the danzantes sang songs. One of them would softly strum his concha. One by one, the others would begin to strum.

Just as I would have decided that nothing further was going to happen, the first would throw back his head, open his mouth, and sing. Two or three of the others would join him. The rest, strumming steadily, would wait until the end of the first verse, or planta. Then they would repeat it, some in high falsetto. They repeated the planta after every verse, and because of this only the leaders needed to know all of the verses.

From time to time, a danzante arrived with flowers and candles. He would go immediately to the altar where he and a capitana would kneel and gesticulate with the flowers and the incense burner. One of the capitanas was Natalia Hidalgo, a plump, dignified woman with dark glasses. Between presentations of the flowers to the Four Winds she chatted with La Negra and me. Apparently, La Negra was a lesser capitana, because she helped Natalia to dress the altar when she and the danzante had finished with the flowers. The dressing consisted of putting the flowers on the altar in tin cans and soda-pop bottles.

Capitán General Manuel Luna came over to greet me and to present his son, Tiburcio, a young man in his twenties with a smile like his father's. La Negra whispered that since he was the jefe's oldest son, he would inherit the position of dance chief.

"He is the first bugle," she explained, "and he has the obligation to tune the instruments and to teach the music and the steps."

Tiburcio began to strum his concha and the others joined him. Then they sang, "The Twelve Truths of the World."

The planta, which Tiburcio sang and then the others repeated, was:

Brothers mine of the Twelve Truths of the World,
I want you to tell me one.

After the others had repeated this Tiburcio answered:

One is the Holy House of Jerusalem.
Where lives and reigns the Father of God forever. Amen.

There were twelve verses, each one line longer than the one before, forming a cumulative song like "The House That Jack Built."[13]

From time to time José would introduce newcomers, telling me that they were of our mesa or visitors from elsewhere. Of one man he said, "He was with us on that day in June of 1935 when our enemies worked against us!" turning toward him, "were you not, my friend?"

The man agreed with enthusiasm. Later I learned what they were talking about, for I was to hear the story of the fiesta at the Tree of the Sad Night many times in the years that I walked with the danzantes.[14]

Shortly before twelve o'clock, Don Manuel bustled into the oratory followed by Bill, who explained, "I was lonesome out there in the car."

When the alarm of the clock rang out at midnight, Capitana Natalia turned it off and one of the danzantes requested Capitán General Manuel Luna to "raise the word." Don Manuel appointed José, La Negra, and two others to "work the flower." Then he went to a corner by the altar and seemed to be looking for something. When he turned, his arms were filled with thin, round sticks about a foot long.

"A bundle of sticks!" I thought.

Somewhere I had read that the Otomí worshipped a bundle of sticks in Preconquest times.[15] Even after José had fitted them into the holes around the top of a short upright pole so they were arranged like the spokes of a wheel, I thought of them as a bundle of sticks. It was not until my next velación that I recognized the object's likeness to the custodial or monstrance in which the Host is elevated in the Catholic Church.

Natalia and La Negra took flowers from the altar, and Natalia and some of the women broke off the long stems. Then La Negra and José sorted the flowers and placed them on a white cloth spread on the floor in front of the altar. Meanwhile, the rest of the group sang to the strumming of the conchas. When the flowers were spread in neat order on the cloth, José and one of the men began to tie them to the crude custodial, or the "bundle of sticks," as I thought.

"What is it and what are they going to do with it?" I whispered to La Negra.

"It is the Santo Xuchil, señora. We will burn candles before it and we will not allow the light to go out for three days."

While the Custodial was taking the form of a fluffy, yellow disk, I whispered to Bill, "José invited us to visit the velación. Perhaps it's time to leave."

Don Manuel Luna accompanied us to our car and invited us to join the danzantes at the Basilica on the night of December eleventh, when the four chiefs we had met in Ameyalco would take the general oath. Bill thanked him and we drove away.

"Well, now that you've been to a velación, what do you think of it?" he asked on the way home.

"I think it's one thing to hear a danzante describe a ceremony and quite another to see it yourself!"

"You're right," he agreed. "No description can equal seeing a thing yourself."

The General Oath

AT THE END OF THE CALZADA DE GUADALUPE, sandwiched between the old and the new approaches to the Laredo highway, stands Mexico's most famous church — the Basilica. It is the home of the Virgin of Guadalupe, the dark Virgin who became successively the Patroness of New Spain, of Mexico, of Latin America, and of the Americas. The Basilica fills the back of a spacious square with the Hill of Tepeyac rising behind it. On the right, seeming to hang from the sky, is the hillside chapel that stands where the Nuestra Señora appeared to Juan Diego in the sixteenth century, while inside over the main altar hangs the miraculous painting that further recalls the story of the Virgin and the Otomí Indian.

Juan Diego, on his way from his native village of Cuauhtitlán to Tlaltelolco, met the Virgin on Tepeyac where she indicated that she wanted her temple built, but when he told the church authorities this, nobody believed him. Then she appeared there to him again and told him to gather roses from the mountainside, and to take them to the Bishop wrapped in his *tilma* — the mantle hanging from his shoulders. When he offered the roses to the Bishop, all were amazed to see the Virgin's likeness on the inside of his tilma. This convinced the Bishop, who immediately began plans for the erection of her temple at Tepeyac.

The region has always been a gathering place for Indians. Before the coming of the Spanish, the Hill of Tepeyac personified the earth goddess, Tonantzin, mother of the gods, and the Indians went there yearly to do her honor. Now they go there every twelfth of December to honor the Virgin of Guadalupe. The Villa (Villa Madero) — the suburb where the Basilica is located — is one of the Four Winds (Los Cuatro Vientos) of the danzantes of the capital, along with Los Remedios, Chalma, and Amecameca.

The church was done over inside and out during the time that we lived in Mexico. I can remember the feeling of great age about it when

I first saw it. There were *puestos,* or booths of vendors, a smelly market, and other buildings huddled close to the wrought iron fence that enclosed the small atrio. Dancing space was at a premium. Chiefs conferred with church officers for weeks before December twelfth, trying to obtain a place in the churchyard, but the dance circles always overflowed to the side streets, the cemetery, and the space behind El Pocito, the chapel with its well of healing waters.

All this had changed by the late 1960s. The puestos, most of the market, and a number of buildings had been razed to clear a square around the church. At most fiestas the wide area at the right of the main entrance was roped off with signs, "Zona de Danzantes," posted at intervals. Policemen herded the public back, keeping them on the opposite side of the rope from the dancers. A policeman at each end of the rope granted permission to those who wanted to leave the dance zone for a few minutes. When they remained outside the rope mingling with the crowd in their bright costumes, a loudspeaker blared from one of the towers, directing them to return to the dance zone. There was a feeling of plenty of room as the worshippers tramped across the great expanse between the south gate and the main entrance to the church, for the atrio was now of grand dimensions.

At the time when we went to the Villa to see the taking of the general oath, however, the section surrounding the Basilica was still cluttered with unpainted booths and shabby buildings. We reached the poorly lighted, teeming plaza at nine o'clock and, following José's instructions, pushed through the crowd to the west gate. A policeman there refused to let us in. José hurried toward him from the inside and spoke to him in an undertone. The policeman protested, then opened the gate just wide enough for us to slide through. We picked our way carefully across the atrio for the ground was covered with sleeping figures. What looked like a bundle in a serape grunted when I stepped on it, and the end of the serape flew up to reveal a scowling face. Finally, we reached a group of friends by the church wall, and I sat with Capitana Natalia Hidalgo on her serape while Bill and José walked about and talked to the men.

Presently, the danzantes began to sing alabanzas, most of them about Juan Diego and the Virgin of Guadalupe, and soon three groups on the west side of the atrio were singing three different alabanzas at the same time. After an hour or two, since Natalia's serape was scant protection from the cold, hard pavement, I sent Miguel, Don Manuel's younger son, to a little grocery store across the plaza to buy an empty wooden box. We placed it near the fence and two elderly women shared it with me, one beside me and the other behind us with her back to ours.

Suddenly, two policemen, scattering danzantes as they came, strode from the back of the atrio toward the front, clearing the way for men in white carrying a stretcher with a woman on it.

"What happened? What happened?" several bystanders asked.

"Woman fainted," was the reply.

The policemen barked instructions for the path to remain clear and the crowd obeyed, thus leaving an aisle for the public to flow through, for no reason that I could see except to stare at the singers.

When the woman beside me left us to repair a banner, she told an Otomí girl to occupy her place on the box until she came back. We were singing when six Latin Americans, two women and four men, came through the gate and turned down the cleared passage that led past the danzantes. A portly, bareheaded man seemed to be in charge of the party. He pointed to the danzantes, apparently explaining them, and the others grinned and giggled. At first, we were unable to hear their comments because of the singing, but we finished an alabanza just as they paused in front of us and we could hear them clearly.

"As I told you," said the portly man in Spanish, "they are carrying on the same practices that they had before the Conquest. They have not changed. Look at them," making a sweeping gesture almost in our faces, "they are pagan, I tell you, purely pagan in their religion."

"Of a truth?" giggled one of the women.

"And tomorrow you will see how they dress: completely uncivilized. As you will see, they wear anything, just anything!"

I turned to the Otomí girl, trying to find words to sympathize without sounding condescending. She raised her large, almond-shaped eyes and I saw that she was moved.

"*Pobre gente*," she murmured sadly. "To be so ignorant!"

There was a stir among the danzantes as Captain General Luna's sons moved from group to group telling them that it was twelve o'clock. It was after twelve, however, before the first smoke cross of the ceremony rose toward the sky. The jefes cleared a space near the front corner of the atrio and sent danzantes hurrying in all directions to bring the standard-bearers. With a great show of authority, they ordered them to "stack arms," but the young standard-bearers, awed by the occasion, moved about clumsily and leaned the banners at awkward angles, so that they fell down and had to be stacked again and again. The officers waxed stern and exacting as, in harsh undertones, they directed the young men until the brightly colored banners were in a firm pile — the new banner with the names of the four jefes written across the bottom standing upright at center front. We had an excellent place a few feet from the stack, but when they were ready for the ceremony, danzantes and the public pushed forward, crowding us back until we could see nothing and could hear only an indistinct drone of voices.

Don Manuel spoke to José, who turned and strode toward us.

"Señores Estony!" he called, "The General wants you here." And he led us to a place near the banners where we could see everything.

It was the time of speechmaking. Elderly Manuel Cortés, the new capitán segundo, did not want to speak but the danzantes insisted, nudging him toward the new banner. He said that he was now an old man and could not be as active in the dance as he had been; that he had confidence in Manuel Luna; that he wanted to join with him, "and why not?" He glared around the circle of faces and backed into the shadows.

"¿Estaís conformes, compadritos?" shouted the man in charge of the ceremony.

"¡El es Dios!" came the danzantes' reply.

Francisco Luciano expressed high hopes for the new group, of which he was the first sergeant, and pledged his best efforts to its success.

Most Mexican Indians are inclined to eloquent and ostentatious speech. Nahuatl is a flowery language, and the Spanish imposed upon it was the courtly Spanish of the sixteenth century. Even small children sometimes sprinkle their conversation with ornate expressions of words of several syllables. Many Indians are splendid orators.

José was an exception. When it was his turn to stand in front of the new banner and address the crowd, he twisted and turned and giggled like a small boy. The other chiefs smiled tolerantly and prompted him in whispers. Finally, he stammered out the final statement of the speaker before him and was voted in.

Captain General Manuel Luna touched upon the records of the four former groups, extolling the merits of each. He praised the new group and painted an inspiring picture of its possibilities. Then he placed his hand on the new banner, lifted his chin, and spoke in a voice that could be heard by the whole crowd of danzantes

"If I am to be your jefe, I tell you now: I shall be jefe! I shall expect you to make real sacrifices for the danza, serving it with all your heart, not just talking about it. When I give you orders, I shall expect you to obey them to the best of your ability. If any shall give his word and then break it, I shall expect him to accept the consequences of his error, according to my decision and that of his compadres, before the whole community. Is there anyone here present who does not want me to be jefe?"

Silence.

"This is the time to speak. After this moment will be too late. If you are not *conforme* and keep silent now, to go from one to another of your compadres talking against me later, you are not fair to yourself or to me. Again I ask: is there anyone here present who does not want me to be jefe?"

Again there was silence.

He finished his speech by making the usual promise to devote his efforts to the success of the new mesa. After they had voted him in, he led the danzantes in an alabanza about the Virgin of Guadalupe, "Madre de mi Amor" ("Mother of my Love").

When the ceremony had ended, La Negra and I went back to the wooden box to sing alabanzas. Presently, José came up with two captains from the Bajío whom he introduced to us.

"Is this the first time, señora," asked the older man, "that you have come to honor the Virgencita on her birthday?"[1]

"No, señor, I was here last year. And you?"

"We come every year, señora. We have been here many times. We even came when it was forbidden to dance here."

"¿De veras?"

"Sí, señora. During the troubles between the government and the church our government forbade us to dance, but we came anyway."

"And did you dance?"

"No, señora. They confiscated our arms."

For a moment I was startled. Then I remembered that the danzantes' arms are their banners, conchas, and headdresses.

"What happened then, señor?"

"They threw some of our mesa in jail. Captain Manuel Luna raised the money to release them, but our arms were torn and soiled and many of them ruined."

Miguel Luna remarked that the danzantes were putting on their uniforms to sing "Las Mañanitas," and the captains hurried away.

The danzantes changed their clothes in the churchyard. First, as he crouched on the ground, a danzante pulled on his colored stockings. Then he removed one sleeve of his shirt and pulled on one of the blouse, or a strap of the upper part of his uniform. He repeated this on the other side. Then he stood up and lifted his skirts over his head and fastened them at his waist. Under cover of his skirts, he removed his trousers. The women proceeded in the same manner, all going about it so casually that nobody paid any attention to them.

Suddenly, La Negra announced, "It is time for 'Las Mañanitas.' Come, señora!"

We entered the church and tried to follow the danzantes to the altar to join in the singing of the birthday greeting, but the crowd was so dense and so unyielding that we had to remain standing just inside. After a time, we saw the banners bobbing toward the door and followed them out.

The morning air was fresh and bracing as we stepped into the graying churchyard where the electric lights shone pale and yellow in the coming day. Concheros circles were forming here and there, and La Negra left me to enter Don Manuel's. Since Bill and I were tired and sleepy, we told José that we looked forward to seeing him the following week and went home.

José did not come for my lesson the next week, however, nor the next. We did not see him until several months later when I wanted something distinctive to model at an exhibition of Mexican costumes and decided to ask him to lend me one of his dance uniforms. I finally found his one-room house in La Colonia de los Doctores and knocked on the door. His sister opened it.

"Come in, Señora Marta. You remember José's señora, do you not?" indicating a slender woman with dimples who was in bed.

"Ay, Señora Celis, I did not recognize you. You have lost weight, have you not?" Though, I did not say so, I had remembered her as older with gray hair.

"Sí, señora, I have been sick. And I have a very bad leg. See!" drawing back the sheet.

José had told me about his wife's accident. They had been at a vela- ción and she had been making coffee, when a frightened dog ran through the patio upsetting the gasoline cans filled with boiling water and scald- ing her from knee to ankle. That had been months ago and she should have recovered before this. José was out, but they expected him soon. I waited, commiserating with the señora about her leg and chatting with his sister.

When he came, he seemed delighted to lend me his costume, unpacking it and showing me how to put it together, how to fasten it, and so on. Later I wore it and enjoyed its distinctiveness. As soon as I reached home that afternoon I asked my next-door neighbor, who was a doctor, what to do for a burned leg.

"I'd like to see the patient," she said. "Bring her in. I'll donate the consultation and you can donate the medicine."

I told José that on a certain day I would go for his wife in our car and take her to a doctor. A few days before the appointed time, he arrived at our house in great embarrassment.

"Pues . . . señora, I hate to ask another favor of you. But, señora, we have made a *promesa* to the Lord of Chalma, my wife and I. And it is this, señora: that twenty-one days from now we will walk to Chalma."

"But your wife's leg! How can she walk to Chalma?"

"The Lord of Chalma can cure her, señora, in twenty-one days." He paused while I thought this over. "Therefore, señora, will you give us the money you would pay the doctor, so that we may take a little gift to the Lord of Chalma?"

I gave him fifty pesos. He came only once after that. His wife was sick, he said. She had walked to Chalma, but as she had been unable to walk back, she had returned to the capital in a truck that had happened to come along. Then without explanation, he came no more.

Months passed. I went to his house, but they had moved. I went to the Basilica on December twelfth, but was unable to find him. I went to other fiestas, but I was no longer *andando con los danzantes*.

Years passed, three of them. Once at the Basilica I saw a demonstration of what José termed *atropellar*. A group of danzantes were peacefully dancing in a circle when two unfriendly groups formed circles on each side of them. These two rival groups began to extend their circles toward the first, dancing vigorously all the while. The inner circle, protesting futilely, first became an oval, then two parallel lines. Finally they gave up and marched furiously off to find another place to dance. I knew a few of the vanquished group and ran along with them. They paid no attention to me. Again I was on the outside peeking in at the Concheros.

Fiesta at San Juan de los Lagos – Train Wreck

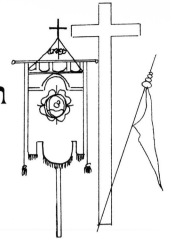

SPRING WEATHER came close on the heels of Christmas in 1945. After the misty rains of a chilly New Year, the sun shone clearly and the middays were almost too warm. Near the end of January I went to a tea in the Lomas de Chapultepec, one of the residential sections of the capital. As we chatted in the living room, someone commented on the efficiency of the maid serving us.

"Yes," agreed our hostess. "I hate to be without her even for a week. — She wants to get off for the fiesta at San Juan de los Lagos."

"San Juan de los Lagos," echoed a small red-haired woman. "What's so wonderful about that fiesta? Both my servants want to go."

"And you're letting them off?" I asked.

"How can I, with house guests coming? I told them that one could go but the other must stay. They're to settle it between themselves and are arguing all day. I don't know who'll win in the long run."

"Our Juana says that the Virgencita is *muy caprichosa*," said another. "So capricious that she sometimes sends a great catastrophe on the people so that they'll think of her and bring her offerings."

"Our *dulce*-vendor," said our hostess, "has asked if he can leave his cart in our backyard for a week."

Many Americans in Mexico speak a mixture of English and Spanish. A dulce-vendor is a vendor of sweets, usually candy, chewing-gum, and fruit or nut pastes.

"Your dulce-vendor?" I repeated.

"Oh, didn't I tell you? There's a dulce-vendor, a nice boy of about seventeen, who leaves his pushcart in our backyard every night while he carries his wares back and forth on the bus. Every morning he stocks his cart and pushes it through the Lomas crying his wares. He gives my children candy and they think he's wonderful! Of course, I said we'd keep his cart until he came back from San Juan."

I went home a little sad for the days when I had been *andando con los danzantes*. José had talked glowingly of San Juan de los Lagos. It was one of the great dance centers he said, along with Querétaro, Chalma, and Tepeyac.

When Nieves, our vivacious and capable little maid, opened the gate for me, she said that there were visitors in the living room.

"Who?" I asked.

Her wavy black hair bobbed around her shoulders with her suppressed laughter, and her generous mouth widened in a smile that revealed a gold front tooth. "Surprise, señora! You would never guess!"

I hurried in to find José, his dimpled wife, and a sturdy baby boy about two years old. José Celis had come back. I was accepted again.

For three years they had been living in Guanajuato where José had learned to bottle by electricity.

"Always he who works the electricity makes more money," his wife informed me.

They had come back to a better job in the capital and José had resumed his position as a capitán of the Concheros.

Finally he came to the purpose of their visit. "Señora, I have come to invite you to go on a march with us. It is to go to the fiesta at San Juan de los Lagos. Twenty of us will go on the excursion train. La Negra and the Capitana Hidalgo will go. Would you not like to go, too?"

"I should love to go! And I have a friend who might like to go with us, the señora Sensibar. You remember her, José, the señora Shayne Sensibar?"

The pilgrim train would leave the Bueña Vista station at five o'clock in the afternoon on Wednesday, the thirty-first of January.

"I shall return Friday for the money for your ticket, señora. I shall buy all the tickets at the same time so that we shall all be together."

Friday he looked at the money I gave him and asked, "Where is the photograph? There must be a photograph of passport size to put on the ticket."

I had never heard of a passport picture for a railway ticket! Again José would come back. "You can have a photograph made tomorrow, just a cheap one, señora, and I will come back Monday."

Monday he had bad news. "All the tickets for the car in which we are going have been sold, señora. I can get a ticket for you in another car, but none of us will be there to take care of you. If someone should take your seat, you would have to stand up. It is a long trip."

"Then the señora Shayne and I will go on the regular passenger train Thursday. Where can we find you Friday morning, José?"

"We will await you between the gate and the main door to the church at San Juan, señora, at ten o'clock *en punto.*"

The Sensibars were friends of ours from Chicago who had recently moved to Mexico City. Shayne, who was interested in folklore, and I left on the Thursday train for a town near San Juan de los Lagos. At Querétaro somebody bought a newspaper and left it on the seat across the aisle from us. Suddenly Shayne dived for it.

"Look at that headline," she cried. " 'Frightful Wreck of Pilgrim Train .' "

The facts were meager, but apparently many danzantes had died.

"Was this the train that José and his dancers were on?" asked Shayne, her hazel eyes serious and troubled.

"I am afraid that it was. The paper says that it left the capital yesterday afternoon. They were planning to leave then."

We left the train at Lagos de Moreno and took a bus for San Juan a few miles away. Soon we could look down on the beautiful white church in the wide valley with the streams of humanity converging toward it. We scanned the countryside for dance banners, but saw none. When we arrived we climbed the stairs from the street to the spacious atrio enclosed by a white wall. As we stood in the gate the width of the spaces between the stacks of danzante "arms" showed that few groups had arrived. At this important fiesta the churchyard should have been studded with stacks fairly close to each other.

"Why are the conchas and banners piled up like this?" asked Shayne.

"They're stacked in the centers of what were dance circles before the Concheros went to breakfast," I told her.

Ten o'clock came, but no José. An elderly couple began to "inspect the arms" of a nearby stack whose banner carried the name of Captain General Cecilio Morales of Guanajuato. José had often mentioned him, and when they had finished I introduced myself and asked about José and his personnel."

"I know nothing definite, señora, but it appears that all perished in the wreck."

They invited us to attend the fiesta in Guanajuato in July, and we chatted until the danzantes came trooping into the churchyard, when they left us to enter their circle.

After a time Shayne and I stopped waiting for José and joined the line of rebozo covered women and bareheaded men who were pushing their way through the tall door into the sanctuary. The high point of the elaborately decorated altar was "San Juanita de los Lagos" about whom I had heard so much, a lovely image of the Virgin in blue and white with a crescent moon at her feet. A few of the faithful knelt at the altar, but most of the public were content to stare as they moved along, without losing their places in the long lines that were weaving through the crowded church. In the jostling, shoving throng, we made a mistake and followed the wrong line, soon finding ourselves in the white glare of the atrio again.

Here and there in the enormous space a few forlorn groups of danzantes were fulfilling their obligations. Inside a circle from Querétaro danced a malinche from the capital and a blond American woman. They danced a little apart from the others, their feet barely moving as they scraped to the various rhythms. At intervals the blond opened her mouth wide and gasped.

"She probably doesn't know it," I told Shayne, "but she's close to sunstroke."

While we were watching her, just as they finished a step, one of the danzantes in the same circle suddenly fell to the ground. Nobody moved or spoke, except a capitán who quickly crossed the circle and bent over the man. Gently he examined him, feeling his pulse and his heart, and drawing his eyelids back. When he had finished, he stood up and gestured to the others. Four danzantes stepped forward, lifted the crumpled figure, and carried it away. Immediately the field sergeant went over to a danzante in the circle and placed a narrow black band around his left arm, while the malinche abanderada turned toward the banner with a black ribbon.

"Did you see that?" asked Shayne. "A man dropped dead in that circle!"

"Yes, I think he did," I agreed.

"Look! They're putting black ribbons on the banners."

"Then he was dead."

As soon as they were properly in mourning the danzantes began to dance again. Only the blond American walked away.

"Why, they didn't even break their circle!" Shayne observed.

"They can't," I explained, "because once a danzante votes 'El es Dios' to dance at a fiesta, not even death of another can interfere as long as he is physically able to fulfill his obligation."

In the afternoon the *penitentes* arrived, most of them on their knees when they came around the corner, a block from the entrance stairs. Friends and relatives walked along beside them, spreading serapes for them to crawl on instead of the rough cobblestones. The last was a blindfolded man, clad only in a pair of faded blue shorts, with a crown of thorns around his head, a cactus plant with long spines strapped to his naked back, and two large safety pins pinned through the flesh of his upper arms. Sweat stood in dewy drops on his torso and trickled from his forehead, but he refused the serapes or to let anyone wipe his face. Blood oozed from his knees as he slowly and painfully crawled up the steps to the atrio. Then the line of penitentes crept through the church door, and we saw them no more.

As the afternoon wore on, other groups of danzantes arrived. One handsome jefe, magnificent in silks, sequins, and ostrich plumes, brought gasps of admiration from the public when he pranced across the atrio.

"Who is that?" I asked a man near us.

"Natividad Reina. They call him King of the Danzantes, señora, because he was in a movie for your paisanos (fellow countrymen)."

The day drew to a close with no word of José Celis and his danzantes. Finally we went back to Lagos de Moreno.

The next day, when we went to the station to board our train, we saw what the pilgrim trains were like, for several cars were in the siding waiting for departure. They were freight boxcars, filled with wooden horses across which rough planks were laid to form seats for the passengers. Pilgrims huddled so closely on them that I wondered that they could breathe. Those unable to secure places on the improvised benches sat in the doorways, hanging their feet outside.

As soon as I reached home, I telephoned the plant where José worked. A man's voice told me that though they knew nothing, they feared the worst. "When we know anything definite, señora, we will let you know."

Then I read the papers. Apparently the pilgrim train had had orders to go into sidetrack at Cazadero to let the regular passenger train for Guadalajara pass. Behind the Guadalajara train was a freight. When the pilgrim train returned to the main line, it was directly in front of the freight, which overtook it and plowed into it. Immediately a fire broke out that burned for more than twelve hours. One car of the freight was filled with sugar. A reporter described the rivers of boiling molasses that flowed over the victims pinned beneath the wreckage. Many who were injured, some fatally, begged the doctors to treat them at once, so that they might hurry on to San Juan to honor the Virgencita.

As I talked to danzantes who had relatives on the pilgrim train, I learned what the radio can mean to the illiterate.[1] A malinche told Nieves and me of her experience.

I was working the *maza*[2] and getting ready to cook the tortillas at my regular place. Sí, señora, I sell tortillas on the sidewalk of a street near the San Cosme Market. I have a little portable *brasero*,[3] and I make and sell the tortillas on the sidewalk. And just as I was preparing my maza, the woman who sells pumpkin seed and peanuts down at the corner came up and threw a newspaper down in front of me.

"There it is!" she said. "There are the pictures on the front page!"

"What is it?" I asked her.

"It is the wreck of the pilgrim train. Was not your Pancho on that train? And your Conchita? And your brother, too? It tells all about it. Read it!"

"Mother of God!" I screamed. "I do not know how to read. Tell me what these horrible pictures mean!"

But she could not read either, señora, nor could I find on all that sidewalk anybody who could read that terrible newspaper. Then I heard that they were telling the names of the dead and the injured on the radio. I started running, señora. Running like a crazy woman. My compadre, Juan, has a *puesto* in Tacubaya and in that puesto he has a radio. I ran and ran toward his puesto. At times I fell down, but always I got up again. At last I arrived and I saw there in the street all around Juan's puesto many danzantes — all silent, all listening. All listening to the names of the injured and the dead at Cazadero.

Sometimes a woman would burst into tears and her friends would lead her away. Once a woman fell fainting on the sidewalk when the radio said the name of her son among the dead.

All the rest of the day we waited, señora. When the hour to close the puesto arrived, a policeman came and said that it was the law to close the puesto, but it was not the law to stop the radio. Juan put out the light and closed the puesto, but he did not leave, señora. All that night, inside the puesto in the dark, he turned the knobs of the radio. And outside on the sidewalk, we danzantes crowded close to listen.

I sat on the ground and leaned against the side of the puesto. After midnight I fell asleep. I was awakened at daylight by the other danzantes shaking me. The names of my husband and daughter had just come over the radio.

Sí, señora. My daughter is the Conchita whose dancing you admired at the Villa last year. She is fourteen years old and she is a good little daughter.

The danzantes told me, señora, that my husband and my daughter would be on the train that would arrive from Querétaro that morning. They said that I must await them at the railroad hospital with food for them.

I took a bus to my home, señora. And there I found my five younger children asleep. My neighbor said that my oldest son had gone to Querétaro to look for his father, his sister, and his uncle. I said a little prayer for his uncle, my brother, because the radio had not mentioned him. My neighbor said that she would feed and care for my younger children but, since she is a widow with children of her own, I could not tell her that I must take food to the hospital.

So I walked to the place where I sell tortillas because, señora, I had not the money to take the bus. My place on the sidewalk was bare! Of course, I did not really expect that my brasero and my maza would be there. I had run away and left them. It would have been a miracle had they remained there. And so, señora, I had no food for my injured, and no way to earn the money with which to buy it. The train would arrive that morning and I had no money!

Then I did a thing of which I am not ashamed. No, señora, I am not ashamed. If I had to live that awful experience over again, I would do exactly as I did then. This is what I did: I pulled my rebozo over my forehead and draped the lower part across my mouth. I walked along the streets of the center of the city and I said, "A charity! For the love of God, a charity! My husband, my daughter, my brother were in the wreck at Cazadero. A charity, for the love of God!"

And God was good to me, señora. Almost everybody I met dropped money in my hand. I bought rice, coffee, and milk. Also, a chicken. I had food for my husband and my little daughter.

No, señora. My brother did not return. But my daughter saw him. She saw him, señora, standing upright on top of the wreckage with flames all around him. She screamed. "Uncle! *Tío mío!*"

But he did not move, señora. She begged the people by her stretcher to rescue him, but they moved her away and she saw him no more. He was dead, señora. They told my oldest son about it later.

Ay, señora! He was killed by an iron rod, a beam, that entered his body at the back and went completely through his chest. It had held him upright in the fire.

A few days after I had called him, the man at the bottling plant phoned me.

"They have found the body of José Celis, señora, and they are bringing it to the capital for burial."

"And his señora? What about her, señor?"

"It appears that she perished by his side, señora — though the message from Querétaro made no mention of Jesusita."

"Made no mention of his wife?"

"No, señora. But I know that she was with him. They will have the velación tomorrow night. Can you and your husband come, señora?"

Bill and I went to the velación in the one-room house in the *Colonia de los Doctores.* Just inside the door was a rusty black coffin flanked by tall, brass candlesticks holding wax candles. Four danzantes stood at the four corners of the casket as a guard of honor. I peered into the shadows for another casket, but saw only one.

José's sister came forward with a pretty speech of welcome. Then she brought chairs for us and introduced an aunt and José's godmother. As they moved away, I saw José's wife waiting behind them.

"Oh, Jesusita, I am so glad to see you! They told me you were killed in the wreck, too."

"No, señora. I decided not to go. It was too hard a trip for the baby." And then she began to cry.

A few days after the funeral, I was having breakfast in bed when Nieves announced that the widow of José was at the gate.

"Bring her in," I told her.

The little dimpled woman, dressed in shabby black, twisted her hands nervously as she crossed the room to my bedside.

Señora, I have come to confess the truth to you. Though José Celis did marry with me — truly he did, señora — he was not living with me at the time of his death. No, señora, he was living with another. He came to my house only to see the baby. And, señora, this other one, the one of whom they told you, she died in the wreck with him. Her name was María de Jesús. She was Jesusita.

I met José when I was very young and I became completely enamored of him — completely, señora, — but he did not tell me about this other one. I did not know of Jesusita until after I had married with him.

Jesusita was a widow when José met her. He was pledged to the danza, señora, and he wanted to learn all that he could because he wanted to be a jefe, a capitán. Jesusita was a capitana and she knew much — much that was good and, also, much that was bad. There was much that she could teach him. Also, señora, she was alone. And so she joined with José and they lived together.

Later I met José, and after four months he told me that he loved me very much and that he wanted me to marry with him. And so I did. See, señora, here are my papers. Here is the marriage certificate, for we were married by the civil ceremony which is the marriage that is recognized by the law. Is it not so? And here is José's *sindicato*[4] card where he wrote my name as his wife. And they tell me that with these, I can collect the money that the railroads will pay for his death.

And now, señora, I have come to ask a favor of you. You see, the brothers of my husband, they do not want me to collect this money. They wish to collect it and to divide it equally, so they say, among each brother and each sister and me, giving me just one small part. But José married with me and I am the mother of his son! I can collect all of this money and I shall do so. Therefore, señora, this is the favor I ask of you: will you take this money and keep it for me?

I do not want it for myself. I will never spend one centavo of it. I have always worked and I shall continue to do so. Sí, señora, I am a washerwoman and I support myself. But this money from the railroad, I wish to save it for my son. When I collect it, señora, will you keep it for me?

Ay, señora! I have suffered, José suffered, too. He was a good man, señora. And this Jesusita, as I have said, she knew much. She knew about the danza, and also — how can I explain it to you? — she knew how to put a spell.

She was very good at spells, señora. Do you remember that my leg was burned? Well, at that time she put a spell on me. I lost the use of my legs. I had no strength at all. Jesusita put a spell on me and she made me suffer until I advised José to return to live with her. Sí, señora, José returned to Jesusita four months before the baby was born. She was a bad woman, señora. Besides knowing about spells, she was a great drinker of pulque. José came back to me when little José was five months old. He had decided that we would go to Guanajuato to live — he, little José, and I.

No, señora, we were not able to live happily in Guanajuato. At first we were and then we were not. You see, as I have said, Jesusita knew about spells and when we were living happily in Guanajuato, she put a spell on José. One night he had a vision. He saw something. He saw Jesusita. He saw her sitting right there in the corner. I could not see her, señora, but José could. She put a spell on him and he could see her sitting there in the corner beside our bed.

We came back here and José returned to live with Jesusita. Ay, señora, I have suffered, but I loved him. I loved him very, very much. I loved him so much that if he wanted to go live with Jesusita, I wanted him to go with her. She was very jealous and she had quarrels and fights with him. But I, I could not fight. I loved him too much.

Si, señora, he came often to my house to see the baby. He loved little José! And my son is very like his father. Have you noticed it? You know how José always walked with both hands rammed in the pockets of his trousers? Little José does the same. Exactly the same.

Sí, señora, I shall continue to *andar con los danzantes* because I want little José to be trained as his father was trained, but I shall not dance. No. Pues, señora, some of the danzantes are nice to me. Very nice. And some prefer the memory of Jesusita. You see, she had a high place among them. She was a capitana and she knew much.

You remember José brought little José and me with him when he came to tell you about the excursion? I knew that Jesusita would go with him on that excursion. It was her custom. At first I planned to go, too. Then I decided that the trip would be too hard on the baby. As we left your house, I said to José, "What will you do? The señora knows me now as your señora, but when you meet her in front of the church at San Juan, I will not be with you. Another will be with you. What will you tell the señora?"

And he said, "I shall explain everything to the señora!" — but I did not really think that he would.

He was planning to live with me after he came back from San Juan. He told me so that day. And the next morning came the news of the horrible wreck.

I went to Querétaro all alone. Ay, señora! And there, lying with a lot of the dead, I found him. I found José dead. He was terribly burned, his arms, his chest, and one side of his face. I identified him and claimed his body and brought him back in his casket.

I found her, too. She was there with the dead. But I did not claim her body. I did not identify her. I could not forget, señora. Had it been only that she had loved José, I would have brought her back. I loved him, too. But that time when I lost the strength in my legs until José returned to her, that I could not forget! And so I left her there and they buried her in a casket of wood furnished by the government. I bought a special one lined with metal so that José would not be decomposed at the time of his funeral.

The brothers of José wished to have the velación at their house but I would not allow it. I insisted that it be in my house. Sí, señora, many danzantes came. Even after you and the señor had gone they continued to arrive. And they are going to raise the cross tonight. Can you come? Sí, señora, the night of the velación, they made a cross of lime and left it there. Tonight they will raise it, and later they will take it to the cemetery and place it at the foot of the grave. It is the custom.

Ay, señora, life is hard, very hard. Sometimes my poor heart can hardly bear the suffering that I have. See, underneath my black dress I have to wear a bright red blouse because of my heart. The black makes my heart sick, and so I have to wear red next to my skin underneath my mourning.

Are you going to Chalma this year, señora? Everyone will be in mourning — the danzantes will all wear black bands on their arms. Sí, señora, I plan to go because they will honor the danzantes who were killed at Cazadero. And José was a capitán. It will be in honor of him. Si, señora. And of Jesusita, too. After all, she was a capitana. Truly I would have brought her back if she had not put a spell on me. I had no strength in my legs, no strength at all! Ay, señora, do you blame me that I did not bring her back?

Sí, señora, there is one who can teach you in José's place. His name is Pancho. He broke his leg and cannot work. He will have plenty of time to tell you about the danza.

I have to be in the offices of the railroad at twelve o'clock, señora. Many thanks for this favor you are doing me. I shall bring you the money as soon as they give it to me. And now good afternoon, señora. *¡Muy buenas tardes!*

She received no money from the railroad that day nor for many days afterward. Brigida the cook, a buxom young woman from a village near Texcoco, had decided opinions about the matter.

"She will never be paid," predicted Brigida. "All the world knows that the marriage by the church is the real marriage, and she admits that she married José only by the civil ceremony. She was no wife!"

One morning in April the widow came to our house in high spirits. The railroad had paid her. Half the money was gone already, but she had brought the rest for me to keep for her. Quite by chance, an agent of the undertaking establishment that had buried José was in the bank when she arrived with the 5,000 peso check. He had immediately come to her assistance, identifying her when she "made her mark," and telling them how she wanted her cash. Then he had escorted her to the undertaking parlor to pay her bill.

"How much did they charge you?" I asked.

"Twelve hundred and thirty-five pesos, señora."

A third secretary of our embassy had died shortly after José. His funeral was in quiet, good taste by the same funeral establishment for less than 900 pesos.

"Are you sure it was twelve hundred and thirty-five pesos?" I asked.

"Sí, señora."

"You have the bill?"

"No, señora. I asked them for a bill, but they said that since I could not read, it was not necessary."

"I think we should call on the undertakers," I told her.

And so the widow, my daughter, and I went down to the under-taking establishment. We talked to a businesslike individual who consulted a file and sent us to the man who had charge of the Celis funeral.

"Señor," I said, glancing from the elegant middle-aged mestizo to the bronze nameplate on his desk, "I feel that you made a mistake with this funeral. I personally know of a more recent funeral by you that made a better appearance and cost less. May I have an itemized bill of the Celis funeral?"

"Why do you want an itemized bill, señora?"

"I want it for two reasons, señor. First, in behalf of my friend, the widow, who, as you know, cannot read. I want to explain each item to her."

"We have done that, señora."

"I believe not, señor. And second, I am writing a book about the danzantes and want to include a complete account of the death of Capitán José Celis."

"When do you plan to publish this book, señora?"

"As soon as I finish it, señor."

"In Mexico, or in the United States?"

"Perhaps in both, señor. And the bill, please?" holding out my hand.

"I cannot give you an itemized bill of the funeral."

"Why not, señor?"

There was a long, thoughtful pause. Then he said impressively, "Because I am forbidden to do so."

I opened my bag and got out a notebook and a pencil. I opened the notebook and poised my pencil.

"Permit me to ask you, who forbids you to give me this bill, señor?"

He eyed the pencil, then became more impressive. "Counsel for the company has advised them not to give itemized statements to anybody."

"Why not?"

"Because, señora, prices are constantly changing and we do not let anyone know our prices for that reason."

"I am not sure I understand, señor. Do you mean, for example, that if someone of my family should pass away and I should engage you for the funeral you would refuse to give me an itemized bill?"

"Absolutely! I would refuse to give you an itemized bill!"

"I assure you, señor, I would refuse to pay you. My lawyer would see you through the courts, and, until you presented me with an itemized bill, you would not get one centavo!"

He shrugged his shoulders and spread his hands. "Ay, we have many problems . . . ." he began.

"And you would have many more, señor, if our hypothetical case were a reality. All the world, following my example would refuse to pay you for your services. And what would counsel for the company advise you then?"

"Madam," with a French accent, "I am not a lawyer."

"Forgive me, señor," writing industriously, "perhaps I should not complain. This is most interesting data. But," looking up again, "on one point I must ask your assistance. Some of my friends with whom I have discussed this case insist that you did not have to pay the government to bring this body from Querétaro. I am under the impression that you did . . . ."

"Oh yes, we did. Yes, we paid the government."

"Will you look that up and tell me exactly how much you paid the government."

"With pleasure. Tomorrow . . . ."

"Will you look it up now, señor?"

Reluctantly he opened a drawer and fished out some papers clipped together. As he sorted them, I stood up and frankly read over his shoulder.

"There! There it is," I pointed, " 'government one hundred and fifteen pesos.' What was that for?"

"It was for fees."

"What fees?"

"Pues . . . various fees."

"And that next item, señor: 'thirty pesos for uniformed attendants.' Why?"

"They were the pallbearers, señora."

"But the danzantes did not want them. They wanted to carry the casket themselves. Why did you send pallbearers to these poor people?"

"Ay, señora, these sindicatos. They make us do so many things."

Knowing little about the unions, I was unable to argue that point, but I had a low opinion of any group who would exploit the Cazadero situation.

"Look at that!" I pointed again. "Twenty-five pesos for *tramites*. What tramites?"

He waved his hand. "Tramites — as you know — tramites!"

"Sí. What tramites?"

"Errands like . . . like taking papers to offices."

"But you have complete funeral equipment here — I have read your advertisements. What offices would you have to take papers to?"

He thought for a moment. Then, "Government offices!" he stated triumphantly.

"Twenty-five pesos in order to pay 115 pesos. Do you send your errand boys in taxis and instruct them to tip the elevator operators?"

"They are very busy, the people in the government offices. On many occasions, señora, we have to send again and again."

"And then you have to charge it to the poor washerwoman?"

Again he shrugged.

"Señor, there is one item about which there can be no explanation. Definitely, it is a mistake. The one about the lot at the cemetery. The widow paid you for the lot before the funeral. I myself heard her statement to that effect to one of your thirty-peso uniformed attendants the day of the funeral. He assured her that it was duly noted. Here —" pointing it out, "you charged her fifty pesos more on it when she received the check from the railroad."

"Ay, señora. You are right. Forgive me! She must be reimbursed." Opening another drawer and taking a fifty-peso bill from it, "You are right. It was a mistake!"

And that was all I was able to collect from him, though we argued in his office for more than an hour.

Often that spring, as the danzantes talked of velaciones, funerals, and Masses for the dead, I heard them say, "It is the custom."

Always my immediate thought was "I must ask José to explain that!"

But José Celis was gone. So were his personnel of twenty-two danzantes, including my friends, La Negra and Capitana Natalia Hidalgo, all lost in the wreck at Cazadero. And in a backyard of the Lomas de Chapultepec, blistered by the sun and beaten by the rains, a little wooden cart was slowly falling to pieces.

Fiesta at Tlaltelolco

TRUE TO HER PROMISE, the widow of José Celis appeared at our house one day with a man who had a leg in a cast and walked with crutches. This was Don Pancho who had broken a leg and, therefore, would have time to teach me about the dance.

Unlike José, who had begun dancing when he was five, Don Pancho had not entered the dance until he was grown. At a crisis in his early twenties he had made a vow to be a danzante for the rest of his life and at thirty-eight was still keeping his vow. Taller than José and inclined to gaunt slenderness, he had the light skin of the mestizo, expressive dark eyes, and longish wavy hair. He used a whistle-like tuner for his mandolin, which he played, he said, because he had little ability with a concha. But he knew the words, and, after a fashion, the tunes of many alabanzas, and was willing to teach them to me. Also, he knew the danza of the Bajío from a subjefe's point of view.

With the rank of colonel in the dance he was a person of importance on weekends. The rest of the week he was a furniture hoister on a moving van — a position that he regarded far beneath him.

Ay, señora! I have sacrificed much to the danza. As of a truth you must have noticed, I am an intelligent man. It is true that I do not know how to read or write but, señora, I have a marvelous memory. So the opportunities I have had to learn to read and write, I have not accepted — because I am afraid I would begin to depend on the little pieces of paper carried in my pocket and lose my powerful memory. Sí, señora, they say that happens sometimes.

With my intelligence and my memory, without doubt, I have the capacity for a better job than the one I now have. But where, señora, could I find a job with a high salary where they would give me eight days or fifteen days off now and then for the obligation of the danza?

I have a *promesa* and every year I must go to a fiesta on Culiacan Mountain in the Bajío. About halfway up there is a cave that is famous among the danzantes, señora, and we always stop and spend the night in this cave. Then the next day we climb to the top of the mountain and have the fiesta there. It is one of our important fiestas and it takes at least fifteen days away from the capital. Do you think any of the big companies would let me go for that length of time every year, señora, as well as to Chalma and to San Juan de los Lagos?

As I have said, I have sacrificed much to keep my vow and comply with the demands of my little father, San Miguel.

Like José, Don Pancho came to me several times with the question, "With what motive do you search for these data?" — which always led to a discussion of Catholic and Protestant faiths. With Don Pancho I hit upon a statement that served so well it became my stock reply: "Don Pancho, why do we go to church, anyway? Is it not because we hope that there is something better after this life and we want to share in it? Now if we are going to the *zócalo* and you go by the street of Tacuba and I insist on going by the street of Madero, should that make us enemies? We expect to meet in the zócalo eventually, do we not?"

Among the things he taught me were the names of various articles of the dance uniform of the Bajío:

> The crown — feather headdress
> The ribbons — streamers down the back
> The cape
> The deep cuffs
> Circular collar
> The scepter — "Carried by the jefe, señora."
> The bow and arrows — "The proper arms for their defense, señora, carried by all the soldiers."
> The quiver — for the arrows
> The talpan — "That which hangs down in front, señora." (loin-cloth?)
> The shield
> The corbatio — ornate little shield dangling over the knee
> The sandal — "Of *encinia* Azteca, señora." (most danzantes call them *huaraches*)
> The tanico — small bag hanging from the belt "in which the ancient Chichimecs carried obsidian arrowheads and stones for their slings."

As I had done with several danzantes, I showed him a reproduction in color of Duran's Calendar.[1]

"Look, señora!" Don Pancho exclaimed as I opened the book. "There is a dance that we used to do in my *tierra*"[2] — a ranch near San Miguel de Allende. "They do the same dance in other parts, too, but we did it better in my tierra than anywhere else."

After describing the various formations along the lines of the calendar, he said, "And, señora, in my tierra, each danzante brought fruit — beautiful, fresh pineapples that we grow there, or some other large, delicious fruit — or sometimes vegetables, if they were large and beautiful. And, as we finished the dance, señora, we paused, covering these lines in this picture, and put our offering on the ground, so that when we marched off this very picture was left there on the ground of the churchyard, formed of fruit and vegetables. Then all the poor of my tierra came forward and took the offering, for it was really for them."

I have never shown that picture to a Conchero who did not see a dance in it.

Don Pancho's ideas of chieftainship were those of a subjefe.

"A capitán has many obligations to his personnel, Señora Marta, but in these days most capitanes forget that."

"What are some of those obligations, Don Pancho?"

"If a soldier is sick, señora, it is the obligation of his capitán to call a doctor. If a soldier is arrested and jailed, it is the obligation of his capitán to raise the money to pay his fine."

"How does the capitán raise the money?"

"By each danzante paying a quota of what is needed, señora."

"Who takes charge of the money?"

"The sargento. He has a list of the money raised and of the expenses paid. When there is money left over he gives it to the family of the unfortunate soldier."

"Is this sort of business discussed in the oratory, Don Pancho, or is it arranged on the outside?"

"In the oratory, señora. After the obligation there is always discussion and voting. That is why it is important for you to know how to address the altar. In the oratory, it is necessary to address the altar before expressing an opinion."

According to Don Pancho, the way to address the altar is, "In the name of God (in the names of all the saints on the altar), the Four Winds, and the Blessed Conquering Spirits who left us as remembrances these *incinias* and obligations of the sainted religion."

Once, after his leg had mended, he missed a lesson.

"Pardon me, señora, but I could not come last time. I was *andando* ["going about," literally, walking] conquering folks for my *Broncos*. You see, I am jefe of a group of Broncos, or *Brutos*, as they are called, and . . . ."

"But Don Pancho!" I interrupted, "I thought you were a conchero."

"I am a conchero, señora. I dance in the circle always. But I am also jefe of the Broncos. They follow me in the dance."

"Broncos?" I repeated.

"Sí, señora. That means Unbaptized Ones."

"¡De veras!"

"Sí, señora. And when my leg was broken, the jefe of the mesa to which I pertain tried to make my Broncos turn their backs on me and follow him. Imagine, señora!"

"How awful!"

"Sí, señora. It made me furious. It filled me with repugnance for him."

"Repugnance?" I wondered if it meant the same in Spanish as in English. "What does that mean, Don Pancho?"

"As we in Mexico use that word . . . pues, señora — it means . . . it means, *indigestion mental.*"

"I see. And are the Broncos similar to the Concheros?"

"Sí, señora. And they are different. They dance to the music of the concha, but always it is tuned in seconds."

"In seconds?"

"Sí, señora. This is the incinia of the Broncos, or the Brutos, who are not baptized; they do not sing alabanzas, the *incinia* of their march is that it is always directed by the tunes of their jefes — that is, the first and second jefes direct them by the music that they play, señora — and they are in accord with the dances of the Conquest."

"How interesting!"

"Sí, señora. They dance in two parallel lines and that gives them four ends, or as we say, Four Winds."

My Spanish teacher came in just as I asked, "What does *incinia* mean, Don Pancho? I cannot find it in my dictionary."

"There is no such word," broke in my teacher. "He means *ensenanza* or teaching."

"Then you should get another dictionary, señora," Don Pancho replied, as if the teacher had not spoken, "for clearly, the one you have is no good. Incinia is a word we use often, like incinia of the Brutos, or incinia of the banners. You know — *incinia.*"

He left almost immediately but the next day he came again.

"Señora Marta," he began before taking his hat off. "That profesora who was here yesterday — it is better you pay no attention to what she says because, clearly, she is an ignorant person. She does not even know incinia which is a good word and one we Mexicans use all the time."

"I am glad you came today, Don Pancho, for I want to ask you more about the Broncos."

"Bueno, Señora Marta. That is why I am here, to invite you to a fiesta at Tlaltelolco Sunday. The Broncos will dance there and you can learn more about them."

The following Sunday I set out for the fiesta at historic Tlaltelolco where the Aztecs made their last stand against the Spaniards. Shortly afterward the Christian church was erected above the ruins of the ancient temple. In the sixteenth century it was a church, a convent, and a college — the College of the Holy Cross (*el Colegio de la Santa Cruz*). Under President Juarez' Reform Laws the property was confiscated, the sanctuary converted into a warehouse for the customs service and eventually the convent and college became a military prison.[3] In 1945 the Avila Camacho government returned the warehouse to the Catholic Church. The old convent and college remained a military prison.

When I arrived at the fiesta the following Sunday the spaces in front of the customs building and beside the church were filled with dancers. I saw nobody I knew near the entrance and strolled about the atrio looking for my friends.

"Buenos días, Señora Marta!" called a voice.

By the customs platform stood María and her husband Juan, danzantes from Peña Pobre and members of a mesa that was in the same capitanía as was José's. While I was greeting them, José's brother, Mateo, came up.

"Muy buenos días, señora!" he said cordially. "Have you seen Pancho yet? Would you like me to find him for you?"

But apparently Don Pancho had not yet arrived. When Mateo came back I was alone.

"Give me that negative!" he snorted, his small eyes snapping.

"What negative?" I asked, completely taken back.

"The one of the picture of my little brother!"

"You mean the picture of José that I gave to your family?"

"Sí. Give me that negative," he insisted brusquely, "and give it to me now."

This was too much.

"Look, Mateo," I said, "José gave that picture to my husband and me in friendship with no mention of anyone else, and . . . ."

"And I want that negative now," he repeated.

"Do not interrupt me," I told him severely. "I had two copies of the photograph made and gave them to the widow and to his family, because I heard that they had no pictures of him."

"Sí. It is the truth. That is the negative I want — and I want it now."

"You will not get it," I snapped; "since you speak to me in this manner you will get nothing. Do you understand? Nothing!"

He opened his mouth to protest.

"And I want to hear no more about it," I added. "Not one word!"

He drew his mouth in a grim line, whirled, and stalked off.

At that time I had gone to no velaciones in the Bajío where danzante altars have photographs of dead jefes on them. Then, too, I was yet unacquainted with *las ánimas* and I had never heard of *la cosa*. A few years later I would have been less angry with Mateo.

Near the customs building I ran into short, darkskinned Juana Velasco de Hernández and her middle-aged husband, Florentino, important in a uniform of yellow silk with red appliqué in fretted design. He was an officer of Manuel Luna's group, and I had known them several months.

"Where is Don Manuel?" I asked. "Is he here?"

"No, Señora Marta," replied Florentino. "He has gone to Chalma to buy a lot."

"To buy a lot? Is he going to live there?"

"No, señora, he has to live in the capital because his work is here. He has worked at a textile factory near San Simón for twenty years. His son Tiburcio works there, too."

"And this lot in Chalma — why has he gone to buy it?"

"It is so that at the fiesta there, each banner (group, or mesa) under his orders will have a place to camp."

Since Chalma, normally a small village, sometimes expands to a population of over 100,000 at fiesta-time, this showed considerable forethought on the General's part.

"There will be a special Mass at the fiesta in Chalma next month, Señorita Marta," continued Florentino. "It will be for those who died in the wreck of Cazadero."

Don Florentino, like many old-fashioned Indians, made no distinction between "señorita" and "señora," addressing me in the form that came to his tongue at the moment.

"On the tenth of June, señora," said Juana, "there will be another fiesta here in Tlaltelolco and they say that the padre will recognize some, and some he will not." (I inferred that he would not permit the unrecognized to dance.)

"In May we will have a fiesta in the little chapel on the top of the *cerro* at Santa Cruz de Ayotuzco," said Florentino. "Have you been to a rehearsal, señorita?"

"No, Don Florentino, and I should love to go to one!"

"I am going to begin rehearsals at Ayotuzco in two weeks. Would you like to come?"

"With much pleasure, Don Florentino, and many thanks."

"I will come to your house Sunday, señorita, and we will arrange it. Now I must return to the circle. Con su permiso, señorita."

After Mass I slowly searched the crowded atrio for Don Pancho. Finally Mateo Celis and a small popeyed man came up to say that he was dancing in the big circle near the other end of the platform and we quickly made our way there. According to Mexican custom, Mateo hissed at Pancho.

Pancho was regally grand in beaded headdress with three ostrich plumes of green, white, and red, a green velvet cape, a dyed green sweatshirt, beaded collar, cuffs, talpan, and corbatio, and brass sleigh bells around his ankles. An impressive shield of Aztec design hung from his arm. He was playing his Chinese mandolin and dancing in the center of the circle. When Mateo finally attracted his attention, he danced gracefully to the edge of the circle, put out a hand to me, bowed low, then danced back to the center.

"Golly, the King of Egypt!" said someone in the crowd behind us.

Shortly afterward Don Pancho left the circle to introduce us to the Broncos who danced their spirited dance in two parallel lines nearby. They were all that he had promised in their striking uniforms of tans, browns, and reds. They stopped dancing and broke their lines to pose shyly with Don Pancho for photographs. Since all had been born in León, they were called Los Broncos de León, though some had lived in the capital for years.

After lunch I came around the corner of the church to find the Concheros gathered in a tight little group beside the wrought iron fence. A Mexican photographer, apparently a professional, had climbed it as far as he could. He clung there by his toes and one arm. With the other he held his camera as high as possible above his head. On the ground below, the danzantes shook their fists and shouted at him. A capitán I knew seemed to be delivering an ultimatum. When he turned and saw me watching them, he shrugged his shoulders, grinned sheepishly, and sauntered away. The others gradually dispersed.

In late afternoon the sky darkened and the wind blew cold. Most of the public and the vendors had gone and the fiesta had almost ended. Florentino's invitation to the rehearsal at Ayotuzco meant that Don Manuel Luna's group had made me one of them and I could congratulate myself that I was still walking with the dancers.

But I missed José.

Afternoon Tea and Rehearsal at Ayotuzco

Don Florentino had more in mind than plans for a dance rehearsal when he came to our house the following Sunday afternoon accompanied by his stepson Juan, José Cortés, Nicolás whose last name I never knew, and two teen-agers, Luciano and Tomás. They had come, said Florentino, to play and sing for me.

As soon as they were seated in the living room, Don Florentino began to question me along the old theme, "Con que motivo . . . ,"[1] while the others listened attentively. Somehow I felt that my future among the danzantes might depend upon my answers, so I elaborated. In addition to my stock reply about going to the zócalo, I told them that I was interested in the history of Mexico and that after reading the old books, was convinced that the dance was of ancient origin, particularly the Concheros who probably were, in my opinion, the modern vestiges of the temple dancers of old Tenoxtitlan.[2]

"It is my ambition," I said, "to write a book about the dance, so that all the world may know it as I know it."

"¡Claro!" ¡Claro!"[3] murmured the five.

"I want to tell the truth in my book, señores."

"Sí, como no!"[4] exclaimed Juan Martínez, Florentino's stepson.

"I tell no lies about my motives," I went on, "and I expect no lies from those who undertake to explain the dance to me."

"¡Claro! ¡Claro!" — and everybody seemed satisfied.

Don Florentino then informed us that there was to be a new mesa in Huitzilapan, the tierra, or birthplace, of Señor Cortés.

"Señor Cortés will be the primer capitán, señora, and Señor Nicolás will be his segundo. We are all going to the ceremony of the blessing of the banner there in the month of August and we have come to invite you and the señor to go, too."

We accepted, of course, and they seemed pleased.

"Señora, you have many photographs of danzantes, have you not?" prompted Don Florentino.

I brought out my box of photographs and they had a pleasant half-hour identifying themselves and their friends.

"Here I am," said Don Florentino, "and here is my compadrito, Manuel Luna."

"See! This is me," Juan pointed to the devil outside a dance circle. It was a picture that Bill had taken from the church-top in Ameyalco the day the villagers put me in jail.

"How do you know that is you?" I asked, looking at the tiny blob.

"By the uniform of the devil," he replied, "because I was the *flaxique* on that day."

"And who is he?"

"He is the sargento who keeps the order, señora."

The conversation then turned to Chalma, for they were planning to go to a fiesta there.

"Do you know, Señora Marta, that the Señor de Chalma is very much a punisher?" asked Florentino.

"No, Don Florentino. Is he?"

"He used to be more so than he is now. In the old days at nearly every fiesta someone received justice. I remember one year there were two señoritas who had lovers. They all started for Chalma but on the way the two men decided to go no further. The two señoritas went on anyway. More than that, señorita, they went on as if they were like all the other pilgrims. And as we were returning home at the end of the fiesta, we came to a river that we had to cross. We heard a great cry and we ran to the edge of the water, but all we could see was a bit of the hair of the señorita that swirled under and disappeared as we arrived."

"How awful! What did you do, Don Florentino?"

"There was nothing we could do, señora. She was gone. Afterwards, when we found out the true state of affairs, we knew that the Señor de Chalma had punished her."

The others nodded solemnly.

Then he returned to their plans for the *mesa real* [the first mesa, or dance group, in the vicinity] in Huitzilapan, and I never learned what happened to the other señorita.

"And I have told the boys," he said, "of a little plan of mine and of my compadre Manuel Luna, he who is our capitán general. We have thought this, señora: that it will give us much pleasure if you and the señor will do us the favor to be the godparents of this new banner that we will raise there at that time. Will you and the señor do us this honor, señora?"

I looked at Bill. He nodded.

"Thank you very much, Don Florentino, for this honor."

He turned to the others. "¡Estaís conformes, compadritos?"

"¡El es Dios!" they replied.

I realized that he had been selling us to them all the while.

Still he had not fully accomplished the purpose of his visit. It developed that feathers, particularly ostrich feathers, were difficult to obtain. The danzantes were going to make me a little present of a crown to wear at Huitzilapan. Even now Juana, Florentino's wife, was at home beading a band for my head.

"Perhaps you would like to help us with the feathers, Señora Marta?"

"With pleasure, Don Florentino."

"They will cost seventy-five pesos, more or less. I will investigate, señora, and let you know the exact amount."

The conversation turned to the difficulties of establishing new mesas. "Everywhere we go, we encounter enemies, Señora Marta. We thought we were going to have a strong mesa at Ayotuzco, but the last time we went there, though many had promised to join us, only three or four came."

Then for the benefit of the other danzantes as well as for us, Don Florentino told us about the Fiesta of the Tree of the Sad Night.

Several years ago, señorita, there was a big disgusto among the danzantes and from that time there have been two main divisions of us — besides those caused by the small disgustos that are natural in the danza, señora, — and always those on the opposite side are working against us everywhere.

There was a man who was a politician, or something in the government, señora, and he wanted to make all the danzantes into something called National Dancers. But how could we be National Dancers and a part of the government when we are not political? We are and always have been religious. That is our tradition. We refused.

Also, this politician said that the saints on our banners were idols and he wanted us to replace them with national heroes, men who had never been danzantes and knew nothing about the dance. Imagine, señora!

At first all refused. Then a few danzantes turned against us and promised to do as this politician said. So he arranged a fiesta in honor of the President of the Republic at the Tree of the Sad Night and ordered us to dance in it.

We had a junta at Tello's oratory and this politician came and talked to us. He said that the government would send us to fiestas in trucks so that we would not have to walk or pay bus fare. Then more danzantes placed themselves under his orders. My compadre, Manuel Luna, and several other jefes and I spoke against all this. And do you know what those Stupid Ones did, señorita? They escorted fourteen of us, including my compadre Manuel Luna and me, through the gate into the street!

But we were not without power, Señora Marta. We sent a commission to call on a Person of Great Influence to ask that the matter be explained to the señor President of the Republic on our behalf. And after that there was a junta at Bellas Artes [National Theatre] and some spoke for the plans of this politician, and some spoke saying that the danza was composed of religious dances, that the church and the government were separate, that a church official could not hold a government post, and that if a government official accepted a position in the church, he would lose his government post. That meant, señorita, that if this politician should place himself over the religious dancers, he would lose his position with the government.

When we left Bellas Artes, we who had been thrown out of Tello's oratory went to the house of my compadre Manuel Luna to listen on his radio to the National Fiesta at the Tree of the Sad Night which, as I said, had been organized by this politician.

My compadre Manuel Luna sat in front of his radio to operate it. The rest of us crowded around to listen. We heard the voice of the politician that we knew so well, saying that he had much pleasure in presenting the Danzantes Chichimecas of the Bailes Nacionales [National Dances]. Then we heard the conchas as though far away and the voices of those who had been our friends singing:

> When our America
> Was conquered
> There in the great,
> The great Tenoxtitlan

Then there was silence. We listened closely, señora.

A voice asked, "Are these the Chichimecas of whom you spoke?"

The politician's voice answered that they were.

The other voice said, "But why are they here? This is a national fiesta and we have a band to play the National Anthem and any other national music we may need. These are religious dancers. This is no place for either their music or their dance. Take them to the church down the street and let them dance there."

And so we won, señorita, but after that there was much odium between those who profane the dance by dancing in national fiestas, where there is no altar, and us.

Once at the time of the fiesta at Los Remedios these enemies of ours said that, because of their standing, they could do us harm. They said that when we arrived at Los Remedios they were going to make bonfires of our arms — that means conchas and banners, señora. But we were not without influence. We went to San Bartolo Naucalpan and signed some papers. Then the military headquarters of San Bartolo assigned some soldiers to escort us to Los Remedios. And when we danced up the hill to the church, preceded by our military escort, our enemies could do nothing.

There have been other similar cases, señorita, but we who dance only after asking permission of a santo on an altar hope that it will not always be thus.

As they were leaving Don Florentino asked if we were planning to go to Ayotuzco the next Sunday.

"Yes, Don Florentino, unless your plans have changed."

"They have not changed, señora. Sunday morning I will send someone to accompany you and show you the way."

"Oh, thank you, Don Florentino."

"For nothing, señora. I want you to see the famous little chapel on top of the mountain. The santo is resting there at present."

The following Sunday we found Ayotuzco nestled in the Sierras and the "famous little chapel" perched on one of the mountains that hovered over the village. When we stopped in front of a typical Otomí home — several one-room adobe buildings around an open space — the car was surrounded by the Hernández family — Capitán Juan of the mesa was there, his brother Telésfero, and their wives. Juana and Florentino went to lunch with them, while Telésfero's wife Lupe, a plump, amiable woman who was to become one of my best friends, shared our basket. As we ate she pointed out places of interest nearby, calling special attention to the mountain down which water flowed into the village.

"It brings the water for our fine crops!" she said.

"What is your best crop?" asked Bill.

"Pulque! Do you know, señor? The best pulque in Mexico comes from Ayotuzco."

After we had eaten Don Florentino suggested that we climb the mountain to the shrine, but because of the recent lunch, or the altitude, or perhaps both, I was unable to climb that afternoon.

"Have no care, señora," he said, bustling away. In a short time he returned with a sleek, well-fed horse, a large comfortable saddle, and an intelligent-looking young man in overalls to lead the horse.

As we started off a *tlachiclero,* or pulque maker, came down the path toward us, his bulging pigskin on his back together with the long gourd used to siphon the honey-water from the maguey. My escort immediately launched into the story of pulque, describing all its processes and ending with, "As perhaps you know, señora, the best pulque in Mexico comes from Ayotuzco."

At first Don Florentino, the dutiful host, walked with the man of the family, entertaining him with stories of strange and wonderful plants along the trail. Then he sent the young Otomí to walk with Bill while he himself led the horse. I was glad, for this gave me a chance to ask him something.

"Don Florentino, what does *andan par' alla*[5] mean? Like when we say of a mesa that they andan par' alla?"

"Señorita, that means they have nothing to do with any priest."

"Nothing at all?"

"Nothing, señora."

"Do they have their oratories and their banners blessed by a priest?"

"No, señorita. They have only their ceremonies in their oratories which they themselves perform without the aid of any priests."

"But they dance at fiestas?"

"Sí, señorita."

He changed the subject to the Santo of Ayotuzco. "As I have told you, señora, this santo is a little bit of a punisher. One time a woman was dancing in the circle and an animal of the woods ran between the dancers and tried to bite her legs."

"Horrible!" I shuddered.

"But the santo saved her. The animal was able to fix his teeth only on her clothes and ran away with part of her skirt." He stopped suddenly on the trail. "Do you see that rock, señora? The one on that ridge that points straight to the sky? That is what happened to a woman who failed to keep a promesa to the santo."

"Oh, no!"

"That is what they say, señora! She completely disappeared and, after a time, the people noticed that ugly shaft of unhappy rock standing there for all the world to see."

"Do you believe that, Don Florentino?"

"That is what those of Ayotuzco say, señora. They believe it! Another time there was a man of Ameyalco who was coming from Ameyalco to make a promesa. The day he started here, bringing his offering of money, he met some friends who invited him to drink with them. And he did, señora. He drank with them!"

"¡Qué lástima!"

"With the result, señora, that he spent his offering money to get himself drunk. He did not arrive at Ayotuzco! He paid no promesa."

"And was he punished, too?"

"Sí, señora. A few days later this man's wife was out on the mountain and there was a loud cry. The people ran to see what was the matter, but all they could find were her clothes. They say that a wolf carried her away to eat her. And the man who spent his offering on drink and failed to keep his promesa was left with many small children and no wife to care for him or them."

"What a pity!"

"Sí, señora. This santo is a little bit of a punisher."

A group of pilgrims carrying banners came down the trail. They halted near the Otomí and Bill, who were ahead of us, and sang alabanzas to the music of a fiddle and two guitars. We dropped coins in the box they carried to collect centavitos for their santo. They had stopped before a pyramid of stones a few feet high; smooth stones about the size of a man's fist piled with careful precision in the middle of the trail.

"What are those stones, Don Florentino?"

"They are souvenirs of the pilgrims, señorita."

Later I learned that they were resting places for unhappy spirits of the afterworld when they returned to earth to pay a neglected promesa.

Eventually the horse plodded over a steep incline and we were in the churchyard. The new chapel gleamed white on one side, and a huge green cross rose above us on the other.

"What is this?" asked Bill, picking up a bit of broken pottery near the foot of the cross.

"*Tepalcate.*" I replied. "Preconquest pottery. The early Franciscans planted crosses on the sites of ancient altars. Also, they buried the idols beneath them."

"Do you mean to say that if I dug under this cross, I'd find an idol?" he wanted to know.

"Probably — if you dug deep enough."

"Well I'd certainly want to make sure nobody saw me. I don't like village jails."

"May I show you the Señor de Ayotuzco, señora?" invited Juana.

She led me into the chapel with its stained glass windows and tiled floor.

"Come to this side, señora. You are on the side for señores. The women must go on the right side and the men on the left. Away from the capital they are very strict about this."

The santo, dressed like a charro and mounted on a white horse, was on the altar.

"He is *muy milagroso!* [very miraculous]," whispered Juana.

When we got back to the Hernández home Telésfero's wife told us that we were just in time for the rehearsal. The danzantes, she said, were already inside the oratory waiting for us. We hurried in and they ushered us to chairs in the back of the room near the door.

On the flower-decked altar was one santo and a number of photographs. The Concheros were seated on the floor along both sides of the room and I noticed a new petate, rolled up, leaning against the back wall. Several men squatted in front of the altar going through the ritual of lighting five candles with drippings from a sixth. I was watching them when a sudden gust of air put out one of the candles. The man who seemed to be officiating raised his head and looked at me — just one quick, suspicious glower, and I knew something was wrong. Telésfero and Bill were chatting in undertones, unaware that anything was amiss. Don Florentino rushed about from one danzante to another. One man shook his head stubbornly as Florentino argued with him. Finally Florentino made a speech about "the señores Estony and their friends," quoting his compadre, Manuel Luna, as sharing his opinion. "They are muy fina gente [very fine people]. They have studied the history of our country. They know about the customs left us by our ancestors. But more than that, they are kind to the danzantes and never refuse them when they go to them with problems. You tell me they are not Catholic but I tell you, they are more Catholic than we are," he paused, then asked abruptly:

"¿Estaís conformes, compadritos?"
"¡El es Diós!" was the danzantes' reply.

The vote was not unanimous but a heartwarming majority. Then he continued to speak to the group about the obligation. He exhorted them to always live up to it, without consideration for their own comfort, warning them that the road would be one of sacrifice, and so on.

When he had finished he started strumming his concha and the Concheros formed a circle around the room and began to dance. The floor was of packed mud, and after half an hour's spirited practice the air was hazy with dust. One young danzante tired more quickly than his fellows and leaned panting against the door. Don Florentino pounced on him.

"Why have you left the circle? No one gave you permission to do so. Go back to the circle and dance."

"But I am tired," protested the boy.

"Seeking your own comfort after one little hour. Dance, I tell you!"

"But I am very tired."

"That makes no difference," snorted Florentino. "You have sworn to be a danzante, to suffer whatever sacrifice may be demanded along the way. You cannot rest now, or at any other time when you are ordered to dance. Go back, I tell you!" — and grasping his shoulders, Florentino whirled him back into the circle.

We began to cough from the dust, and Don Florentino suggested that we sit outside where we would be more comfortable. Soon the rehearsal was over, and the señora Hernández invited us to have some pulque.

"The best pulque of the capital comes from here. You must not go away without trying it."

She ushered us into her kitchen, a one-room house of fair dimensions with several metal portable braseros on the floor along one wall.

She and two other women slapped tortillas out of a bluish corn dough, and cooked them on a griddle over a brasero. A young man brought a pail of fresh pulque and, pouring it into cups and *jicaras,* or small gourds, offered it to us. For pulque, I suppose it was good, but we sipped it sparingly.

Meanwhile Telésfero entertained us with a lesson in Otomí. He would touch an object — a cup, a gourd, or my bag — and say the Otomí word for it. We would repeat it after him, and he would correct our pronunciation.

As they took the tortillas off the griddle they passed them around, piping hot. We sprinkled salt on them, rolled them into cylinders, and ate them. They were delicious, but I had to overcome a prejudice against their bluish color.

When the sun had disappeared behind the mountain we took our leave. The Hernández family, including the grandmother and the children, accompanied us to the car, thanked us for coming to their humble village and urged us to come again. Their "¡Adios!" and "¡Vaya con Dios!" followed us as we drove away into the fragrance of the night.

Godparents of a Flag — Huitzilapan

HUITZILAPAN IS ANOTHER HILL VILLAGE, not far from Toluca in the Sierras. When we arrived with our picnic lunch for the baptism of the flag, Don Florentino was waiting for us in the door of the oratory, an ell of the Cortés' house at the edge of town.

"Where is your crown, Señora Marta?" he wanted to know.

Bill handed him the bundle containing my new headband and feathers, and he hurriedly put my headdress together. After presenting it to the Four Winds, he placed it with the other headdresses hanging from the frame around the top of the altar which, for a danzante altar, was rather bare. On it was an image of the Virgin in a handsome *nicho*, a boxlike receptacle for carrying images, an oil painting of the Virgin, and a few photographs, probably of dance chiefs who had died.

"What a lovely Virgin!" I exclaimed as we paused before the image.

"That one is San Juanita de los Lagos," explained Florentino. "And this," indicating a plump white-haired woman, "is the señora Torres who has loaned it to us."

The woman beamed and lifted the image from the altar to give us a closer view. Then she invited Florentino and me to call on the Virgen-cita upon our return to the capital, and I told her that we would be happy to do so.

When we had finished in the oratory Don Florentino asked us to assemble in the road in front of the house where he arranged the procession. Bill and Florentino went ahead so that Bill could take pictures as we moved along.

We marched down an ancient cobblestone trail, flanked by a cobblestone fence curbing stunted trees. Just ahead of us frisked the flaxique, or red devil, his mask hanging down his back or pushed back on his head most of the time. The danzantes played their conchas and sang alabanzas as we marched.

El Diablo

The trail turned sharply and we began to climb, leaving the stunted trees behind. Another procession came up a converging trail and merged with ours, each member reverently kneeling in front of the Virgin before taking a place in our ranks.

At last we reached the end of the trail, which wound two and a half times around the conical mountain, and drew near the white church perched on the top. The first thing I saw as I passed through the gate in the whitewashed wall was a huge green cross in the center of the atrio. The Franciscans passed this way, I thought, wondering what idol was buried at the foot of it.

I sat on the rim of a tomb and rested while the fiesta got under way. The man with the fireworks "bull," who had joined our procession somewhere along the trail, now trundled it into the church to be blessed. A group of *pastorcitas* followed him in to sing their greeting before the altar.[1] All around me I could hear Otomí, but could recognize none of the words Telésfero had taught me in Ayotuzco.

The flaxique came up and, in his role of jester, kissed my hand and made a pretty speech while the bystanders laughed and applauded. As he turned away Don Florentino leaned across the tomb and spoke in an undertone.

"The flaxique — the one dressed as the red devil, señora — he is one of the traitors who danced at the Tree of the Sad Night on the occasion of which I told you. He has since reformed his opinions, but I have no confidence in him."

Then we went into the church and took our places for the ceremony. I marched in the center, wearing my headdress and carrying the candles. Bill, frowning and solemn on my right, carried the Huitzilapan flag. Don Florentino, empty-handed, walked on the other side whispering instructions. Behind us came the danzantes singing alabanzas. Straight down the center of the huge church, empty of pews, we marched to the altar rail. The priest, murmuring indistinctly, dipped the sprinkler into the brass bowl held by his assistant and sprinkled the flag with holy water. I strained to catch the language of the ceremony — Latin, Spanish, or Otomí? Suddenly in the midst of swirling smoke and the ringing of bells, I heard him say something in Spanish about ten pesos.

Don Florentino stiffened. "But, Padre," he protested in a loud whisper, "it is voluntario. I cannot tell them to pay ten pesos because they know it is voluntary. I have already said so. They know that they can pay what they wish."

"They will pay ten pesos!" murmured the priest angrily.

"But Padre," insisted Florentino.

Bill nudged me. "Tell Florentino," he muttered out of the side of his mouth, "that we will gladly pay ten pesos, if he will shut up."

"Don Florentino," I interrupted. "We will gladly pay ten pesos."

"Only if you want to do so, señorita. It is voluntary and that means that you pay whatever you want to pay, and nobody can do anything about it."

"I can destroy this flag," intoned the priest while he sprinkled it. "That is what I can do! I can tear it down!"

"We will pay ten pesos," I said quickly.

"But, señorita," persisted Don Florentino as we marched back down the middle of the church, "the baptism of a flag is always a voluntario, and the priest has no right to demand a definite amount. Pay no attention to what this priest says, señorita. No attention at all!"

When we reached the back of the church, Bill gave the flag to the alférez, and we followed Don Florentino through a side door to a room where we found a man in a black robe waiting for us. Bill paid him ten pesos and he noted it in a ledger.

Then the priest who had officiated stepped briskly through a door in the back.

"Have they paid?" he asked.

"They paid ten pesos," murmured the man with the book.

"The señorita said ten pesos was what they wanted to pay," Florentino informed him.

The priest was cordial now, thanking us and asking if he could be of any service to us.

"Yes," answered Don Florentino before we could reply. "The señorita is ill and she is tired. You can kindly send a seat so that she may sit and rest herself."

The priest nodded and Florentino led us out. Before we had gone many steps two men carrying a black wooden church bench began making their way through the now crowded church. When they reached the back they placed the bench against the wall.

"For the señora," one of them announced to the worshippers who started toward it.

Then the Concheros began to form a circle in front of us, just inside the church door.

"Come to the center of the circle a little moment, señora," called Florentino.

He stood beside me and spoke to the danzantes. "The señora Marta de Estony is the *madrina* of the flag of your mesa. That means, compadritos, that she is your godmother in the dance. As you can see, compadritos, we are in front of an altar. I am now asking you to promise to respect the señora Marta always, to listen to her counsel, and to protect her even at the risk of danger to yourselves."

He paused, then asked, "¿Estaís conformes, compadritos?"

"¡El es Dios!" they replied heartily.

They danced a few minutes, then came out of the circle in three straight lines, and backed out of the church. We got up to go too. The two young men immediately took up the bench and followed us with it to the atrio. I entered the circle and danced a step or two. Then, shaking hands all around, we took our leave.

We went back to the oratory where we had left our picnic lunch. Then we spread our serape under a tree across the road and unpacked our baskets. There was a pleasant breeze, the birds were singing, and the air was bracing. We were leisurely enjoying our food when a young woman from the oratory joined us.

"I have brought you something for your lunch," she said, handing me an egg. "It is very fresh, just laid. See, it is still warm."

I thanked her profusely and bent over the lunch basket. She sat down on the log beside Bill and watched us.

"Somebody has to eat that egg," I mumbled. "It would constitute an insult not to eat it. Somebody must eat it. I can't because I would be sick."

"I'll eat it," said Bill.

He opened the shell at one end and downed its contents in three great efforts. He smacked his lips and praised the flavor in Spanish while the woman beamed and giggled. Then she accepted our invitation to join us at lunch.

The next week when Don Florentino and I went to the Torres home, we found that San Juanita was out. — I think that she is properly called "Santa Juanita," but she is "San Juanita" to the danzantes.

"¡Ay, señora! She has gone to visit some friends who have an oratory in another colonia," the señora Torres explained.

"Would the señora care to see the secretaria of the Virgencita?" suggested her daughter.

"I should love to see the secretaria," I assured her, wondering what the secretary was.

"Bring the secretaria," ordered the señora.

The girl brought out an oval brass ball about the size of a large grapefruit. It hung from her neck by a long heavy brass chain.

"What is that?" I asked.

The señora touched some hidden spring on the ball and a door dropped open, revealing a tiny replica of San Juanita de los Lagos. She was exquisite in blue satin with white lace and perfect in every detail.

"It is the secretaria of the Virgencita. The secretaria is always carried on long hard marches, señora, like that of Chalma. She is placed on the altar beside the Lord of Chalma. When the secretaria returns she is placed on our altar beside San Juanita. The good that the secretaria derived from the Lord of Chalma then passes to San Juanita."

That was the first time I had seen a "secretary," or "pilgrim," as it is sometimes called in the Bajío. I was to see several similar brass ornamental balls a few weeks later, swinging by heavy brass chains from the backs of pilgrims along the Ocuila Trail to Chalma.

Fiesta at Chalma

CHALMA, an isolated village in the southern part of the state of Mexico, is in the Tierra Caliente, or Hot Country. Almost completely surrounded by mountains, it lies in a deep canyon beside the Chalma River, with several trails leading to it, but the traditional as well as the most difficult, according to the danzantes, is the Ocuila Trail.

In ancient times Chalma was the seat of worship of Oztocteotl, the Otomí cave god, apparently a variant of Tezcatlipoca, or Smoking Mirror, also known as Heart of the Mountains, the war god, the magician, the guardian of the souls of the Mexicans, and the patron of the warrriors. Oztocteotl's image was in a cave on the mountainside high above Chalma when, in 1535, two friars accompanied by villagers found it smashed on the cave floor and a Christian image in its place. Fifty years later the church and convent were built in the canyon.

For the fiesta there in May of 1945 Bill placed Brigida and me under the care of Don Pancho and the widow of José Celis, who was going with little José, or Pepe as they called him, and her two daughters by a previous marriage, fourteen-year-old Elena and twelve-year-old Felisa. As we were leaving the capital in a hired car, a woman with a baby in her arms stopped us and told a sad tale of a promesa and the difficulties of getting to Chalma. Don Pancho and the chauffeur invited her to join us. With the chauffeur's brother to help drive, we were eleven in one Ford, and the roads almost impassable. But, say the pilgrims, you simply do not ever refuse aid to anyone going to Chalma.

We reached Ocuila at half past ten by the widow's new wristwatch, but it seemed like two o'clock on a hot summer afternoon in Florida, except that the heat was dry, so dry it almost crackled. We left there about noon, Brigida and I on horses, Felisa and Pepito on one donkey, Elena on another, and our luggage on the third. The widow walked with the stranger who carried the baby while Don Pancho led my horse. Ocuila is divided in the center by a shallow stream, on one side of which the road from Santiago ends, and on the other side the Ocuila Trail to Chalma begins. Grownups on foot crossed by stepping-stones, while the children and animals waded across.

When we had left the village behind I discovered that the mountainside was alive with people in the stifling heat. On the sandy trail, among the trees, and along the dry gullies left by last year's rains, trudging figures moved steadily along the trail — men and women, young and old, sick and well, all bent on honoring the Lord of Chalma. Occasionally a merchant's pack animal jostled along, loaded with produce to be sold at the fiesta. Wilted vegetables, chickens, turkeys, pigs — even a goat bleated by, tied to a burro's back.

Except for a fair-skinned man in riding trousers and a khaki shirt the pilgrims were Indians. Several groups carried santos and bells. Many carried *mulas*, the traditional canes of the pilgrims. Sturdy young oaks, straight and slim, are peeled and scraped clean of bark, then their small roots clipped and bent at angles to the taproot, like animal ears. Now they are "mules," but before the Conquest they were called "deer" and had to do with magic.

In the dappled shade of a tree beside the trail a man writhed and groaned. His face was scarlet and he kept saying that he had "such a fever!" I had no medicine except salt tablets. I gave him several and some bottled drinks that I bought from a vendor taking his wares to Chalma on a burro. When he seemed better we left salt tablets with him and went on.

Though those accompanying the sick were silently sober, most of the pilgrims in the swirling dust were gay. According to a long established custom they shouted greetings, trying to guess each other's names.

"¡Adiós, Concha!"

"¡Adiós, Pedro!"

Shouts of laughter rang out when anyone correctly guessed the name of someone he had never seen before. To Don Pancho's delight, his name was guessed several times. He always congratulated the guesser with a flowery little speech.

As the afternoon wore on the heat grew almost unbearable. My wooden saddle was small and uncomfortable and my throat was dry. I wet my handkerchief from the canteen and spread it around my neck. Don Pancho, leading my horse, tried to find the smoother spots in the rough trail while I frankly clung to the horn of the saddle.

Suddenly he halted. "Look! Look, señora! This is something I have wanted you to see."

To the right of the trail just ahead was an enormous cypress.

"It is not as large as the one at Tule, señora, but it is much more famous among us, los Indios Mexicanos."

I could believe it, for not only was this cypress of great size, but it was hung about the trunk and lower branches with an amazing variety of objects — shirts, hats, blouses, handkerchiefs, scarves, a guitar, a banjo, and dozens of tiny bags; some of silk, some of cotton, and some of maguey fibre, most of them white but a few of gay colors.

"What is it?" I asked in wonder.

"The *ahuehuete* of Chalma. The famous ahuehuete of the Ocuila Trail. All the world knows about it."

"And what are those things hanging on it?"

"Remembrances, señora. Remembrances left by the pilgrims."

He led my horse past the tree and around the other side. Water literally boiled up between the gnarly, twisted roots, falling over the embankment and rippling away to the canyon beyond. I had read that the ancient Mexicans in times of drought planted baby cypresses over the mouths of dried-up springs. As the tree grew the roots reached down and loosened the earth that blocked the passages and, in time, water shot up between them. Was I looking at one of those? That would make it four hundred years old. I regretted that I knew so little about trees.

Beyond the ahuehuete the trail became a shelf overlooking a shimmering, sweltering valley. The heat coming up almost pushed my ears from my head. I drank from my canteen but my throat seemed as dry as before. Then we left the shelf and climbed a steep incline to Chalmita at Ocuila Pass, where the trail descends sharply into Chalma. The fiesta began here, with the flimsy wooden stalls against the cobblestone fence that rimmed the pass on one side, and the cluster of tents and thatched shelters for campers on the other. The trail was wider and was paved with worn cobblestones.

When we reached the top of the descent, soldiers with guns ordered us to dismount. Yesterday, they explained, two sick women had been on their way down the hill on horseback when the horse of one slipped and fell and, dragging his rider with him, rolled over and over down the hill. Seeing this the other señora, who had a bad heart, fell dead. So the authorities had decreed that all should come down the descent on foot.

The air was sharp with the odor of burning charcoal from the fires of the portable braseros in the food stands. While the others unloaded the burros, Brigida and I crossed to the shade of a tent on the other side of the trail. Just below, on a hill overhanging the valley, was a small graveyard. Two large green crosses leaned across the cobblestone ramp forming the entrance to it, and beside them was a sign: "It is prohibited for women to descend into the village of Chalma wearing trousers."

I read it aloud, and Brigida sprang to her feet with a gasp. She was wearing overalls!

"What is the matter with the señorita?" asked a man stretched in the shade of the tent. "Why is she agitated?"

"She is worried about the sign," I replied.

"What sign?"

"The one beside the crosses."

"Well," looking across the mountains, "what does it say?"

I realized that he could not read and again I read it aloud.

He chuckled. "That is for foreigners, for they are the only ones here who can read."

"Where is the convent?" I asked.

"Just over the fence, señora," Brigida replied. "If you lean over the fence there, the steeple will be almost under you."

The sixteenth-century convent was built in the angle formed by two mountains. Later I was to stand in front of the church, looking at the horizon beyond the steeple. The horizon was Ocuila Pass.

When the others finished unloading we started down the hill. Pancho held my arm while the others, with the help of Miguel, a danzante from Toluca, struggled with the luggage. About halfway down Pancho steered me to the porch of a house in the bend of the trail.

"Sit here, señora, while we take the luggage down. Then I will return for you."

I was drowsing when he came back. He grasped one arm and Miguel the other, and with my feet hardly touching the ground, they helped me down into Chalma.

We stopped before a building with a sign stating that this was the headquarters of the danzantes of San Miguel de Allende. In front of us was a flight of stairs. We began to climb one flight and then another. On the third floor we went through an open hallway to a narrow gallery that ran across the front of the building. Pancho guided me to a door.

"Have you set up her camp bed?" he asked.

"We are doing that now," replied Brigida.

The next I knew I was lying on the floor and Pancho was snatching my hat off. The smell of charcoal was in my nostrils. Finally I was stretched out on the camp bed.

People came from everywhere with pitchers and jars of water. Brigida wet a towel and put it around my shoulders. Then she tilted a jar of water above my head and emptied it. I drank long and satisfyingly from the thermos. By this time I was sopping wet and feeling better.

People continued to come with water. Mine were the only folding camp bed and chair at the fiesta, they said. Some, I felt sure, came just to examine them.

We were in the room where the banners were kept, stacked against the back wall, each with a strip of black cloth streaming from it. Near the foot of my bed, as I lay with my head toward the door, was a mound of coarse building sand, for the building was new. The floor, covered with fine, gray earth, was unstable and full of cracks. Brigida and the widow began to unpack, spreading serapes about the floor for the children.

Suddenly, with a thud, Don Pancho fell to the floor and lay still.

Again people rushed in with water.

"Stand back!" shouted an elderly man with thick moustaches. "Air! Give him air!"

He snatched up Brigida's bottle of rubbing alcohol and put it to his lips.

"No! No!" I cried. "That is not for drinking. Put it down!"

He lowered the bottle and through his teeth blew a fine spray in Don Pancho's face. Pancho groaned and opened his eyes.

"What happened?" he asked.

The old man laughed and said, "You fainted."

He was Refugio Pinedo of Querétaro, I learned, with the rank of ambassador among the danzantes. His wife, María, tall and thin, sat on my frail camp chair and admired it while he questioned me as to where I had been and whom I knew in the danzante world.

As soon as the Pinedos were gone, the brothers Barreda, joint jefes of a large dance group, arrived to express their sympathy. I began to suspect that an argument of some sort was going on and, when Cecilio Ramírez came on the heels of the Barredas' departure, I felt sure of it. All were capitanes and could make decisions. I wondered if somebody had doubted my illness.

Sometime during the evening the widow left the room to return shortly with Refugio. "Señora, did I go to the Mass for José with you?"

"You did," I answered wearily, for I was not up to settling an argument.

"Did I sit beside you in the church?"

"Yes, of course."

"There," turning to the old man, "now you can tell them!"

Brigida insisted that I eat something and I managed to chew a bit of chicken. Then I wrapped myself in the large sheet that did double duty, since it was both under and over me, and rested on the camp bed.

When night came the Otomies in the front corner of the room prepared for sleep. All five — two men, two women, and a boy — stretched out on a big petate. The younger woman lighted a candle, planting it in some of the coarse sand near the foot of my bed. Every now and then a sudden gust would put out the candle and immediately, all through the night, she would get up and relight it, yawning and sighing as with slow, heavy movements she stamped down the sand around it to hold it upright. Somewhere I had read — I forget where — that the Otomies were afraid of the dark, peopling it with spirits, witches, and the like. But that was in the sixteenth century!

On the other side of my bed the widow and her three children were spread out on serapes. Brigida had put her serape under my bed, and every time I turned, she said, "It is all right, señora!" We were all wearing the same clothes we had worn on the trip. Apparently nobody changes at a fiesta — except the danzantes when they dance.

Don Pancho lay across the open door on a large sheepskin.

"Señora, if you want to sleep comfortably on these marches, get a sheepskin like mine! It is easy to carry and it serves both as a mat and a covering."

"How is that, Don Pancho?"

"When it is warm weather I turn it upside down and lie on the skin which is cool. And when it is cold I sleep on the fur — for it is pure wool, you know."

On the gallery outside charcoal fires burned on portable braseros. One glowed just in front of our door where friends of Pancho's camped. He finally asked them to let the fire die down, since the smoke disturbed the sick señora.

The capitanes visited their banners from time to time, striking matches and waving flashlights as they adjusted the silken folds. It seemed that every time I opened my eyes, I saw either a capitán fiddling with a banner, or the Otomí woman with the candle.

When I fell asleep voices were singing:

Da la una y dan las dos	It is one, it is two
Dan las tres de la mañana.	It is three in the morning.

I had been asleep a short time when I woke to a jangling world. Cecilio Ramírez, in full dance regalia, strode in playing "La Hora de Caminar," a *paso de camino* — which meant that the danzantes were about to leave for the circle to dance. I sat up. Don Pancho was gone. Cecilio's noise was directed at the young Otomí boy, evidently under his orders and, therefore, slated to dance in his circle. He called the boy, told him to dress, advised him to hurry, and marched out — all without missing a beat on the concha.

The boy dragged himself from his petate and began to pull on the brightly colored stockings of his uniform. Every now and then he yawned and remained motionless for a time. I thought perhaps I could keep him awake by talking to him.

"Are you a Conchero?" I asked.

"Sí, señora."

"How old are you?"

"Fourteen."

"Are you an Otomí?"

"Sí, señora."

"And the four who are with you? Are they Otomies, too?"

"Sí, señora."

"Can they speak Spanish like you?"

"No señora. They speak only Otomí."

Cecilio came in again playing his concha loudly. When he saw the half-dressed danzante in conversation with the foreign woman he scolded him, threatening to refuse to "recognize" him (to let the boy dance in his circle) if he were not in uniform in five minutes. The boy hastily put on his dance regalia and slipped out.

Soon I heard voices and the striking of matches up and down the gallery as braseros were lighted. A puff of smoke wafted through the room as the widow sat up and spoke to Brigida. The younger Otomí woman got up and blew out the candle. The day had begun.

Shortly after daylight, Pancho and the other danzantes came back to breakfast. Brigida had bought the privilege of heating water for coffee on one of the braseros on the gallery. She and the widow unpacked our baskets and soon we were eating.

The Concheros trooped in, group after group, to ask about my health and to see if they could help us.

"Buenos días, señora. How do you feel this morning?" "Have no care señora, you will feel better today." "How may I serve you, señora?"

Costumes of silk, brocade, and leather, of many textures and colors, passed in review as the danzantes paused in the doorway to speak to me.

Meanwhile the widow had gone out on the gallery to buy the privilege of heating water for my thermos. She came back crying.

"What is the matter?" I asked.

"¡Ay, señora! Do you know what they are saying? They are saying that I did not attend the Mass for José on his Saint's Day. You know that I did. We went into the church together, did we not?"

"Of course! I said so last night. Who says that now?"

"Two señoras out there on the porch. ¡Ay, señora!"

"Bring them here. I will talk to them."

"¡Ay, señora!"

"Go with her, Brigida."

Brigida led the widow outside and a moment later they came back with a thin, middle-aged woman.

"The other one refused to come, señora," Brigida explained.

"Señora," I said to the woman, "it appears that someone has made a mistake. They tell me that someone has said that the widow of José Celis did not attend the Mass in his honor. That is not true. I myself went with her into the church. She went with this señorita," indicating Brigida, "and me."

"Don Cecilio said she did not attend the Mass," said the woman, drawing her lips into a grim line.

"Impossible! How can Don Cecilio say that when with my own eyes I saw him approach her, and with my own ears I heard him tell her to leave her place between us and sit in the front pew with the family of José?"

The woman fidgeted uneasily but said nothing.

"And let me tell you, señora," I added, "that the Mass was very badly managed. It was given out that the hour would be six o'clock in the morning. As it was quite impossible for my husband to go at that hour, this señorita and I went alone at six o'clock. None of the danzantes were there. None of the friends of José were there. The morning was cold. We had to sit on cold stone steps. Nobody knew when the Mass for José Celis would be said. Another Mass was said. And another. And still another. Then the widow arrived."

"Sí, señora," broke in the widow. "They told me to come at eight-thirty."

"And they told us to come at six!" snorted Brigida. "What a barbarity!"

"Telling some to come at six and others to come at eight-thirty! Whose fault was that?" I demanded.

"Of a truth, señora!" replied the woman defensively. "I do not know."

"But the danzantes arrived at nine o'clock. Only a short time before Mass was said. *They* knew the correct hour. How was that?"

"I do not know, señora. Truly, I know nothing about the affair — nothing at all!"

"If anyone should mention the Mass in honor of José Celis to you again, please have the kindness to tell them that my husband and I consider that it was badly managed. So badly managed as to be lacking in respect for our friend, José Celis. Will you tell them that?"

"Sí, señora. Sí — sí, señora." stammered the woman, as she hurried out.

"Oh, the señora," chortled Brigida. "She can do anything, if you make her mad enough."

Don Pancho came in about nine to say we could now call on the priest, and I crawled down the stairs and staggered across the churchyard to the convent. We had to wait an interminable time in the sacristy before a priest arrived to talk to us. He was youngish, tall and dark, and was, he said, a provincial.

"Is this the first time you have come to Chalma, señora?" he asked brusquely.

"No," I told him. "I was here seven years ago. I came with the doctora, Frances Gillmor, a writer from the States, and a captain who was a friend of the presidente municipal of Malinalco. At the president's request we were given rooms here at the convent. Could you let us have a room at this time?"

"Who was the padre when you were here before?"

"There were three, I think, but I remember only one name — Padre Antonio. Pardon me, I must not forget the letter I should like for you to read."

I handed him a letter from a canon at the Basilica, explaining my interest in Mexican history and folklore. I was sure it would thaw the provincial but he read it without comment.

"Come with me," he ordered.

I thought he was taking us to a guest room but he led us to a library where a middle-aged priest was seated.

The priest rose and greeted us politely.

"Do you know this padre?" the provincial asked me.

"I do not believe so," I answered slowly.

He turned to the priest. "This señora says that she was here seven years ago and that you let them have the guest suite on the top floor. There were three of them: this señora, another woman, and a friend of the presidente municipal of Malinalco."

"His name I do remember," I interrupted. "He was Señor Figueroa."

"Was Figueroa the presidente municipal seven years ago?" the provincial asked the priest.

"He was," nodded the priest.

"You remember them?" the provincial asked.

"I remember them well," the priest replied quietly.

The provincial was surprised, but no more than I.

"And they were given lodging here?"

"They lodged here."

"Are you Padre Antonio?" I asked.

"I am Padre Antonio."

"I am sorry, Padre," I apologized. "I did not recognize you, but I am ill. And seven years is a long time."

The provincial started out.

"Very well, señora," he flung over his shoulder, "you shall have a room. I shall send you the key."

Without a backward glance, he strode away. Pancho and I hastily took leave of Father Antonio and followed him. He waited at the head of the stairs and shook hands with us, asking us to excuse him as he was very busy and saying that the key would be waiting when we returned with our luggage. I was tempted to sit on the stairs and let the others bring the luggage but the traffic there was so great that I went back with Pancho.

The widow was again in tears.

"¡Ay, señora! What do you think they are saying now? They are saying that I did not carry the cross of lime to the cemetery as I should. ¡Ay, señora!"

"The cross of lime?"

"Sí, señora. The night of the velación when they raised the cross they gave it to me. And now they are mad because they say I should have taken it to the cemetery."

"What did you do with it?"

"I gave it to José's sister because she wanted me to do so. She wanted José's brothers to take it to the cemetery, and I wanted no more quarrels, so I gave it to her. ¡Ay-y, señora!"

"Come," said Pancho briskly, "we are going to the convent. The provincial has placed a room at the disposal of the señora and we are all going there."

"To the convent!" crowed Felisa.

"We will shut the door and shut out all quarrels," Pancho went on, turning to the widow. "There you will have no cause for tears. Hurry! Let us pack. The key is waiting."

Since Brigida had packed while we were gone, we were soon climbing the convent stairs again. The place was filled with people. Family groups camped beside the stairs, in corners, in corridors, behind doors, in front of closed doors, and on galleries overlooking patios. They even camped on the roof of the *portales,* or colonnade, along the side of the convent.

We stepped over people napping on the gallery and followed a young man in gray uniform to a room off one of the corridors. It was a spacious room with an iron bed, a table, and a chair in it. Opposite the double door to the corridor was another like it. When I took the key from the young man he bowed and, turning to Don Pancho, offered to show him the toilets.

As soon as they had gone, Brigida threw open the other door to reveal a balcony that overhung the roof of the portales. It was occupied. Two couples and a baby camped there. Three portable braseros sent charcoal smoke into our room the minute we opened the door, and a hen, tied by one leg to the balcony rail, turned an eye at us and gave a startled cackle.

Down the long hall past the stairway were the toilets, seven of them, built in a row down the side of a long room with an underground stream far below them. Outside the door stood a young man in gray, the keeper of the key, who graciously unlocked the door upon one's arrival and carefully locked it when one left. He, or a companion in similar uniform, was on duty day and night.

The widow's daughters enjoyed their tilts with these guardians of the toilets, who always challenged their right to enter. (Apparently the toilets were for the exclusive use of persons attached to the church.) The girls always replied that they were with the foreign señora, at whose disposal the padre had placed the room down the hall and the convenience of these toilets. Then they stood by with disdainful air while he unlocked the door. When they came out they always marched by without so much as a glance in his direction. All this they related in detail as soon as they reached our room, to the wicked enjoyment of the widow and Brigida.

I tried the bed in the corner and found it comfortable. Then I offered the use of my camp bed to Brigida, who in turn offered it to the widow. They finally decided to let Pancho use it.

Brigida invited the widow and her children "to see something of the fiesta" with her "and leave the señora alone to rest and sleep."

As soon as they were gone the younger woman on the balcony began to encroach. At first she lay down with her head and shoulders in our room. Since the balcony had the morning sun, I thought she only wanted the shade. I dozed off then awoke with a start. Something was banging my bed with such force as to shake it and start my headache anew. The woman was seated on the floor with her back against the foot of the bed. She held the child facing her in her lap and, apparently to amuse it, was throwing her head back and banging the foot of the bed with resounding whacks.

"Do not hit the bed," I said sternly. "I am ill and it disturbs me."

Apparently the woman did not understand Spanish, English, or any word of Nahuatl that I could remember. Again I dropped asleep, and again was awakened by the banging. This time, by waving my arms and shouting, I managed to drive her to the other side of the room. While I was scolding her, Elena, the widow's older daughter, arrived with Pepe.

"Pepito was tired," she said. "My mother told me to bring him here and let him rest."

She sat on a pile of blankets with the child and again I went to sleep. I was brought back to consciousness by one plaintive note in the air. I thought it had come from the balcony and sat up to look for the woman. She was no longer there and I lay down again. For the next hour and a half I alternately dozed and wakened to the sound of one sad note.

At two o'clock Brigida, the widow, and Felisa hurried in.

"The hour to eat has arrived," said the widow. "The danzantes have stacked their arms and broken the circle. Pancho should be here soon."

Elena still sat on the serapes playing with Pepe.

Within a few minutes we heard the tinkle of bells drawing near; the door opened, and in marched Pancho in full uniform — sweeping plumes, sparkling beads, green velvet cape, and brass sleigh bells around his ankles. He put his mandolin on my camp bed and was removing his headdress when the little note smote the air again. Pancho whirled and looked at the baby. With a roar of indignation he swooped down and snatched something from the child's hand.

"Why did you give him that to play with?" he yelled at Elena.

Pepe burst out crying. This waked the baby on the balcony, who added his wails to Pepe's and set the hen squawking. Meanwhile Pancho stormed at Elena, fairly dancing in his wrath. The widow plucked at Elena's sleeve and rebuked her. Pancho paused in his tirade to stare; clearly he had expected harsher measures. Elena curled her lip, placed a hand on her hip, and turned her back to her mother. This was more than Don Pancho could bear. With a bitter cry, he hurled himself at the dufflebag and pounded it in helpless rage. Elena and Felisa stared flabbergasted. Then they skittered from the room bound for the toilets.

Don Pancho sat on the camp bed and wiped his face with his handkerchief. Brigida eased over to my bed to explain the situation in an undertone. When the widow told Elena to take Pepe back to our room, Elena had refused to go, saying that she was no nana, or nursemaid. She had been so disrespectful that the widow had wept. While quarreling they had passed near the circle where Pancho was dancing and he, seeing the widow in tears, had asked permission to leave the circle for five minutes. Brigida had explained what was the matter and Pancho sternly lectured Elena on filial obedience. Then he had advised the widow to be firm and send them to the room without further argument. Elena, awed by Pancho's grandiloquence, had brought the baby back but she resented his interference. Her revenge had been to give the child the one thing that Pancho had said they should not play with; the precious tuning whistle that tone-deaf Pancho had to depend on to tune his mandolin!

After lunch two women whose acquaintance Brigida and the widow had made that morning came to visit them. The baby was asleep, Elena and Felisa were "seeing the fiesta," and Pancho was dancing. I rested on the bed while the four women, seated on serapes on the floor, talked in low tones.

I caught a phrase that aroused my curiosity.

"What did you say?" I demanded, sitting up.

"That the married ones do not sleep together at the big fiestas," repeated one of the strangers.

"Of a truth?"

"Sí, señora," Brigida assured me. "I have always heard that, too. That the married ones do not sleep together at the big fiestas."

"It is the fast," explained the other stranger, as had the chroniclers of the sixteenth century.

"Yes, it is the fast," agreed the first.

That afternoon when it was cooler, I crept downstairs and sat on my camp chair halfway between the main entrance of the church and the circle where Don Pancho was dancing. The widow had been right. Each danzante wore a black arm band and black ribbons hung from the conchas.

The atrio was jammed with people, men in white calzones from the distant villages, and women in all types of dress: heavy wraparound skirts from Toluca, straight slim skirts from the south, and skirts pleated all around from Jalisco; white cotton blouses from Morelos and Guerrero, and the cerise, pink, and blue China silk from the Otomí highlands;

rebozos of all colors, knitted shawls, and triangular Otomí scarves. For every gaily dressed woman, there were three black-clad figures in mourning.

Two lines of people going to church extended across the atrio into the distance beyond our view. Inside the church there was singing, followed by the loud ringing of altar bells announcing the end of the service. People passed out of the church through the opening between the lines. A man in a gray uniform, similar to that of the young man who kept the key to the toilets, acted as traffic cop, directing the outgoing lines toward the center so that as the crowd came out, those in line moved up and inside. Within a few minutes the church was emptied and filled again, and another service was under way. The length of the waiting lines was unchanged.

"Señora, look!" Brigida nudged me.

Near us stood Francisco Servín, who had worked with my husband for years. With him were Mariquita, his wife, and Celia and Nahum, their children aged sixteen and eighteen. They had been looking for me, Servín said, because the señor (Bill) had commissioned him to look after the señora. They had slept last night in the atrio, along with hundreds of other pilgrims, and they readily accepted my invitation to share our room.

As we chatted with the Servíns a friend of the widow's came up. She was quite upset, she said, being on her way to a funeral. The four-year-old daughter of her *comadre* (relationship between mother and godmother) had been stung by a scorpion and the *pobrecita* (poor little one) had gone to be an angel. Because of the twenty-four hour law governing burials, they would have to leave the body in one of the graveyards of Chalma. There were expressions of sympathy from all sides, after which she went away, accompanied by the widow and her children.

Since I was finding it difficult to keep from resting my head on my knees, Brigida suggested that I go back to our room.

"How would I ever get through the crowd?" I asked surveying the compact mass around us.

"I will manage it," she replied.

I stood up and she folded my camp chair, tucking it under her arm.

"With your permission," she said loudly.

Instantly the sargento from the circle of dancers was by my side.

"Are you leaving?" he wanted to know.

"The señora is ill," Brigida told him. "She cannot keep upright in her chair. She must return to bed."

"Come," he said.

He guided us into the dance circle, escorted us across it and walked before us, shooing the pilgrims out of the way, to the foot of the stairs of the convent. Sometimes it is convenient to be walking with the danzantes.

Upstairs the odor of charcoal smoke filled our room. The occupants of the balcony were cooking supper, as were dozens of other groups perched on the roof of the convent colonnade. Over the valley a blue haze formed with the deepening shadows that brought an early twilight.

Pancho came up for a taco and quickly returned to the circle, for they were going to dance in the moonlight. I wanted to go down and watch them, but the others — the widow and her children had returned from the funeral — advised against it. Instead I had a small meal and lay down on the bed.

The Servíns came up about nine o'clock and spread their blankets in front of the balcony at the foot of my bed. Brigida offered them food from our pack, but they politely refused, saying that they had eaten.

"Where?" I asked.

"At a puesto in the street," Servín answered "In the street in front of the church are many little food puestos, señora. We had hot tacos and café con leche."

How I longed to roam the streets and trails and watch the people!

Two main classes make up the crowd at a fiesta; those who spend money, and those who cater to them. The first furnish a spirit of light-hearted gaiety, much like the carnival spirit of the United States. They come to pay *mandas,* to fulfill *promesas,* to give thanks for past blessings, to pray for the future, and to catch up with the latest news of the people and places that hold their interest. To the second class, the fiesta is a matter of business, an affair of centavitos and daily bread. They come early and stay late, bringing their produce by burro-back, and setting up their stalls beside the cobblestone streets and along the trails used by the pilgrims. Some, equipped with portable braseros and gasoline cans of *maza,* bake tortillas on the spot and, filling them with meat and spices, roll them into cylinders. This is the taco, the mainstay of the Indian traveling public. Others bring fruit and the flower of *jamaica* (roselle?) to combine with sugar and cool spring water in refreshing drinks.

To these add the attachés of the Church: the priests, the men in uniform, the black-clad women selling tracts or collecting alms, and the laymen, officers of the *cofradia* or some other church organization, who confer with the priest between services, and hurry importantly across the scene from time to time, like a stage manager at the theater on opening night.

Then, too, especially if the fiesta is near the capital or another city, there are the petty criminals who follow the crowds everywhere, the pickpockets, the women with a sad story, and the slicker looking for a sucker. It takes all of these to make a big fiesta!

It must have been midnight when Pancho came in. We could hear the jingle of the sleigh bells long before he opened the door. He made a great fuss about the camp bed. He had turned over his precious sheepskin to the widow, who had finally permitted the wheedling Elena to sleep on it. The camp bed was less comfortable, according to Pancho.

I spent a sleepless night. Every time I turned over the springs creaked and the hen on the balcony let out a squawk that waked the baby to a blast of crying. About daylight I slept soundly.

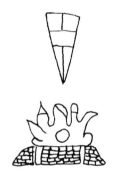

Sunstroke at Chalma

THE ODOR OF CHARCOAL SMOKE awoke me and I knew that I was ill. The Servíns had gone, the babies were asleep. The widow was moving quietly about, dressing herself in the best that she, Elena, and Brigida had among them.

"Where are you going so early?" I asked.

"Ay, señora, it is the Mass for those who died at Cazadero!"

I tried to sit up, but sank back on the pillows. "Are you sure?"

"Sí, señora," Brigida broke in. "Pancho came back from the circle to say that the padre has announced it for five-thirty this morning."

"This is why I came to this fiesta in the first place," I told them.

"Ay, señora, do not try to go," pleaded Brigida. "You are sick!"

Then sleigh bells announced Pancho's arrival. He was sorry that I could not go to the Mass, but was sure that I would be better that afternoon.

"But Pancho, I came to Chalma just to attend this Mass!"

"Señora, I shall place all that the priest says here," tapping his head, "and I shall tell it to you afterward. Now try to sleep again and this afternoon you will be better." He turned to the others, "Come, it is the time to go into the church."

But the widow held back whispering to Brigida.

"Since you are not able to attend the Mass, señora," said Brigida, "would you do the widow of José Celis the favor to lend her your *chal?*"

"Yes, but I have forgotten where I packed it. You will have to find it."

"I have it!" and she held up my black lace scarf.

My memory of that day is hazy. I grew steadily worse as the heat increased. Brigida thought that we should consult a priest and sent Celia Servín to bring one of the uniformed young men to whom we gave a message for the cura, but the morning wore on and no priest ever came.

Later I opened my eyes to find Pancho beaming at me from the foot of the bed. "Señora, I have permission for only five minutes, but I wanted you to know that the danzantes have named a commission to go to the padre and arrange for a special prayer for your recovery. All the danzantes gave money and now the padre will pray for you. I said you would feel better this afternoon, remember? And now I must hurry back."

The widow came in with another woman, taking up a collection to help with the burial of a woman who had dropped dead in the river.

"What was the matter with her?" I asked.

"She was hot and very tired," said the widow, "and when she arrived here, she went at once to the river and walked into the deepest part. She fell and when the men lifted her out she was dead."

"You are molesting the señora," Brigida told them sternly. "Here are five pesos from both of us. Now let the señora rest."

Sometime during the morning Brigida came to my bed with a bottle.

"Señora, will you let me massage you with alcohol?"

She poured alcohol into her palm and rubbed me lightly.

"Ay, señora, your face is so red . . . ."

There was a light tap at the door. Brigida started toward it, but before she reached it, it opened and a priest came in.

"¡Ay, Padre," Brigida gasped with relief, "how good that you have come!"

The priest, hands folded in front of him and a benign smile on his lips, advanced toward the bed. I raised my head and looked at him. He was neither the provincial nor Padre Antonio. Halfway to the bed he halted in midstep as his smile changed to an expression of shock. His nostrils twitched. He spun on one foot and made for the door, his robe swirling around him.

"¡Ay, Padre! One little moment, Padre," Brigida called after him. "Please, Padre. Please!"

But the padre was gone.

"¡Ay, señora, he is gone! Why did he leave us like that?"

"Because my face is red and this room smells like a whisky factory!"

"¡Ay, señora," Brigida moaned, "what will the señor say? Your face is red and you have much fever — ay, what shall I do? Here, take some water, señora. The señor said you should drink eight glasses of water. And take some salt tablets!"

I drank water and took salt tablets and Brigida rubbed me again with alcohol. Then I dozed. When I waked the others were there. Don

Pancho, puzzled because I was worse, told of the danzantes' arrangement for the special prayer and urged patience.

"Patience is not what she needs," said Servín.

Like many organizations in Mexico City, the laboratory of the Bureau of Entomology had held classes in first aid at the beginning of World War II. Servín had done so well in the final tests that Bill had ordered a first aid manual in Spanish for him. He now stood by my bed and ticked off on his fingers the symptoms of several ailments. I am sure he knew nothing about my first sunstroke two years before, but after checking my symptoms with Brigida he settled on sunstroke.

"I am afraid that I shall be no better until I leave this awful heat," I told him.

"Have no care, señora. I will see that you leave here soon."

Cheered by this I lay back and closed my eyes. I have often said that I do not care where I am buried, but within the last twelve hours I had discovered that I did not want to be buried in Chalma.

Servín handed the larger jars to the young people and sent them for water. "Not river water," he instructed them, "but cold water from the spring."

When they came back he had Mariquita and Brigida wrap me in a sheet that had been dipped in the water. How delightfully cold it was!

After the second sheet he turned to Mariquita, "Now, if the book is right, the señora will have a reaction and complain of chill. She should have a stimulant. Get some black coffee, very hot."

How she managed it I do not know, but when I told them I was cold she handed me a cup of black coffee, very hot. I was better. I noticed that the people of the balcony had taken their three braseros, their baby, and their noisy hen elsewhere. I was calm and relaxed.

Servín took my foreign relations card and the canon's letter to "the Authority," the officials of the nearby county seat, Malinalco, who had set up an office in Chalma to keep order during the fiesta. We had hoped that they would order me out of the heat but they were not in. Servín left a message explaining our situation and asking their assistance. We sent messages to the cura too, asking his advice. Perhaps he did not receive them, for no cura came. For some reason one does not turn one's back on the Lord of Chalma; I could see that our whole party felt that I should not leave unless either the officials or a priest told me to go.

"Señora," said Servín, banging the back of his chair with his fist, "Authority or no Authority, cura or no cura, we are going out of here when the sun is low."

"But Servín, how can we? I could never climb that horrible descent from Chalmita."

"Have no care, señora. If necessary my son and I will carry you in a chair."

I knew that Don Pancho had planned to be in Chalma on Thursday, for early on that morning the danzantes would take the big green crosses to the top of one of the mountains to "plant" them there, and he was to take part in the ceremony.

"Don Pancho," I said, "Señor Servín thinks that I will be able to go to Chalmita when the sun is low. I know you want to stay here. Señor Servín has worked with my husband for eleven years and has his complete confidence. Why not let Brigida and me go home with the Servíns, and you stay here?"

"Impossible, señora! That is impossible."

"But, Don Pancho, that would have the approval of my husband. He knows Servín well and trusts him completely."

"Señora, you do not understand. I know Señor Servín is a fine person. All that you say is true. But, señora, when we left the capital, your husband placed you in my hands. He has confidence in me and I have an obligation to him. I cannot fulfill that obligation until I deliver you and the señorita Brigida safely to his hands in your home."

And though Servín argued a little with him, he changed from dance regalia to ordinary clothes and began to pack his belongings.

I stood up and Brigida put the convent sheets and spread back on the bed. Then I sat on it, leaned my forehead against the cool metal headboard and closed my eyes in dreamy relaxation. The others packed our things, shooed the intruding horde back to the halls, or argued about this or that. I no longer cared. For the first time in two days, I was cool.

Suddenly I was aware of movement near me and opened my eyes to find two well-dressed mestizos in front of me. The Authority had come! With the help of Servín, I explained the situation to them.

"Señora," said the presidente municipal, "we agree that you are very ill. We can see that. It is urgent that you leave here and we order you to do so — if that is what you want. We will do all that we can to help you. You have only to command and it shall be done."

"Could you," I asked, "set aside that law about no horses on the descent and let me try to make that hill on horseback?"

"Certainly we can set aside the law. We *are* the law. You may use one of our horses." Turning to Servín, "How do you propose to get the señora downstairs? No horse can come up here."

"There is a camp bed there," nodding toward the luggage. "We can use that as a stretcher."

"A camp bed? You have a camp bed? Then we will take her all the way on that. She is too weak to sit on a horse, anyway." Then he sent his companion for the comandante and a squad of soldiers.

At the mention of the camp bed as a stretcher, Don Pancho had disappeared. When the bed had been set up and I was on it, he came in with six other men — he told me later they were danzantes — who, with Servín and Nahum, lifted the bed and carried me out.

The soldiers with guns walked ahead clearing a way through the crowd. The eight men, four on each side, with the side rails of my bed across their shoulders, walked slowly and steadily through the corridor and down the stairs. As they carried me along the portales someone behind us called me. By putting my arm through the canvas loop at the head of the bed, I was able to pull myself up until I could look back. A man in military uniform was following us.

"¡Señora! ¡Señora Marta! Do you remember me? I am Figueroa. I knew you when you were here before. I count among my treasures the charming letter you wrote me."

He had been presidente municipal seven years ago and I had written him after our return to the capital, thanking him for his kindness to us. He was now sergeant of the squad of soldiers.

At the edge of the churchyard the comandante addressed the crowd. "The señora is ill because of the heat. She must be carried to a higher place. Who will volunteer to help carry her?"

Instantly there were twice as many volunteers as were needed. One was Miguel, the danzante from Toluca, who had helped me down the descent when we arrived. Carefully they raised the camp bed to their shoulders and, marching steadily, followed the soldiers. I glimpsed a long second-floor porch on one side of the convent. It was filled with people, leaning over the banisters looking at me. They quickly faded from view and I floated on, easily and comfortably, above the heads of the public, who, I knew, were crowding to the edge of the trail to see what was passing.

Then I saw a sea of straw hats rise in the air and halt at half-mast. I knew what was happening. They thought I was a cadaver. They were lifting their hats out of respect for the dead. Again I managed a hold on the loop above my head and, raising myself, looked at them. To a man, their jaws dropped and their eyes popped. I lay back and floated on.

The upper part of the trail, which winds up the hill like a cobblestone shelf, was filled with pilgrims coming down on their knees, accompanied by their helpers with serapes. The soldiers scattered them like straws before the wind. I protested, but was unable to make myself heard above the shouts of the comandante and the answering jeers of the bystanders.

"Do not molest yourself, señora," said Don Pancho who walked beside my bed. "It will do no good. The military always conduct themselves like that!"

When we reached the top of the ascent, they set my camp bed down in the middle of the trail and a throng immediately surrounded me.

"¡Ay, it is the señora!" — and María, with whom I chatted at the fiesta in Tlaltelolco, was bending over me. "Ay, señora. Are you ill?" — then she disappeared.

Pancho motioned to the comandante, "Shall we take her up there?"

"Why?" demanded the comandante.

"To get her out of all this," nodding toward the scowling crowd, "and, also, the air is better."

"They lifted me again and we moved up an incline. I wondered where I was and raised myself to look. I was in the graveyard! The one by which the green crosses had been leaning the day we arrived.

The presidente municipal appeared beside my camp bed.

"Are you all right, señora? What do you wish? We will take you on to Ocuila if you like."

I thanked him and told him that by morning I would be able to ride a horse to Ocuila. Pancho assured them that he would see that I reached my home safely, since he was a friend of my husband and my husband had placed me in his care. Then the presidente municipal and each of the soldiers politely wished me well and disappeared down the trail toward Chalma.

Servín arrived, but finding me resting comfortably, went back to help with the luggage.

The crowd at the foot of the ramp leading from the trail to the graveyard had grown larger and was now beginning to mutter.

"I will speak to them," said Pancho, starting toward the entrance. Then he quickly turned back and knelt by the bed.

"Señora," he whispered impishly, "all your life you are going to remember that the best rest you ever had was in a *campo santo* (cemetery)!"

He strode to the top of the incline and made a speech "The señora is here because she is sick. The cura knows she is here. She came here because the cura wanted her to." (This was news to me.) "The señora is not a hiker. She is not a tourist. She has lived in Mexico for eleven years and she is a friend to all the Mexicans. She is interested in our history. She has made archaeological studies in many parts of our country and she is well-known as a friend of the Mexicans. She is not haughty. She is *muy corriente* [very democratic]. From the highest to the lowest, she greets all. Though she is a foreigner, she is very Mexican. She is here because the heat of Chalma made her sick and the cura wanted her to come up here where the air is cooler."

Big drops of rain put an end to the speechmaking. María and her husband Juan ran up. María threw a bedspread over me and Juan offered his tent on the other side of the trail as shelter for the "pobre señora."

Again they hoisted me and, with many a bump and a bang, for there were fewer people carrying me and they were hurrying to get me out of the rain, we crossed the trail to the enclosure by which Brigida and I had rested the afternoon we arrived. Headfirst they shoved the camp bed under the tent. A fine mist enveloped me. The tent was made of sugar sacks sewn together and was not waterproof. They hastily covered the top of the tent with mats woven of the leaves of rushes.

The rain was only a shower. Soon the danzantes were stirring again, busily preparing for the night, for we were all to be the guests of María and Juan. They brought a tall, slim tree and tied it along the ridgepole of the tent, extending it to twice its original length. Then they tied bedspreads along the new pole to extend the tent to twice its size. Instead of the blankets and sheets that we had brought, most of the pilgrims at Chalma carried rush leaf mats to sleep on and bedspreads for covering.

They placed my bed across the open end of the long, narrow tent because Servín insisted that the señora have air. Somebody's poncho made a waterproof roof above my head.

Juan, our host, sat on a wooden box and prepared lights for the night. He broke the glass chimney of a tin candleholder in the form of an antique carriage lantern. María almost lost her temper. She had brought that candleholder in her rebozo all the way from Peña Pobre. Besides, it was one of a pair. Juan gazed sadly at his handiwork. After a moment he laughed.

"Now I can be comfortable," he cried gaily, "for there is nothing more for me to break!" Apparently the candle lantern was not his first offense.

Finally María, an attractive woman about forty years old, laughed too, and told him to hang what remained of the candleholder in the center of the ridgepole. Then she began serving hot coffee, her round jolly face beaming with good humor, and we had supper.

María and Juan occupied the opposite end of the tent. Then came two other guests, Mario, a slim young man with lively dark eyes and a wide mouth, and a tall, angular young woman who seldom smiled. Next came the widow and her children followed by the Servín family. Brigida, as usual, put her roll of blankets under my bed.

After supper María and Juan sat on their bed, a rush mat spread over soapboxes containing uniforms and supplies. The other guests sat on their blankets. I lay on my camp bed and Brigida sat beside me.

Mario was a comedian. He stood up, daintily holding the sides of his trousers, and faced his audience.

"I am a señorita," he announced.

Then he tripped mincingly over sleeping children to a place where the hanging bedspreads had separated. Crooking his little finger like an affected woman, he pulled a bedspread back.

"I am on my balcony, talking to my *novio* [fiancé] in the patio below," he explained.

Then followed a ridiculously funny monologue, a combination of Shakespeare and *carpa*, or street show, that made everybody roar with laughter. The younger woman, after watching our reactions for a time, got up from her place among the blankets, and went over and touched his shoulder.

"Sit down and hush your foolishness," she said in a low voice, then went quickly through the bedspreads, bent on an errand outside.

"My grandmother who takes care of me," said Mario without dropping character, "has just gone out. Now you can come up and see me."

Later when one of the women expressed a wish to take a walk, Don Pancho gallantly offered to accompany her and they went out between the bedspreads. Then Mario did a monologue about them. He placed them upstairs in a house across the street. He did not explain the setting this time but it was quite clear; he pretended that they were before a lighted window and did not realize that he could see them. He watched with avid attention, his lips parted, his eyes glittering. Then he whistled wolfishly. Once he made a remark that I did not understand and the others, except the Servíns, guffawed.

"Be careful, Mario," cautioned Servín. "Remember the señora is here."

Mario immediately pretended to be shocked at what he saw across the way.

"Please close the curtain," he called. "If you must behave like that, do so in private. Close the curtain — please!" Covering his eyes as if to hide a scandalous sight.

Don Pancho and his companion came back in a few minutes and the others told them about Mario's skit at their expense.

"That was neither funny nor courteous," said Pancho severely, glaring at Mario. Mario cowered in exaggerated fear and shame behind María's apron. Then he retired to the other end of the tent to sit between María and Juan, where he and María performed a piece about a bad little boy. María was the mother, and Mario the bad little boy whom she tried to send to the market for some baking soda. He offered absurd excuses for not going. She insisted, adding article after article to the things she wanted. With each item, he offered new and more ridiculous reasons for not going, accusing her of wanting the materials for other purposes than those she named, and so on. Even Don Pancho was restored to good humor, laughing as uproariously as the rest.

After the bad little boy skit, Don Pancho suggested that we put out the light and compose ourselves to sleep, as he wanted to get our party started to Ocuila by five o'clock the next morning. María put out the candle and quiet settled over us. The wind had risen and thundering gusts swept across the peaks like giant horses galloping over the world.

"¡Los Cuatro Vientos!" murmured Pancho. "How they dominate all!"

I could understand the ancients' worshipping them as I listened to the thunderous blasts of the roistering night.

"A mountain is burning!" Nahum Servín suddenly called out.

"So it is," agreed Don Pancho, sitting up.

Brigida rolled out from under my bed. "Now, señora, do not get up. Stay as you are and I will tell you all about it."

"Is it the church?" I asked.

"No, señora. It is the mountain on the other side of the church from here. The church stands black against the light of the fire."

"It must be a big fire," I commented.

"All the forest on that mountain is burning. Tomorrow there will be black, burned posts where today there were trees. Well, I knew this was going to happen. I saw a ball of fire crossing that mountain just after dark — and everybody knows what that means."

"Did you?" asked several of the others at the same time. "What color was it? Where did it go?"

"What does it mean?" I asked.

"The *Bruja* [witch], señora," said Brigida.

I had suspected she believed in the witch!

"What color was it?" persisted a voice — the widow's I thought.

"This ball of fire that I saw crossing the mountain was blue. But the Bruja's daughter would hardly be there without the Bruja, too, being present."

The others agreed.

"Did you hear about the child that the Bruja ate?" asked one of the men.

"Yes, I heard," replied Brigida.

"What child?" I asked.

"A little girl lost herself from her mother, señora," answered Brigida, "and wandered off on the mountain. The Bruja found her and ate her, leaving only the mangled remains of her arms and legs and a few other parts of her body. The parts that were missing they have not been able to find even yet."

"That was the Bruja," another voice spoke with conviction.

"What is a blue ball of fire," I wanted to know.

"The blue ball of fire," said Brigida, "is the Bruja's daughter. The Bruja herself is a red ball of fire."

"And the tree that you admired," added Don Pancho, "the ahuehuete of the Ocuila trail, the one covered with the offerings of the pilgrims, is an incinia of the Bruja."

"How is it an incinia of the Bruja?" I asked.

"Those little bags, señora," explained the widow. "They were offered so that the spirit of the tree would protect the child from the Bruja."

"Would protect what child from the Bruja?"

"The child whose umbilical cord is inside the bag," said Don Pancho impatiently.

"Umbilical cord? Do you mean to tell me that each one of those little bags on that tree has an umbilical cord in it?"

"Each little bag has the umbilical cord of a newborn baby inside it, señora," said the widow. "It is the custom."

"But the hats and the banjos and the other things — what were they?"

"Thank offerings, señora," said Don Pancho.

"And the Bruja really ate a child?"

"Of a truth," replied one of the men. "They had the funeral this afternoon."

The Servíns had remained silent during this discussion.

"Don Pancho," I called, "there is something else I wanted to ask you. Why do danzantes go to Ixtapalapa when they come back from the fiesta at Chalma?"

"Because, señora, when the Christ walked among these mountains He was very tired when He came down from Chalma, and He went to Ixtapalapa to rest. So do the pilgrims of today."

The others murmured in agreement.

The mountain was still burning when I went to sleep.

"Wake up, señora — wake up. It is four-thirty!"

Brigida shook me. We were already packed, she said, and as soon as I had coffee we would be ready to leave. María was cooking, filling the air with the odor of frying bacon. I had breakfast and a cup of coffee, sitting on an empty box to drink it while they packed my bed. Then we thanked Juan and María and said good-bye to them and their guests. Though I am always looking for them, I have never seen any of the four since.

When the mules arrived I saw that they had rented a *camuca* for me. A camuca is a seat with a footrest similar to that of a wheelchair. It is fitted sidewise to the mule's back and is supposed to be "as comfortable as a rocking chair." Only the very young, the old, and the infirm use the camuca. I was low in spirit as they helped me into this one.

I wrapped a blanket around my knees, for it was cold, and we started down the trail for Ocuila.

The morning was cool and cloudy and the people along the trail quieter than those we had seen going to Chalma. Before eight o'clock we were on the edge of the village where the owner of the mules surprised us by insisting that we dismount.

"The mules were hired to go to Ocuila, were they not?" he argued. "Well, this is Ocuila."

"Only the first two houses of Ocuila," I told him.

"It is Ocuila," he stubbornly repeated.

"But I am not going to cross the river on those stepping-stones," I said.

"No, the señora is sick," Brigida informed him. "She would fall off into the water."

"That does not interest me," he replied.

"Stay where you are, señora," Brigida advised me. "The others will be here soon. We will just sit on the mules."

"Then I will take you back to Chalma," snorted the man, flipping the reins over the head of Brigida's mule and turning him around as if to lead him back. Brigida slid to the ground and I was following her example when Don Pancho hurried up the trail. He grasped the situation immediately — or perhaps he had heard by the grapevine what was taking place — for he scolded the man roundly. Since Pancho had arranged for the mules, their owner naturally looked upon him as the person of authority in our party.

"Help the señora to remount," Pancho ordered.

The man obeyed but after Pancho had run back up the trail in response to a call from the widow, he refused to help Brigida.

"Give the señorita the reins," I ordered when she managed to climb on the mule unaided.

Without tossing them over the mule's head, but pressing them together in one hand, he handed them to her, both on the right side. This was the final straw!

"What is the matter with you, man?" I shouted, for I have never been able to speak under pressure of anger without raising my voice.

I swung my mule beside hers, took the reins and, tossing them over the mule's head, gave them to her properly. Without a word, the man caught up the lead rope of my mule and started toward the river. But I had not finished.

"Why are you so contrary?" I wanted to know, as people along the way halted to listen. "You have nothing to lose by doing as you are told. You will be paid. You were amiable enough this morning in Chalma when we rented your mules. Why have you changed? What nationality are you, anyway? You cannot be Mexican, for I have lived in Mexico eleven years and I have not found in all this republic a Mexican who would not be glad to help two ladies — and one of them sick!"

All along the trail people stood grinning. The man stared straight ahead and plodded on, but I thought his already red ears were a shade darker. When we reached the little plaza on the other side of the river, he helped Brigida dismount with such gallantry that she completely forgot the canteen hanging from the saddle horn.

Servín had a compadre in Ocuila who invited us to rest at his house — I slept on the camp bed most of the time — until pilgrims bound for Chalma arrived in a car that might be available for the return trip to Mexico City, for there were no cars for hire in Ocuila. In the late afternoon Servín obtained a station wagon to take us to Tianguistengo, where we hired two taxis to take us to Mexico City.

A few days later when I consulted our family physician he confirmed Servín's diagnosis by stating that I had had a sunstroke in Chalma. He added that the treatment I had received, including the change to Chalmita, probably had saved my life. The next week Don Pancho came to our house and, standing in the center of our living room, repeated with appropriate gestures what the priest had said at the Mass for the dead at Cazadero.

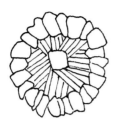

Velación in a Cave – Guanajuato

GUANAJUATO, the picturesque and predominantly colonial capital of the state of Guanajuato, is situated in a teacup formed by mountains. Nieves and I went to the fiesta there by train, arriving at twelve o'clock "in true danzante fashion," as she described it.

"Tomorrow morning," she said, as she guided me to a small inexpensive hotel, "I shall find my uncle who dances with the Broncos and send him to locate Cecilio Morales for you."

The next morning I awoke as she came in with toast, boiled eggs, and coffee that she herself had prepared in the kitchen.

"How did they let you?" I asked.

"I just told the cook I would get your breakfast. She has practically no resistance."

After breakfast Nieves' uncle, in spotless blue jeans and pink shirt, arrived.

"Sí, señora," he told me, "I know Don Cecilio well. I will be glad to go to his house and ask him to come to see you."

Within half an hour he ushered Cecilio in. We discussed the wreck at Cazadero, the fiesta at Chalma, my sunstroke, and danzante affairs in the capital. I told him again of the book I was writing. As he was leaving, he told us that his personnel would be rehearsing that afternoon down the street from the hotel across from the cemetery, and that we might attend the rehearsal if we liked.

At the door he turned back. "My wife and I will call for you and the señorita tomorrow afternoon, señora, if you want to go to the velación in the cave."

Of course we wanted to go! That was what we had come to Guanajuato for.

Nieves' parents came to see us that afternoon. They were clean, neatly dressed country people. They lived on a ranch outside Guanajuato. I gathered that it was not large and that it was their own. They were planning to go with us to the cave the following afternoon and would bring food for us, they said.

That afternoon Nieves and I took a taxi to the rehearsal of the danzantes, but we had no sooner arrived than a summer downpour stopped the dancing. When we returned to the hotel Nieves' mother was waiting with a basket of food from her sister-in-law's kitchen: chicken, rolls, lettuce, rice, peas, and avocados. Enough for breakfast, too, for the fare at the hotel was depressing.

The next afternoon Don Cecilio and María, his wife, and Gregoria, their twelve-year-old "borrowed daughter," arrived at our hotel at about three o'clock and Nieves' parents a few minutes later. Don Cecilio went out almost immediately to buy charcoal to take to the cave and Nieves' father went with him to call a taxi. By three-thirty we were on our way with four or five serapes, food for two meals, charcoal, and numerous bundles belonging to María.

We drove through Guanajuato to the Hormiguero, or the Anthill, a flat-topped mountain overlooking the town where everybody would picnic the next day. On the Hormiguero we turned in the opposite direction from the picnic ground and drove as far as we could. Then we got out and walked, and the taxi went back to town.

Señor Sanchez, Nieves' father, loaded with bundles and having little patience with tradition, took a shortcut across the grassy plain, but we trudged on and on along a shelf of a mountain by the traditional trail of the pilgrims. We passed the entrance of a mine of *pura loza*, a pink, green, and beige building-stone that breaks off in sheets. We walked slowly, we four women and the little girl, for the señora Morales was recovering from an attack of pneumonia. After about an hour we passed the opposite side of the mine of pura loza. Here the opening was low and the rock was rose-colored. The señora Morales walked ahead a few yards, then stopped and pointed up the mountainside.

"There it is," she said.

We looked straight up, or so it seemed to us, and saw the cave, the paintings at the mouth of it standing out garishly in the late afternoon light.

"How will we get up there?" we asked.

"We will climb," she replied.

And so we did, for an hour or more. As we neared the top, the way led over the bare rock face of the mountain. Water had worn puddly little holes in the surface and these furnished toeholds. Finally we pulled ourselves over the rim of the cave and lay there resting, gazing out over the trail we had just climbed and the green valley far away.

In front of the cave to our left rose a craggy, squarish elevation called Los Picachos, capped by a crenelated rim of rocky crags of even height that gave it the appearance of a pink castle from a fairy tale. This, said Nieves, was the top of Bufa Mountain. The trail to the cave lay between Los Picachos and a peak of similar formation to our right. Not far below us the trail divided, one branch leading to the mouth of the cave and the other winding to the left (to the right as one climbed), around, behind, and up to the top of Los Picachos. The feat of the young and venturesome of the region, said Nieves, was to climb at daybreak on the day of San Ignacio de Loyola to the top of Los Picachos, and look down across the rolling plains to the tumbled and twisted terrain beyond with white specks of mining villages peeping over its lesser green folds.

The cave itself was divided into two parts, the outer part having flaring flanges with natural low platforms underneath them on each side. On the wall of the flange to the right was painted the likeness of San Ignacio de Loyola, on that to the left, the Virgin of Light. Halfway to the back were the remains of what might have been a dividing wall at one time. Now only a curved abutment from the cave wall and a step-down of two feet marked the dividing line. The top of the inner room rose in a high dome.

As we rested at the mouth of the cave, Cecilio Morales and another man arrived. Don Cecilio carried the image of San Sebastián in a bundle strapped to his back, while his companion carried a wooden box holding an ivory image of "the prince and archangel, San Miguel," or Saint Michael.

Don Cecilio and three other danzantes carried the bundles to a low natural platform near the center of the back wall in the inner room. In the wall on each side, irregular holes had been gouged out and filled with blocks of wood. Nails had been driven into the wood from which hung oil lanterns. Don Cecilio tied cords to a nail in each wall and sus-pended a long thin roll of canvas over the platform. Then he unrolled it, revealing a painted altar front in rose and blue, with a large, oval opening in the center, like the proscenium arch in a theater. Next he hung a rose-colored bedspread behind the oval opening. He placed San Sebastián in the center, a photograph of Padre Jorge on the left, and San Miguel in his *nicho* with a glass door on the right. He put a paste-board box containing *estampitas* (stamps or prints) of the church at the back of the altar, and a plate from María's lunch basket, filled with copal, near the front on the right.

Don Cecilio and I talked while he slowly and lovingly laid bunches of flowers and greenery here and there.

"Padre Jorge," he said, "was a friend of the Indians and even in death he has not deserted them. His tomb is muy milagrosa and is visited by hundreds every year!"

He laid herbs and greenery around the front of the altar. Later I noticed that the disciplina was hanging over the edge but I had not seen him place it there. It looked new and unused. Probably it was the one "used for show," as José Celis had said.

Nieves' parents sat in the outer cave by the dividing wall. They had spread serapes on the floor and had unpacked the lunch basket. Hot coffee from the thermos was particularly good in the evening chill now creeping through the cave.

When darkness had fallen, Nieves and I stood at the outer rim and watched the tiny lights twinkling like fireflies along the trail below. These were the miner's lights strapped around the heads of danzantes climbing toward us. When a newcomer would finally emerge through the opening of the cave, an appreciative murmur of "¡Qué sacrificio!" would come from those already assembled.

In the inner room the men sat on the left and the women on the right. Doña María invited Nieves and me to sit beside her near the altar, saying that they were about to begin their exercises. I was surprised to see a portable brasero in the corner where María had spread her serape and petate.

"This is what we had to buy the charcoal for," she explained.

There was also a jar of water and several brown bowls.

As I looked at the altar I recalled what Don Pancho once told me, "The most important things on a danzante altar are the *benditas ánimas* [blessed spirits] of our ancestors — the photographs, señora. Always they are the most important things there."

I looked at the photograph of Padre Jorge and decided that he must be one of the benditas ánimas. I noticed later that he figured in one of their alabanzas.

The flag bearers came forward with the banners, now shorn of their wrappings and set up on metal standards, and presented them to the Four Winds. Each flag bearer knelt in front of the altar, lifted the standard high and made the sign of the cross three times, while the capitana rang her bell and the congregation sang. Then, remaining on his knees, he turned to face the opposite direction and again made the sign of the cross three times. He repeated this to the right and to the left. Then once more he faced the altar and presented the flag to the capitana who took the incense burner and made smoke crosses with it, censing the flag and the flag bearer. Then he placed the flag against the wall beside the altar, while all the capitanas rang their bells. After the flags, the danzantes presented their conchas in the same manner.

Don Cecilio began the velación by calling on San Sebastián, San Miguel, the benditas ánimas, and the Four Winds. The segundo chanted a litany and the group responded. Then we formed a procession and marched to the mouth of the cave where they placed flowers under the paintings of San Ignacio and the Virgin, singing alabanzas all the while, except for a short prayer to San Ignacio. After this little ceremony we marched back to the inner room.

After we were settled on our rush mats again, we sang several alabanzas, including, "Santo, Santo, Santo," that José Celis had taught me, and one about the miracle of the Señor de Villaseca when he "freed a married woman" from her irate husband. In this alabanza, the woman is taking lunch to her lover when the husband walks up and asks what she is doing. Terrified, "with her mouth dry, dry," she answers that she is taking flowers to the Señor de Villaseca. The husband lifts the napkin with the point of his dagger and lo, the tortillas have changed to flowers and the salt to incense. The Señor de Villaseca is a santo in a church near one of the mines in the outskirts of Guanajuato, Nieves told me. The alabanza is a favorite of the danzantes.

By now a second group of danzantes, with a florid blond chief, had set up an altar in the outer cave, beside the platform of San Ignacio. They were singing alabanzas also, but they sang in the high-pitched, nasal voices that I was accustomed to in the capital.

Throughout the evening danzantes continued to arrive in groups of five or six. Don Cecilio and most of the other danzantes would go to meet them. I know now that an interesting little ceremony took place as the two groups met, but since María did not go with them, Nieves and I remained in our places on the petate beside her.

This outside welcome took place when several from another mesa arrived with their banner, candles, and flowers. One group brought an image of the Señor de la Conquista that joined San Sebastián, San Miguel, and Padre Jorge on the altar. A woman of another group carried a bundle wrapped in gray flannel about the size of a football, that was treated as a santo and placed on the altar with the others.

"What is that?" I asked Doña María.

"If it is for me to tell you," she said impishly, "never will you know."

I remembered that before the coming of the Spaniards, the image of the wind god, Father Snake — also known as the Four Winds — was always carried covered up. Naturally, I was eager to learn more about the gray bundle on the altar. I made several attempts to question María but she always gave the same laughing reply: "If you wait for me to tell you, you are never going to know."

New arrivals knelt in front of the altar and presented their offerings to the Four Winds. When one group had finished, I saw four green objects like huge artichokes, or undersized pineapples, on the front of the altar.

"What are they?" I asked María.

"Have you seen them at velaciones in the capital?"

"No."

"You will see many things here tonight that you have not seen in the capital."

"But what are they?" I persisted.

"You will see." But the woman on the other side of me whispered that they were plants of the sotol, a species of spoon cactus, that had been brought in from the mountainside and that would be used "to dress the Santo Xuchil."

"Oh, is that *cucharillo* [spoon cactus]?" I turned to María.

"That is cucharillo. Now you know." We lapsed into silence.

In describing the Preconquest fiesta of Xocotl, Duran mentions pineapples made of maza. Could his dough pineapples have been dough spoon cacti?

At exactly midnight, Don Cecilio made an announcement that I did not understand, but I gathered from María's remarks that they were going to dress the Xuchil, and that the segundo would have charge. A capitán carefully spread a clean white square of cloth on the cave floor in front of the altar. Then he picked up one of the tiny pineapple-like magueyes and, taking hold of the top of the prickly green "handle," peeled downward, snapping off last the white "spoon" at the bottom. He took them off slowly because, as the woman next to me whispered, he was praying all the while.

"Each *penca* is a prayer," she murmured, "and he has to say it."

He placed a penca, or a spoonlike petal, in the center of the white cloth in front of him and one at each corner, forming a square; one penca in the center, one at the upper left, one at the lower left, one at the lower right, one at the upper right, one in the center, and so on until all were used. When he had finished he slowly and reverently gathered up the five piles and placed them on a plate. He then offered them to the Four Winds while the danzantes sang.

Then the segundo and the capitanas began to slit each penca along the outer edge as children sometimes slit the petals of a rose. When all the pencas were slit, the segundo knelt and slowly placed them upside down on the white cloth, forming a beautiful white cross. Its broad base lay at the segundo's feet and its top at the edge of the altar. Streamers extended from the cross beams to a point on the middle strip in much the same way the paper decorations drape the big green crosses that top many of the mountains near the capital.

When the cross was finished Don Cecilio laid two highly polished reed poles about three feet long across the penca cross, crossing them in the center in a large X. He placed the small box of church estampitas on one side. The capitán set an incense burner among the pencas at the base of the cross. They placed the two skeins of stout cord beside it, one on each side. Then they put a plate from María's lunch basket a little to the upper right beside a tall, lighted candle. Another candle was burning on the opposite side.

One by one, first the men and then the women, got up, walked over to the base of the penca cross, knelt, picked up the incense burner, and made the sign of the cross three times to the Four Winds; first facing the altar, then the opposite direction, then to the right, then to the left. After replacing the incense burner, each got up and dropped a coin into the plate before returning to his or her place on the cave floor. I had taken a peso bill from my purse and asked María to place it in the plate for me.

"Place it yourself," she urged. "They will be very pleased."

"But I do not know how to make the crosses to the Four Winds. We do not have that custom in my country."

"We should like to see how they do it in your country," she said. "Go ahead. Do it exactly as they do it in your country."

Here was a dilemma! I could not admit that it was never done in my country nor could I refuse to do anything at all. Furthermore, whatever I did must surprise them by being no less than grand, if I and my country were not to lose face.

When I first came to Mexico I had the good fortune to live next door to Dr. Samuel Young, a charming Chinese gentleman, who taught me to kowtow. I now got up from the mat and, with all eyes on me, walked to the foot of the white cross on the floor. Deliberately I stepped back two long paces. I closed my eyes and crossed my arms to my shoulders, the left over the right with the peso bill held in my right hand. Then I doubled into a kowtow that laid my forehead on the floor. After a moment I raised myself to my knees, opened my eyes, and stood up. Slowly I stepped forward, extended my right arm and let the peso bill flutter to the plate. Then I marched majestically, I hoped, back to my place beside María.

Not only were they surprised, definitely they were impressed. Don Cecilio got to his feet and made a speech full of flowery, danzante language, the object of which I missed, but I gathered that he was "throwing flowers" at me because the others looked at me, nodding and smiling.

"¿Estaís conformes, compadritos?" he asked.

"¡El es Dios!" echoed through the cave.

Then he ceremoniously presented me with three estampitas from the cardboard box. I think there was more to this than appeared on the surface, but I shall probably never find out all its ramifications. When I stole a glance at María she quickly looked in the opposite direction.

Don Cecilio and El Segundo took the two skeins of stout cord from beside the white cross and, in the same reverent manner as was used in forming the cross, proceeded to take the pencas, or cactus petals, from the cross and tie them to the two long reed poles. While the danzantes sang, they slowly tied pencas, the slit side of the petal out, to the reeds.

María meanwhile was cooking a concoction on the little portable brasero beside her.

"What is that?" I wanted to know.

"*Atole*"[1] she answered. "Do you like atole?"

"It is one of my favorite drinks."

"Then you shall have some. What Mexican dishes do you like?"

"I like most of them — atole, mole, guacamole, enchiladas, tacos, tamales, tostaditas, pollo almendrado, chiles jalapeños, and ate de guayaba con qeso cremado."[2]

The women around us laughed.

"I am glad you like atole, señora. I shall give you some while it is hot."

In the bottom of her bowl was what looked like corn meal dough. From time to time, she broke it into tiny pieces and kneaded it between her fingers, as my grandmother used to do before feeding ailing baby chickens.

"What is that?" I asked, but she pretended not to hear.

When I saw her drop a finger full into the steaming chocolate atole, I was more curious than ever.

"Tell me," I insisted. " What is that?"

"It is to give it flavor," she said, looking away from me.

"But what is it?"

"Just maza, nothing more."

"Maza?"

"Sí," she answered vaguely, and began to talk in an undertone to the woman on the other side of her.

Day was breaking when Don Cecilio and El Segundo finished tying all of the "spoons" around the poles, which now looked like giant blooms of white stock, or white feather dusters. They leaned them against the front of the altar, crossing them in the same manner that they had crossed the bare rods over the penca cross, in a large X.

Now Don Cecilio made an announcement: "Today we will dance on the Hormiguero. We will dance because the government has ordered it. It will not be worth your while for you to tell me that we are religious dancers and that it is not our custom to dance in national fiestas. We .were forced to register under a government department or cease to exist. As you all know, we registered. Now as part of a government department we are ordered to dance or pay a big fine, bigger than we can pay. There is no remedy. We will dance."

Then followed a discussion as to hours, future marches, and so on, in an informal manner. While this was taking place, María served the atole.

"This is for the señora," she announced, filling a half-pint metal cup.

"Oh, not so much," I protested. "Leave some for the others."

"There is plenty," she assured me, and I wondered at the smiles of the other women.

"Try it," she said. "Drink it while it is hot!"

Since it was now bitterly cold in the cave, I needed no further urging. Never have I tasted anything so nauseous! I lowered the cup and tried to keep my face expressionless.

"Do you like it?" asked one of the women.

"Sí," I mumbled, and strolled toward the front of the cave where Nieves was eating sandwiches with her family.

"Would you like some of my atole?" I asked her.

"You do not like it, señora?"

"No, it makes me sick. But they will be offended if I return any of it. Drink it — if you can."

"Thank you, señora. I love atole and they did not offer me any."

She raised the cup to her lips. A still, thoughtful look spread over her face. She moved toward her father.

"My father loves atole," she murmured.

"Be sure to take the cup back to Doña María," I cautioned.

A few minutes later a tourist from Chihuahua who, while trying to climb to the Picachos had missed the trail and landed in the cave, gratefully accepted the cup of atole from Nieves' father. He drank a sip, then lowered the cup, a still, thoughtful expression on his face. Casually he strolled toward the mouth of the cave. That was the last I saw of the cup of atole.

The second group of danzantes in the front part of the cave seemed a little ahead of Don Cecilio's group in the ceremony. Their chief stood in front of their altar holding the two decorated rods. One after another of his congregation stood in front of him while he went through peculiar motions. I stood fascinated, watching him. Up, crossed over the head, down in rapid, sweeping movements, swirling around the body to the left, to the right, up encircling the neck on the left and on the right, over the head again, and so on. I did not know it then, but this ceremony is called "cleansing," and instead of the decorated rods, bunches of certain flowers, small branches of plants, and even candles may be used. Apparently all of their group presented themselves to be "cleansed," forming a line and marching in front of him one by one, while with red face and heavy breathing, he bent and swished and tiptoed, making a great work of it.

Nieves' father suggested that now that daylight had come, we might go. Nieves wanted to go, too. She thought that the danzantes' hospitality was waning. Our belongings were already packed and they were only waiting for me to agree. I went back, shook hands with María, left messages for Don Cecilio, who was still speechmaking, and told the other women that I would see them at the Hormiguero.

In the silvery light of early morning we dropped over the rim and started down the trail. It had rained in the night and the rock was as slippery as glass. Every time I stepped, I slid a foot. Furthermore, the niches that had accommodated a toe coming up were far too small for a heel.

"Stop here and wait for me," said Nieves' father. "I am going down with these things, but I will leave them at the foot of the descent and come back for you, señora."

How I envied him! Hung all over with serapes, pots, and a basket he went hoppity-skip over the rocks.

"Stay with the señora," the mother called to Nieves, "and I will go with him to watch our things while he comes back."

Some young people, bound for the Picachos, came up the trail.

"How soon did you get up to be going back now? You must have climbed up in the dark. How did you ever do it?" they wanted to know.

When Nieves' father came back unencumbered, he stood with his back to me and told me to put a hand on each shoulder.

"Now follow me, señora. When I move my left foot, put your left foot in the spot where my foot was. And follow my right foot with your right foot in the same way."

And so I did, but it was slow going until we reached the shelf and Nieves' mother.

It was a beautiful morning as we dawdled along expecting the danzantes to overtake us. Birds sang and exotic flowers nodded over the edge of the trail. Nieves scrambled up the side of the trail to pick an unusual flower.

"Señora," she said, as she slid down, "who do you suppose is up there above us? The danzantes! Strolling along a perfectly easy trail up there!"

Then it dawned on me; they had gone up this trail not because it was the only trail, but as part of the sacrifice. Once the sacrifice was made, they were free to go back by any route they liked. And we, in our ignorance, had made a double sacrifice!

Soon Don Cecilio, followed by the others, came down a slope, crossed the shelf, and went down another slope toward the plain below. He greeted us perfunctorily as they hurried on. We trailed along behind them. When we reached the Anthill, the danzantes disappeared among the tents that now studded it. Nieves' father told her that he and her mother would leave our bundles at our hotel and go home, as they had promised to bring the rest of the family to the fiesta later.

The housetops of Guanajuato gleamed in the valley below us, for we were standing on the rim of the cup that enclosed the town. On the other side of us stretched the grassy, rolling Anthill. A truck came to a stop behind us and two men unloaded a huge block of ice beside a cold-drink stall. Cars crawled up the steep hill bringing early risers to the picnic. Suddenly the flap of a tent near us opened and Don Cecilio and María, dressed in velvet and feathers, stepped out.

"Do you want to take a photograph, señora?" he asked, smiling affably.

After I had photographed them María insisted that we come to their tent and rest. We found the other danzantes there dressing. We chatted a few minutes, then went back to the hotel for we were both sleepy.

After breakfast the next morning Nieves and I set out for Don Cecilio's house. We found it without difficulty, for he was a pottery maker and everybody seemed to know him. He lived in a beautiful old house at the end of the street, and he and María seemed pleased to see us. They invited us into their oratory, their largest room, and stood by beaming as we admired it.

"This is the *custodia*," said María. I had never heard a danzante call it a custodia before.

"Yes, but it is different from the way we dress the Sainted Xuchil," I told them.

Don Cecilio exchanged glances with his wife and both laughed delightedly.

"I told you," she reminded me, "that you would see many things here that you had never seen in the capital."

"It is the truth," I agreed. Apparently that was the right answer.

I turned to Cecilio. "I need your help, Don Cecilio, with a book I am writing."

He made no reply.

"They tell me," I continued, "that you inherited your position in the dance from your grandfather. Also, that he left you some rare and ancient documents."

He looked at me while María stared at him. The silence stretched on uncomfortably.

"Will you read this letter from a padre in the capital?" handing it to him. "It explains my motive in searching for data."

Don Cecilio took the letter silently and read it. Then he reread it without comment. Abruptly he got up and left the room, his footsteps resounding loudly as he went quickly down the steps to the street gate. Doña María sat silently twisting her hands. I wished we had not come.

"If it is not convenient for Don Cecilio . . . ." I began.

María got up and without a glance in our direction went into the other part of the house. Nieves and I huddled on the long, backless bench along a blank wall of the room and talked in whispers. We wanted to leave, but I hated to lose the letter Cecilio had taken with him. We tried to talk about the altar, but there were many things on it that we were unable to recognize from where we sat. We dared not walk over and frankly examine it.

I looked at my watch. "Don Cecilio has been gone forty minutes," I said. "Where can he be?"

"Probably gone to see the priest about that letter," said Nieves.

We fixed our attention on the Xuchil. It had eight "rays," and even Nieves recognized the fact that the decoration was different from that of the Xuchiles we had seen in and around the capital. Essentially, it was two concentric circles of heavy green moss and curling cucharillo.

In the very center was the picture of a cross, similar to the estampitas of the church. Just as we stole nearer to see it better, we heard footsteps on the stairs and raced back to our places on the bench. María must have heard them, too, for she came in just as we reached it. Then Don Cecilio entered from the porch.

"It is well!" he told us with a smile as he stepped into the room. "Bring the documents," he ordered María, adding a name that I did not catch.

"Not those," she protested.

"Get them," he insisted.

She walked slowly into the next room and, near the door where we could see her, knelt before a metal trunk and began to fumble with the lock. Finally she stood up.

"It is locked," she announced. "I do not know where the keys are."

"Find them," he told her.

Don Cecilio suggested places she might look for the keys and in one of these she found them. She stooped and unlocked the trunk. Then she moved her hands through the contents until she found a notebook and a letter.

"Not these," she looked pleadingly at her husband who gave her a long stare.

"Those," he said finally. "The señora must be permitted to examine them. There is no remedy."

"Don Cecilio, if it is not convenient . . . ." I began.

"It is convenient," he informed me curtly.

"The señora may copy them?" Nieves asked.

"Sí, with all pleasure," he replied standing up and bowing. "With your permission," and he left the room. María followed him.

Nieves copied the framed rules on the wall while I copied what looked like the most important entry in the notebook. I was just starting on a letter when Don Cecilio came in. I hurried, for I was nervous about the affair. He sat quietly across the room and made no effort to interrupt our writing. When I handed him the papers, he smiled amiably.

"Have you copied all that interests you?" he asked.

"Sí, señor, and many thanks to you."

We admired his house, the oratory, and the altar. They became genial hosts again. I invited them to come to see us when they came to the capital, and they urged us to return soon. On that happy note we left them.

The week after we came back from Guanajuato, Captain General Manuel Luna, who by this time was our good friend, came to see us.

"Did you climb to the cave señora? And did you stay for the fiesta the next day?"

"Only a little while. Then we went back to the hotel."

"Then you did not see the contest?"

"What contest?"

"They had a contest to see who was the best dancer, and prizes. The government arranged it. It was a national fiesta, you know. Poor Cecilio."

"Why poor Cecilio? What happened?"

"He did not win. Natividad Reina won."

"Ay, poor Don Cecilio!" said Nieves.

"Cecilio has never done artistic dancing. He is a religious dancer, but the government cannot be expected to know that. They say that he who won turned his body over in the air without touching the ground, playing his concha all the while. We call such things artistic dancing. Did Cecilio burn five candles before the velación, señora?"

"Yes," I replied, "and none went out."

"They have that custom, I have heard. Do you know, señora, four candles bear the names of jefes who have died, and from the way those candles burn, they think they can tell whether the dead chiefs approve of your presence. The fifth one is yours. If the fifth candle goes out they think that you have come with evil intent."

"Fortunately all the candles burned brightly."

"¡Ay, qué bueno! Señora, did they offer you some atole?"

"Sí, Don Manuel."

"Did you drink it?"

"It was awful, Don Manuel!"

"They put little pieces of sour maza in it."

"So that is what gave it that horrible flavor!"

"They keep their maza until it is quite spoiled and put it in their atole. They call it *chicuatole* and, with them, it is part of the sacrifice."

"¡Qué sacrificio!"

And I meant it.

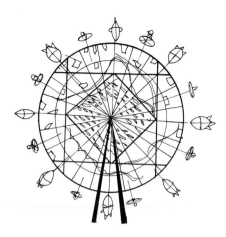

Fiesta
at San Miguel
de Allende

SAN MIGUEL DE ALLENDE, like Guanajuato, is in the Bajío and has begun to compete with Cuernavaca and Taxco as an arty tourist town. Brigida and I were little interested in its art or its tourists, however, when we accepted Don Pancho's invitation to the fiesta there on the Day of San Miguel in 1945. Don Pancho, who had been born on a nearby ranch and received into the dance by Capitán General Ruperto Granados of San Miguel, was sure that the dance had originated there. From what he and other danzantes had told me I expected to learn a lot at this fiesta.

We went by train, arriving shortly before daybreak in a downpour that had dwindled to a drizzle by the time we reached the square in front of the Hotel Posada. Pancho engaged a man to carry our luggage and left him with Brigida and the bags, while Pancho himself escorted me into the wet night "on a little matter of business." He was quite mysterious and, I thought, excited. I tried to get my bearings. I could see that we were nearing a church. Its spires were silhouetted against the leaden sky.

"We are here," he said, and I could make out the figures of danzantes in the murky light. Then I realized that we were inside a dance circle. As I peered around me in the mist, Pancho began to make a speech. He had brought with him from the capital a new silk flag of Mexico to be used to the honor of San Miguel. He waxed eloquent as he expressed his hopes and ambitions for the glory of the Saint and the well-being of the group as they danced beneath this symbol of their country. "And now the foreign woman, who is the companion of the danzantes in their devotions, will do us the favor of unfurling the flag for the first time."

This was a surprise as well as an honor. No wonder Pancho had been excited! He stripped the wrappings from the rolled-up flag and handed it to me. It was heavy and I handled it awkwardly, but I finally unfurled it. A malinche with a spreading headdress knelt in front of me to receive it. I was panic-stricken. I had forgotten the order of the crosses to the Four Winds! And I doubted my ability to make the sign of the cross with the heavy flag. I hesitated. Then I simply placed the standard in the girl's hands, bowed profoundly, and backed out of the circle.

As we walked away, I was afraid Don Pancho might feel that I had failed to live up to my big moment, but he seemed pleased, dwelling at length on the beauty of the flag and on the amazement of certain danzantes of a foreigner so honoring him as to unfurl it for him.

We found Brigida and the luggage man sitting on the suitcases in the muddy street. She said she would have waited three more minutes and then she would have gone to look for us.

"The señora did me the honor to unfurl my flag for the first time," the beaming Pancho informed her.

"And you did not show me the courtesy to invite me to see her do it!" she exclaimed angrily.

"But somebody had to stay with the luggage," protested the surprised Pancho.

"And what will the señor think when he asks me about it and I have to confess that I was not present?"

"Where shall I take these suitcases?" came the plaintive voice of the luggage carrier whose name, it developed, was Pancho — a fact that Don Pancho made much of in an effort to bypass Brigida's wrath.

"And I shall call you *Tocayo* [namesake]," he said heartily.

We made the rounds of all the hotels and boarding houses in the town. Pancho, of course, would sleep at the oratory, but Brigida and I needed a room. The Posada Hotel was full and so were all the others. We were tired and sleepy and damp.

When we had trudged miles, I remembered the advice of a Mexican friend of mine. "Anywhere in Mexico, when you are in difficulty of any sort, you can go to the church — and they will be glad to recommend people or places to you."

"Go to the church," I told Don Pancho, "and ask them to recommend a place for us to stay. Take my card from the Mexican government and show it to them."

"That is unnecessary, señora," he protested as I handed it to him. "The priest knows me. He baptized me. I have only to explain to him, and all will be well. He will help us find a room. Then we will get a car and come back for you."

Brigida and I sat on the curb in front of the Posada and waited. Meanwhile daylight came and we watched the town wake up. After what seemed ages, Don Pancho came into view followed by his Tocayo. Don Pancho was upset. They had gone to the convent and had asked for his friend the priest, but the sacristan had appeared at the gate to say that the priest was busy. Pancho then showed the sacristan our cards, explaining that I was writing a book, and asked him to recommend a place for us to stay.

"And, señora, he answered me in a very haughty manner. He said, just as if I had asked for a room at the convent, that there was no room there as the convent was filled with visiting priests and that he could not recommend a place for us because all the hotels had been taken possession of by your countrymen so that there was no room for anybody."

"¡Ay, qué lástima!" cried Brigida.

"I do not like sacristans," Don Pancho informed us. "Always they are bigger than their positions. Had they told the padre my name I am sure he would have ordered them to let me in. The padre would have recommended a place to us. He would have helped us. He is the priest who baptized me. He is my friend."

Through the kindness of the servant who was mopping the patio of the Posada we finally obtained a room in the home of Señor Martínez, a widower who lived with his three daughters and a fourteen-year-old son on the street of San Francisco. It was an attractive rose-colored colonial house with a charming patio, two sides of which were arched colonnade. We put our luggage in our room and went to a restaurant for breakfast. On our way back we detoured three blocks for Don Pancho to show us where the cuartel general was located. Then he left us at the Martínez door, promising to let us know when the dancing started.

We were surprised that the Martínez family knew Don Pancho's dance jefe, Capitán General Ruperto Granados.

"Everybody knows him," the younger Martínez daughter assured us.

"So they do," Señorita Paz agreed. "He is an Indito and an old man now, but the whole town respects him."

About two-thirty Señorita Consuelo ran in to tell us that danzantes were coming down the street, and everybody dashed to the balconies on the front of the house to watch them. Down the hill, between white and rose-colored buildings at the other end of the cobblestone street, danced the Concheros. Their silk and satin banners and their brilliant feather headdresses formed an island of color in a sea of white-clad *campesinos* (farmers) who hemmed them in on every side and moved along with them in the tropical sunlight. As they passed beneath our balcony Don Pancho, dancing in the center of the first line of three, glanced up and saw us.

"We will await you at the cuartel general," he called. "At the cuartel general!"

Brigida and I hurried to meet them there, but we missed a turn and were soon lost. By the time we found the oratory, the danzantes had gone. The son of the General was there with two women and several men, two of whom had been drinking.

"Where are the danzantes?" we asked.

"I do not know," the General's son answered curtly.

"They will come back soon," said one of the women, and we decided to wait.

I was chatting with the women when I realized that Brigida was having an argument with the General's son on the other side of the room.

"You should be helping her instead of talking in this manner," Brigida said angrily. "She is writing a book about the dance and . . . ."

"She will get it," broke in the General's son with a sneer. "She is a gringa and she will get it all. From the blossom on the end of the branch to the roots down in the earth, she will get it."

"Where I come from," Brigida told him, "we do not treat strangers in this manner. We welcome people from another country. We have manners where I come from."

"Where you from?" the drunk in the corner asked, raising his head and fixing his bleary eyes on her.

"From Tepetlaoxtoc," she told him.

"Eh?"

"Brigida," I called to her, "we will go," and started toward the door.

"Pay no attention to what he says, señora," whispered the woman to whom I had been talking. "His father will be very angry with him. Do not go. He is not the General. He is only the General's son."

"We will go," I insisted. "He is the General's son and some day he will be the General."

"I will not," he stormed. "My father lives out his life at the beck and call of people who care for nothing but themselves. I will not do that. Never! I will not be pope to a lot of Indians. Not I."

Without further ado we started out.

"But you will come back to the velación, will you not?" the woman almost wept, as she followed us to the door.

"Yes, come back to the velación," seconded the General's son gruffly. "My father wants you to come."

As we turned a corner Brigida saw Don Pancho hurrying across the next intersection, and called him.

"I have been looking everywhere for you," he said breathlessly. "We are going to make our entrance from the Camino Real. Hurry, señora. It is not far."

The Concheros had gathered on the road from the railway station to town, and were forming a long line, three abreast. The Capitán General Ruperto Granados, tall and thin, at least eighty years old, but straight and supple, invited me to dance with them.

"Say yes, señora," instructed Pancho. "It will be easy. Just a paso del camino. You can do that."

The General escorted me to the middle of the line beside an elderly woman with gray hair whose name, I learned, was Altagracia Gonzales. I did not learn the name of the young man on the other side of me, for he spoke to nobody the whole way.

First we marched, then began to dance a paso del camino.

"Do not tire yourself, señora," cautioned Altagracia. "You and I are not expected to lift our legs high. Let the chiefs do that — or those who would be chiefs — if they could."

About halfway to town we passed several men carrying large wooden frames filled with what looked like waxy magnolias.

"What are those?" I asked Altagracia.

"Those are the *frontales*,"[1] she answered. "Have you not seen them before? They are also called Xuchiles."

"Is that the cucharillo?"

"That is the cucharillo."

The Xuchiles I had seen had been decorated custodias of the oratory, while the cucharillo of the capital is usually a border around a door. These frames were too long for a door. Upright, they would be taller than a two-story house.

"The cucharillo is the decoration of the Bajío," said Altagracia, "and it is bigger and better here than in any other place."

We danced into the town and up the street that leads to the square in front of the Church of San Miguel. Around the square we danced. I was glad I had not lifted my feet high, for I was now so tired I could hardly lift them at all.

"You dance well," Altagracia cheered me, "and we have almost finished. Do not falter now."

The people on the balcony of a building at the corner threw bunches of pink cosmos at Don Pancho, three trios ahead of us lifting his feet high with nimble grace. They threw cosmos at me, too, but I remembered José Celis' definition of "to call attention" and made no sign that I knew it.

After four times around the plaza, the Concheros danced through the streets to the oratorio general, or cuartel general, as they also called the oratory. A crowd was there. The Capitán General received flowers and candles and offered them to the Four Winds, murmuring as he did so.

"Do you hear him, señora?" whispered Pancho.

"Yes, but I do not understand him," I whispered back.

Pancho chuckled. "Know why? Because he speaks in Otomí. I told you that you would hear Otomí, did I not?"

Then Tata Ruperto, as most of them called him, made an announcement. Those who wanted to, might rest for the dancing tomorrow. The others would stay for the velación.

I turned toward the door and saw that Brigida had arrived. She had not danced, she said, but had walked behind the Concheros. Altagracia brought chairs for Brigida and me. Then she bade us good night for she was one of those who needed rest for the dancing tomorrow.

The two drunks who had been in the oratory that afternoon were still there. One lay on the floor near the altar and wept, his woman kneeling beside him, gently wiping his face with a handkerchief. The other now dragged himself from his corner and fell prostrate in front of the altar, begging the saint to forgive his sins. Tata Ruperto called two danzantes and gestured toward the drunk men. Gently and kindly they led them away.

While they did this, some of the crowd snickered. Don Pancho turned to me, his eyes flashing with indignation.

"Is it not better, señora," he asked in ringing tones, "that a poor sinner have his little hour of redemption before the altar drunk than never to have it at all?"

"I think so, Don Pancho," I answered.

"Then why do people laugh?" he asked furiously.

"It is the way of the world," said Brigida and the danzantes near us agreed, while those who had laughed busily tinkered with their conchas.

From time to time groups of danzantes arrived bringing santos which the capitanas placed on the altar. I had counted eight when I suddenly discovered, at the front of the altar, a gray flannel bundle like the one I had seen in the cave at Guanajuato.

"What is it?" I whispered to Brigida.

She did not know, nor did the woman on the other side of me.

When I asked Pancho he quickly changed the subject. "Do you see that photograph, señora?" pointing to the one beside the altar. "That is the father of Tata Ruperto, Carlos Granados, or Lima Dulce, as he is sometimes called. He was a famous dance chief and they say that that photograph is muy milagroso."

In the coming years I was to find that the danzantes invariably changed the subject when I questioned them about The Bundle.

The altar was across one end of the long room. Near the end of the wall on the left was a door to the street and opposite it on the right was a door into a patio, which was filled with women grinding corn on *metates*, patting tortillas into shape, or stirring huge pots cooking on portable braseros.

The Concheros did not sit together in one big group, as they do in the capital, but cross-legged on the floor in separate little groups. One group would sing an alabanza, at the end of which their leader would call, "El es Dios." This was a signal for the next group to sing, moving around the room counterclockwise.

A blind chief from León came in with his personnel. Another chief introduced him and announced that the group would sing, with the blind chief leading. They had sung one alabanza when Pancho politely asked permission to sing one in honor of those who had died at Cazadero. Some of the group from León seemed reluctant to grant the permission, but the chief stood up and magnanimously requested Pancho to proceed.

An old friend of Pancho's sat beside him, playing his concha and singing with him as Pancho played his mandolin. It was a ragged performance and, I believe, completely spontaneous. (Pancho could never sing it again, though he tried repeatedly after we returned to the capital.) They sang a religious ballad telling the story of the wreck and eulogizing those who "now rest in glory." At times they achieved a fine level of poetic expression, at others I was afraid they would falter in the middle of a stanza. As soon as they had finished, the group from León sang again.

Apparently Pancho had expected something, I do not know what, at the end of his alabanza, for he sank into a dark, bitter mood, glaring at danzantes across the room, and whispering to his old friend beside him.

Suddenly Pancho leaped to his feet. "My General!" he cried, "I came back here to the annual fiesta with much happiness, feeling that I was coming home, back to my oratory, back to My General. But, My General, I have been very disappointed. Oh, I have seen the harsh looks and I have heard the insults that have been whispered! And this afternoon because some of the public who were watching us threw flowers at me and at the foreign señora who is a friend of the danzantes, some of you whispered that I was haughty and proud, and danced only to make an exhibition of myself. Oh, I have known the looks of envy and the talk of hatred that were among you! And now, My General, I feel that perhaps it would be better for me to retire myself and leave this oratory forever. So that is what I tell you now, My General. El es Dios." He was almost crying as he finished.

In a voice trembling with emotion, the General gave his decision. "My son, you will never retire yourself from this oratory until the conquest of your general by death!"

Sometime in early morning, the General, who had just returned after a short absence, picked up a saucer of small cigarettes from beside the disciplina on the altar, and passed them around the room.

"Gracias, no," I said when he passed them to me.

"It is a little custom we have, señora," Pancho explained while Tata Ruperto continued to hold the saucer in front of me, "that all of us smoke together at this time."

I took one of the tiny cigarettes and so did Brigida and, when the others began to smoke, so did we.

"It is long past midnight," I murmured to Pancho. "When will they dress the Xuchil?"

"They did that at midnight at the other oratory. Did I not tell you? This general is so great that he has to have two oratories to take care of the crowds."

"¡De veras!"

"Sí, señora. This is the oratorio real. Tonight he has done those at the oratorio segundo the honor to ask them to dress the Xuchil there. They will bring it here tomorrow."

"I see."

"The wife and the son of the General are over there and that is where he was when he was absent from here."

"So," I remarked, "the son is with his mother."

"No, señora. The son's mother is dead and my General has married with a younger woman. The son is with his stepmother at the other oratory."

The General now began the closing ceremony, leading the Ave Marías in Spanish. I was too tired and relaxed to follow, and when the others began to file into the back patio for their "little waters" of orange leaf tea and coffee, we left.

When we reached our corner, Brigida had the bad judgment to repeat to Don Pancho some remarks against him she had overheard in the oratory. Raising his eyes to heaven Don Pancho, in a voice that at five-thirty in the morning must have waked the whole neighborhood, recalled the abuse he had suffered at the hands of both visiting and local danzantes since he had stepped from the train at three-thirty the morning before.

"I am not going to tolerate it!" he roared. "I will accompany you to your door, as the señor would want me to. Then I am going back to the oratory and tell them what they are. Sí, señora, I must go back and deal with them. For my *amor propio* [self-esteem], I must go back."

Though I longed to curl up on the pavement and sleep, I pulled myself together and tried to quiet him.

"Look, Don Pancho! Which is of importance to you, that you exchange insults with a lot of shameless ones, or that your general extend his fame by having a great success of the dancing today?"

"Pues — the dancing, of course."

"Then consider the dancing. Brigida is tired and sleepy or she would probably explain to you that she heard those remarks before you tried to retire yourself and your general gave his decision. Did you hear what he said?"

"Sí, señora," — brightening visibly.

"And can anyone be in doubt now as to what your general thinks of you?"

"No, señora!" — proudly.

"Wait until tomorrow and you will find that everybody is your friend because the General is your friend."

"You are right, señora, I will wait until tomorrow and see what they have to say. I will wait until tomorrow — but only until tomorrow."

"That Pancho," grumbled Brigida as we climbed the stairs, "taking our time at this hour of the morning to tell us about all the things he knows he is not going to do!"

I had been asleep only a short time when a yell from the other bed woke me.

"¡Ay, señora!" Brigida flounced from her pillow and threw the covers wildly. "I have had such horrible dreams! The whole time I slept I dreamed of frightful things. ¡Ay, señora!"

"Something you ate, perhaps," I suggested.

"But, señora, they were such dreadful things. Ay, I suffered much!"

"How do you feel now?" I asked.

"I feel *muy curiosa* and very sad, señora. What could I have eaten that would make me so sad? I know what caused it! Remember those cigarettes we smoked? Marijuana! That is what they were, señora. We smoked marijuana!"

"Have no care," I soothed her. "It is something you ate. Indigestion often makes people sad."

"No, señora. I have always heard that they smoke marijuana in the Bajío. How could I have forgotten it!"

"But I smoked, too."

"And what did you dream?"

"Nothing."

"But you felt something extraordinary, did you not?"

"Just tired. And a little dizzy while Pancho was talking about returning to the oratory. My feet seemed a long way from my head."

"That is it!" she pounced upon this symptom. "Sometimes you think you are very tall when you are really short. Sometimes you think you are walking when you are running. That Pancho! 'A little custom we have.' Wait till I see him again!"

"Look, Brigida! You will have no more arguments with Pancho on this trip. No more arguments! Do you understand?"

"Sí, señora," — becoming a servant again.

After a late breakfast we gathered the cameras and strolled toward the Church of San Miguel. At the corner of the square we met Pancho in dance costume.

"Señora," he called, "would you like to take a little picture of me beside the statue of my little father, San Miguel?"

"Pancho," Brigida glared at him, "did those cigarettes we smoked contain marijuana?"

"One little moment," I intervened quickly. "Whatever they contained we have smoked them. Let us forget last night and live in today. Don Pancho, I think if you stood by the statue of San Miguel, it would make a very good picture."

"Not standing, señora. Kneeling."

Then I saw the Xuchiles, three of them, standing upright between the statue of San Miguel and the main entrance to the church. In their whiteness, they were even more beautiful standing tall and slim than they had been stretched flat on the Camino Real. I stood admiring them until Pancho became impatient.

"Can you take me like this, señora?" he asked, kneeling before the statue.

"Pancho," I told him, as I squinted into the camera, "it is impossible to get both you and the statue from here. San Miguel is too high. I shall have to go outside the churchyard and take the picture through the iron bars of the fence. That means that you will be very small in the picture."

"Then take one of me from here first, señora. I shall know that I am in front of San Miguel even though he does not show in the picture. Will you do me the favor to take it as I am now, señora?"

I was beside him with the light meter trained against his costume when we heard a peculiar noise and looked up to see a priest striding toward us, his robe snapping and snarling as he came.

"What happens?" he shouted angrily. "What are you doing?"

"It is all right, Padre," said Pancho. "This is the señora of whom I told you. It is all right, Padre. She is not a tourist. It is the señora who came with me."

The priest halted, breathing heavily, and glared at me.

"We have had too much trouble with the Protestant propaganda," he said brusquely, "to allow any photographs by strangers without special permission."

"But I asked her to do me the favor to take a photograph of me here, Padre. May she take it? She is not a tourist. May she take it, Padre? May she?"

The priest stared at me a long moment before he grudgingly consented. He fairly glared before he whirled and marched away.

"Is that your beloved padre, the one who baptized you, Pancho?"

"Sí, señora. I do not understand why he talked like that. He is very good and kind. I never saw him like that before."

I took one picture of Pancho kneeling before the statue and then went across to the corner of the square to get one of him and the statue. A soldier in uniform passed by.

"Make her pay plenty for that picture," he called to Pancho. "She is a gringa and all gringos are rich."

Pancho drew himself up haughtily. "The señora walks with the danzantes," he snapped. "She is the respected friend of all of us."

By this time the fiesta was getting under way. A large dance circle with a banner dedicated to the Señor de la Conquista filled the atrio. Don Ruperto's group formed their circle outside in the square in front of the broad stairs leading to the gate. Pancho placed us in the edge of the circle, insisting that Brigida dance, too — which threw her into a fit of happy giggles. We had danced only one step when the General came over and escorted me to a place in the center, among the flag bearers and the captains. This was an honor, for since before the Conquest, the center of the dance circle has been reserved for important people.

I danced beside a young flag bearer from Comonfort, who wore a simple costume of white rayon with appliqué of the same material in blue. His crown was of blue and white ostrich feathers in a band of

Xuchiles (also the *frontales* or the *cucharillo*)

blue rayon trimmed with sequins. He seemed worried and, between steps, poured out his troubles to me.

"Look," he exclaimed, "there they go! Those who ascend the steps. They are our companions and they put themselves contrary with us in everything. We do not put ourselves contrary with them, but they do with us and that is not the *conformidad*, is it señorita?"

I hastily agreed, for the General was coming toward me again.

"Señora," said the General, "this next step is not difficult. You dance it like this," dancing a few steps. I tried to follow him and eventually he was satisfied with my efforts. Several times after that he gave me special instructions before a complicated step.

"We all agreed to wear uniforms like this one that I have on," continued the young man from Comonfort when we had finished that step. "We agreed, señora, because this is the conformidad. Now they have appeared here today in uniforms very different and very elegant!"

The sargento indicated another danzante, who came to the center of the circle and played the firma. The others joined him and danced the steps that form the cross. Then he played alone for a moment until his dance tune was clear to all.

"El es Dios," he cried as he lifted his right foot and began his step. So we danced again, stepping as he stepped as nearly as we could. After we had repeated the figure eight or ten times, again he called out, "El es Dios," and retired to his place at the edge of the circle.

The flag bearer on my right continued his story. "And look, señorita, they have left this group that is their own, and have entered the circle of others, and they did not ask permission of us, or even tell us that they were going to do this. How can they think that they are danzantes when they behave in this manner? This is not the conformidad."

We danced another step and paused again. "These companions of ours, señora," he continued sadly, "have completely abandoned us. They are now in the atrio dancing in another circle."

"¡El es Dios!" cried the dancer who had marked the step and we stopped dancing. Brigida plunged across the circle to my side.

"¡Ay, señora!" she gasped, pulling my arm. "Come quickly! There is going to be trouble."

"Wait," I protested, "I must ask permission to leave the circle."

"No, no, señora! There is no time. Come now!" She pulled me out of the circle and urged me toward the walk that bordered the plaza. "Hurry, señora," she begged. "Those women who stood behind me while I danced are mad at you. They said awful things about you! The fat one said you would get out of the circle if she had to force you out."

"What fat woman?"

"Come, señora. Let us run. Let us run to the house of Señor Martínez!"

"Now look, Brigida, I came out of the circle because you wanted me to, but I am not going to run anywhere and you are not either. The idea!"

"¡Ay, señora!"

"What fat woman is mad at me? The one with the blue rebozo? I do not know her. We will go over and talk to her."

"No, no, no, señora! You do not know these people. They are bad! You will get a knife between your ribs."

"What silliness!"

"And what will the señor say? Ay, señora!"

Pancho, summoned by Brigida's frantic gestures, came up and she explained.

"The fat woman is the wife of My General," he said. "She takes the part of the son against the father. They are having trouble."

"Let us go over and talk to her," I suggested.

"¡Ay, señora!" Brigida's voice rose to a squeak. "There she is behind you!"

"Introduce her, Pancho," I murmured, as the scowling fat woman approached.

"Señora Marta," Pancho said grandly, "this is the wife of My General, Ruperto Granados."

"Oh, señora!" I exclaimed, pumping her hand. "Much pleasure to know you."

Her jaw dropped and her eyes widened.

"I have been wanting to meet you," I went on before she could recover. "Your husband has shown us many favors at this fiesta, and I want to extend an invitation to the two of you to come see my husband and me at our home when you come to the capital." I took a card with our address on it from my pocketbook.

"The señores have a nice home," Pancho informed her, "in front of the Military College, and they always welcome the danzantes."

The woman took the card and clasped it to her breast.

"Ay, señora," she cried apologetically, "I did not know that it was you." Turning to Pancho, "I did not know that she was the señora who came with you."

"The señora came to this fiesta at my invitation," Pancho assured her, "because My General had given me permission to bring her sometime."

"Now we must go," I told her, shaking her hand again. "I hope to see you and your husband soon *en su casa* [in "your" house, meaning *my* house] in the capital."

"¡Ay, señora! A thousand thanks, señora, a thousand thanks."

That day at lunch, I mentioned the priest and his objections to the photographs. I was surprised at the reaction of the Martínez family. At first I thought they were afraid I would get an unfavorable impression of their town, but I soon realized that their concern was that the priest should think badly of me, a guest in their house. They urged me to call on the priest and present my credentials. Finally I consented to do so, and Señor Martínez called his son, Guadalupe.

"Go with the señora. Take her first to your uncle, the priest. Kiss his hand and tell him that you come to introduce a writer who is not a tourist. Ask him to present her to the señor Cura."

That was the first that I knew that Señor Martínez had a brother-in-law who was a priest. Guadalupe led Brigida and me to a house several blocks away on a side street. The priest himself answered our knock.

Guadalupe solemnly announced, "My father sent me to bring this writer. She is not a tourist."

When his uncle learned from my letters that I was interested in Mexican history, he led me to his small but excellent library. For the next half hour we had tea and enjoyed looking over his rare books.

"Señora," he said, "I think you should show your letters to the cura. I am sorry that I cannot accompany you, but I will send Guadalupe with you."

When we reached the cura's house we found a group of white-clad campesinos seated on the steps outside the door.

"Is the cura in?" Guadalupe asked them.

"Yes," they answered, "we are waiting to see him."

A servant informed us that the cura would see us later and asked us to be seated on a wooden settee in the hall.

"Now that you are in the house of the cura, señora," said Guadalupe, "I can be of no further service to you, so a very good afternoon to you." I think he was glad to be rid of us.

Finally we were admitted to the priest's office.

"Good afternoon," I said, placing my foreign relations card on the desk before him. "Señor Martínez, in whose home we are staying, has asked me to show you some letters I have."

He picked up the card and read it carefully. Then I handed him the letter from our friend in the capital, whose position in the church commands respect. While Brigida and I sat on the bench against the wall, he sat behind his desk and read of my interest in the archaeology and the folklore of Mexico.

"This completely meets with my approval," he exclaimed, bouncing to his feet. "It is just that so many people come here who say that they are well documented and when one comes to read their credentials they are quite worthless. Had you presented your documents when you first arrived nothing would have happened."

From his guarded answers to my questions, it was evident that there would be no sprightly discussion of Mexican history and historians such as I enjoyed with Guadalupe's uncle. Then, too, the white-clad Indians were still waiting outside. After a few minutes we took our leave.

That night the Martínez family invited us to go to the church plaza with them to see the firing of the castillos and to watch the promenade. Birds, animals, angels, and saints sprang into fiery outline as the castillos were burned. Wheels spun, sending sparks in every direction, as whistles, cleverly attached to the wheels, wailed like fire engines. The married people and the children crowded near the castillos, while the young people of the town promenaded.

Around the square they strolled, the boys clockwise and the girls in the opposite direction. From nearby booths they bought bright-colored confetti, which they threw at each other, laughing and shrieking in gay excitement. The Martínez girls promenaded and, after a time, insisted that Brigida promenade with them. She was delighted. Her eyes sparkled and her dark face shone. Her money rapidly disappeared, for she ran from the line of girls to the confetti booth every few minutes. There were other Indian women there, but they were servants, walking discreetly behind the young ladies of their employers' houses. Brigida was a girl among girls, and her happiness was complete. On benches along the walk inside the little park sat the black-clad chaperones, saying nothing, seeing everything, and smiling on the gaiety of the young people.

At a loud cry from the *mayor domo* who managed the fireworks, everybody — married couples, children, young people, chaperones, even the confetti vendors — crowded around the last castillo. The mayor domo touched a fuse and a medley of all that had gone before burst into fiery picture. The children laughed and clapped their hands and appreciative murmurs came from all sides. At the very last came the climax; in the center, surrounded by showers of sparks, to the tune of whistles and sirens, glowed the likeness of San Miguel. The *publico* applauded! Then it was over, and everybody went home.

In all the throng I had not seen one danzante. Where were they? Was I missing some rare and secret ceremony by watching the publico at play? I turned to voice my misgivings to Brigida, but her happy, shining face silenced me.

Pancho arrived at the Martínez home early the next morning.

"Señora, I should like very much to go to the ranch near here where I was born."

"Fine! If we can get back in time for the Mexico City train tonight."

"We cannot do that, señora, but we can go to the ranch today and get back in time for the Mexico City train tomorrow."

"But Don Pancho! I told the señor that we would go back tonight ·and he will meet the train. He will be very worried if we are not on it."

"¡Ay, señora! You would love the ranch. Everybody would quit work in our honor and tonight they would make fiesta."

"If I should send a telegram now, as you know, Don Pancho, he probably would not receive it until tomorrow."

"And tomorrow," he went on, "we would ride the horses and play games. And they would cook *mole con guajolote* [mole sauce with turkey]. You love mole, do you not, señora?"

"¡Ay, señora!" Brigida breathed ecstatically.

"I have to go home, Don Pancho, but you can go to the ranch. Brigida can take care of me. We will simply get on the Pullman and sleep until we reach the capital. And my husband will meet the train. You see, we really do not need you."

"This is the same argument we had in Chalma. Do you not realize, señora, that when your husband places you in my care on a trip, I must go everywhere you go until you return to him?"

"That is foolish, Don Pancho. I see no reason why we should not return to the capital without you."

"If you and the señorita Brigida should return to the capital, and if the train should be wrecked and I should not be there to drag you to safety, do you think, señora, that I could ever face your husband? No, señora, if you cannot go with me to the ranch, then I will go back to the capital with you tonight."

That afternoon we went to the oratory again. We were early and Don Ruperto showed us the Santo Xuchil. Like Don Cecilio's in Guanajuato, it was decorated with spoon cactus.

As the danzantes arrived, they presented baskets of fruit and flowers to the Four Winds in front of the altar. When there were fifty or more, all in full dance regalia, they formed a procession in the street outside and, carrying their offerings, marched to the church. Brigida and I marched in the rear.

When we arrived at the plaza in front of the church, the procession moved up the wide stairs, across the atrio and inside the church. Halfway down the long nave they stopped before a low railing, evidently placed there for the purpose, where a priest in rich vestments awaited them. He received the offerings and blessed them, sprinkling holy water on each basket of fruit and flowers. Brigida, Pancho, and I had a seat not far from the railing, but we were unable to see all that took place because of the line of danzantes across the church. Don Pancho sat between Brigida and me and murmured explanations as the ceremony progressed, adding to the buzz that filled the church as people chatted in undertones.

"These offerings," he said proudly, "are in honor of the already fallen dead, that is, the first conquistadores of the dance. They are in memory of the chiefs of the tribes in the past. So are the Otomí dances offered at this religious fiesta."

"¡De veras!" Brigida murmured conversationally.

"You understand, señora, do you not, that the given name of these people is Otomí and the surname is Chichimec?"

I nodded, though I knew the anthropologists did not agree with him.

"Following their custom," he went on, as if repeating something he had memorized, "they have set up an altar midway in the church, in the center, and a priest attends it, interceding for those danzantes who have bidden farewell to this world. This is the way the dead are remembered by their heirs, according to the ancient custom."

"Aren't those yellow flowers cempaxochitles [marigolds]?" asked Brigida.

"Sí, señorita."

"But the cempaxochitle is the flower of the dead," I said. "In fact, this entire ceremony reminds me of the velación of the dead in the capital — which, of course, is in the oratory and is at night."

"It is similar to that ceremony," he agreed, "because it is for the repose of the spirits. Here in San Miguel they dress the Xuchil on the Day of San Miguel and at Easter."

"Do they?" I asked in surprise. "I thought it was at Easter and on the Day of the Dead."

"No, señora. In the capital they do dress the Xuchil at Easter and on the Day of the Dead — but they do not take their offerings to the church as they do here."

"San Miguel seems quite different from the capital, Don Pancho."

"It is, señora. Have you noticed the priest? Do you know that he is a very special priest who has come here just for this ceremony of the danzantes? Not all priests know how to take part in this ceremony. Of a truth, he is very special!"

The danzantes were now taking the fruit and flowers from the improvised altar.

"What are they going to do with them now, Don Pancho?" I asked.

"They will take them to the cemetery and to the tomb of Carlos Granados."

"Was that Don Ruperto's father?"asked Brigida.

"Sí, señorita, he whose picture you saw by the altar at the oratory. They call him Lima Dulce."

"Why?" asked Brigida.

"Because he ate a sweet lime just before he died."

"¡Pobrecito!"

"Señora," continued Pancho, "the graveyard where he is buried is very far from here. My General thinks it would be better for you and the señorita Brigida not to try to walk there."

Brigida started to protest but I touched her arm. We would do as the General wished.

Señor Martínez had wired for reservations for us on a train that was due in San Miguel de Allende at ten o'clock that night. It was a train from the border, he said, and would probably be filled with tourists from my country. That evening the railway office notified him that the train was now expected at three o'clock in the morning. Pancho had taken our bags to the station earlier and would meet us there. The younger Martínez girls invited us to wait for the train at their house and came to our room to wait with us.

We lay on the beds and talked. The girls knew many delightful tales of that region. They told us of witches, miracles, and ghosts. Brigida's eyes grew round with excitement. Two-thirty came too soon. Señor Martínez and the girls insisted on taking us to the station where we said good-bye with many thanks and promises of visits in the future. We had been with them for three days when we were not involved in the fiesta and they were now old friends.

As soon as they had driven away, Don Pancho materialized from the shadows to escort us to the waiting room which, like the platforms of the station, was filled with Indians, many of whom were asleep on the floor on their serapes. We sat on our suitcases in the corner of the waiting room until Pancho had a better idea.

"Señora, it is very warm in here and the air is bad. Let us go to the platform. You and the señorita Brigida can put on your coats and sit on the suitcases out there. You will be more comfortable."

It was a windy, starlit night. We drew our coats about us and talked. We sat there for hours, losing all sense of time, as Don Pancho told us the things we had not known about the fiesta we had just attended.

"The General Ruperto Granados was much upset when he learned that you had come, señora. He said, 'This is not the time to bring the foreign señora here because of the Campaign Against the Protestant Propaganda. She is your guest; therefore she is the guest of all of us. I shall have to send someone to follow her everywhere to see that no harm comes to her.' You did not know that somebody followed you everywhere you went, did you, señora?"

"Of a truth?" gasped Brigida, while Don Pancho enjoyed our surprise.

"Sí. And My General said, 'She will look like a tourist, she will dress like a tourist, and everybody will think she is a tourist.' And I said, 'Have no care, My General, have no care! For this señora, when she wants to can make herself look like *pura campesina.*'"

Both laughed at my reaction to looking like a country woman.

At five o'clock in the morning the train arrived. We managed to board it in three minutes and eventually Brigida and I obtained a section on the Pullman, she in the upper berth and I in the lower beneath her. We slept all the way to the capital.

Raising the Cross

WE CAME HOME from San Miguel de Allende to find that Nicolás, the segundo of the mesa at Huitzilapan, had passed away in our absence. Don Florentino had gone to Nicolás' house on danzante business and had found him seriously ill, apparently with pneumonia.

"I saw at once that he was badly off, señora. He clung to me and said, 'Do not leave me, compadrito!' That is what he said. And so I stayed until the end. It was the same day, señora."

"But how sudden, Don Florentino! He must have been sick only a day or two."

"Sí, señora, That is the truth. We are going to raise the cross on the night of the fifth. I hope that you can come, señora."

I had missed this ceremony when José died and wanted to see it, and so on the night of the fifth, just nine nights after Nicolás had died, Florentino, Juana, Brigida, and I set out for Nicolás' house.

We found the oratory in the little adobe house on the outskirts of the city already filled with danzantes. Don Manuel Luna sat on a low bench along the side wall. He nudged the boy beside him, "Get up and give the señora your seat!"

I looked about for a cross, perhaps a highly decorated one, but saw none. A narrow, homemade table about five feet long stood in front of the altar, filling the most important place. It was loaded with flowers in containers, probably tin cans, swathed in black crepe paper.

The danzantes were playing and singing when we arrived, but I thought I heard an undertone of moaning. Then across the flower-laden table I saw two women dressed in black, sitting on the floor, their backs to the opposite wall. Both were weeping and moaning. In the lull between alabanzas they burst into loud wails.

"Who are they?" I whispered to Don Manuel. "Is either the widow of Nicolás?"

"Neither. I know her," he whispered back, then added, "How do you like the altar?"

Slowly I looked at the jumble of objects on it. Near the front was a picture frame holding a dark blur.

"What is that?" I asked.

Don Manuel hesitated. "That, Señora Marta, is the Jefe Viejo (Old Chief)."

"And what is the Jefe Viejo?"

"It is a little print that was made by the church in the 1880s. Every dance oratory has one."

Near the Old Chief was an alarm clock. At twelve o'clock when the alarm pealed forth, Don Manuel leaned over and turned it off. Then he stood and named two danzantes to "work the flower," and Don Florentino to "raise the cross."

The two danzantes removed the flower containers from the table and some of the women began to break the blossoms from their stems and put them back on the table. From time to time the two danzantes would pick up a blossom and carefully place it at another spot on the table, but the bench where we sat was so low and the table so high that it was impossible for us to see what they were doing. After a time they slowly and carefully lifted the table and placed it against the wall on the other side of the room. The two women in black immediately crawled under it, leaned back against the wall, and burst into fresh wails.

"Hush them," Don Manuel told a capitán.

The capitán crossed the room and spoke to the women. When he came back, he told Don Manuel that they were professional mourners hired for the occasion.

"Then they are outside our authority," Don Manuel murmured regretfully.

I had been so interested in the two women that I had not noticed what lay on the floor under the table. Now that they had moved the table, I could see it plainly; a cross! Not the cement cross I had visualized, nor any concoction of lime I had imagined, but a cross of dry, loose lime about five feet long. It looked as if it might have been poured smoothly and evenly in a trail about a foot wide. Definitely, it is one thing to hear about a dance ceremony and another to see it yourself!

Don Florentino knelt at the foot of the cross and placed an empty shoebox beside him. With an *escobeta*,[1] or little straw broom, and a piece of white tissue paper, he slowly and reverently gathered up the lime, much as a housewife sweeps the dust into a dustpan, and emptied it into the shoebox. He worked from the foot toward the top of the cross while the danzantes sang, "María, A donde Vas?" ("María, Where Are You Going?"). When he had scraped the last of the lime into the pasteboard box, he meticulously placed the piece of paper, the tiny broom, a little bottle of holy water, and a wad of cotton on top of it. Then he lifted the box and presented it to the Four Winds. The raising of the cross was completed.

Afterward I questioned danzantes from both the capital and the Bajío about this ceremony.

"When the altar is arranged according to tradition, señora," said one, "the Old Chief is in the center, the disciplina at the right, and the Xuchil at the left. The rest of the things, like the santos and the photographs, depend on the mesa."

"When someone dies, señora," explained another, "members of the family, or of the mesa to which the deceased pertained, immediately make a cross of lime the length of the deceased on the floor in front of the oratory. Then they stretch the body over it. This is for the Passion of Christ — and, also, to preserve the body, señora."

"How long do they leave it there?" I asked.

"Here in the capital they usually leave it thirty minutes, but in my tierra they used to leave it twenty-four hours."

"What do they do with it when they take it up?"

"They wash it and prepare it for burial. But first they cover the cross with a table or a large box. That night they have the velación. Then comes the funeral followed by the novenario when the family and friends recite the rosary in the oratory for nine nights."

"Yes, I know. Is the cross of lime on the oratory floor all this time?"

"Sí, Señora Marta. And the spirit hovers around the house all this time, too. Then they raise the cross, and the following day they take the box with the lime, the holy water, the tissue paper, the little broom, and the cotton to the cemetery and bury it at the foot of the deceased's grave. In some regions they also bury a plate of vinegar and an onion. That same day, señora, they have a Mass for the dead in the church."

A year or two later Capitán Manuel Cortés, one of the four chiefs who had given the order to get me out of jail in Ameyalco, passed away, and Nieves and I attended the raising of the cross. Don Manuel Luna and his sons had already left for the ceremony when we arrived at the Luna house on the appointed night, but Doña Ester directed our taxi driver to a certain palm near a certain corner in the suburb of Jamaica where, she said, we would overtake them. I was a little doubtful about this, but when the car stopped, Don Manuel and the danzantes came out from under the palm to greet us. Then we sat with several other women not far from the palm on a hunk of something covered with sacking. I was unable to learn what it was, but it was solid and steady and not too hard. The moon was low and bright, enabling us to see each other's features, and casting patches of black near the buildings along the sidewalk and around the palm where the men stood talking in low tones. We women sat in silence, saving ourselves for the night-long vigil ahead.

After we had waited about an hour, the group of eleven slowly moved across the road into the black shadow of the buildings. Recent rains had made mud puddles in the primitive sidewalks and we had no flashlights. Following Don Fidel Morales, we turned off on a narrow, winding street and stumbled past dimly lighted doorways where stolid figures stared at us. Then we came to an open square in front of a house with a single electric bulb shining brightly inside the narrow, open lane to the patio that served as an entrance. This was where Capitán Manuel Cortés had lived and here was his oratory.

We stopped in front of the house to make our entrance. The two capitanas, youthful Lupe and elderly Francisca, lighted their incense burners. Then both sprinkled the charcoal with copal. About this time Nieves discovered that she had brought no scarf to cover her head — for women's heads must be covered during an entrance. Someone gave her a large handkerchief and we were ready.

A group of danzantes carrying a banner and lighted candles marched out to meet us. After an exchange of speeches between the leaders they joined our ranks to accompany us inside. Don Manuel began to sing to the strumming of the conchas and the others joined him. The capitanas began to ring their altar bells and to blow upon their incense burners. Banners waving and smoke swirling, we marched in.

The oratory was a small room at one side with only canvas between it and the entrance. The canvas had been lifted from the bottom and stretched out across the entrance to the wall on the other side to afford shelter in case of rain, as well as to enable those in the patio to see what went on in the oratory. Our leaders marched in and knelt beside the table in front of the altar. The rest of us knelt with them, those in the rear, including Nieves and me, kneeling in the patio. We were still kneeling when the street door opened to admit a man carrying a stout pole across his shoulders from each end of which hung a gasoline can filled with water.

"*Golpe! Golpe!*" he called, and we scrambled out of the way, for all over Mexico that means, "Get out of the way, or you will be hit!"

When Nieves and I stood up after the entrance, a danzante invited us to sit on a plank bench along the opposite side of the patio. We were no sooner seated than the street door opened and a ragged vagabond stepped inside and sat down beside Nieves. She edged away.

"I am as good as you are," he told her. "Why should I not sit here?"

A danzante came over and took his arm.

"Let me go!" shouted the vagabond. "I am ragged and I am not clean, but is that my fault? This is my country and I am as good as they. Why should I not sit here?"

Finally, the danzantes mentioned food and hot coffee in the kitchen, and he went with them.

In a few minutes the street door opened again and a drunk reeled in. He, too, wanted to sit by Nieves. The danzantes made short work of him. They grasped him by the arms and shoulders and forced him outside.

"I do not like it here, señora," whispered Nieves.

Soon it began to rain, coming down with great force, spilling over the inadequate canvas into the patio and on the bench. Our friends seized the opportunity to shove us into the oratory up by the altar where we would have an excellent view of the ceremony. As we stood by the altar, the long table, for Capitán Manuel Cortés had been tall, was on our left. I could see the cross of lime by stooping and peering. Between the table and the altar were two Mexican flags on pedestals. At each of the four corners of the table stood a tall brass candlestick with a lighted candle. Early in the evening I noticed that the usual quiet reverence was lacking in the crowd. The chiefs inside the oratory were continually calling "Silence!" to the danzantes in the patio. Once or twice between alabanzas I heard sounds of argument out there. I was glad that Nieves and I were inside.

A round-faced young woman with a coronet of black braids walked into the oratory while we were singing and sat in a chair against the opposite wall. I smiled at her and she stared back coldly. Nieves, who was our maid in the mornings and a student at a business academy in the afternoons, was practicing shorthand while we sang. Holding my notebook of alabanzas, she stood between Don Fidel Morales, who led the singing, and me. After he finished a verse and while he waited for the others to sing the planta, she would read the words of the next verse to him in an undertone. Now and then there would be a slight difference between Don Fidel's version and hers, and she would scribble a few notes on the margin of the notebook.

Suddenly the young woman with the braids stood up and, bristling with hostility, eyed us.

"Look at them!" she shrilled. "One of them sings and looks inno-cent, while the other writes in a book. They are partners. They are here to see what they can see, and to hear what they can hear. They probably work for the newspapers. Throw them out! They were not friends of my dear uncle. He never knew them! Throw them out, I tell you! Throw them out!"

In the horrified silence that followed, I leaned forward and spoke to Don Manuel near the foot of the table.

"Capitán General Manuel Luna," I said, "do me the favor to inform this woman that Capitán Manuel Cortés once helped to get me out of jail!"

"Señora Marta Estony," Don Manuel replied slowly and clearly, "please pardon the disorder you have observed here tonight. We have come here to pay our respects to our departed brother, but some seem to have forgotten why they came."

The young woman with the braids rose on her high heels and clattered out.

At twelve o'clock Don Manuel named Don Fidel and a capitán "to work the flowers," and the capitanas set to work breaking the stems "three fingers" from the bloom. They placed the blossoms in a circular line around the edges of the tabletop and the two men took them from there, one by one, to form a cross of flowers in the center, working together, Don Fidel on the right and the capitán on the left, moving from the head of the cross at the end near the altar to the foot at the opposite end. Every now and then Don Fidel would stop and peer under the table to make sure the flower cross on the table coincided exactly with the cross of lime underneath. This was what I had missed at the ceremony for Nicolás.

Before they had finished the cross of flowers, argument broke out anew in the patio. Don Miguel Herrera, a gentle old man with drooping gray moustaches, had been the segundo of Don Manuel Cortés' mesa. Apparently the deceased, having no son in the dance, had left his posi-tion to his segundo. Now Captain Herrera had decided to place himself under the orders of Captain General Manuel Luna. When Don Manuel called him to the foot of the table and introduced him as the new chief, loud objections came from the patio. Don Manuel made a placating speech, suggesting that they have a conference at another time to express their objections. He urged them to "respect these ashes" and to be careful of their language "in the presence of the defunct," gesturing toward the cross of lime. He then called for the report of those who had done "the work of the flowers."

Don Fidel reported that they had finished and that "well-done or not well-done," they now offered the results "in memory of these ashes." Don Manuel accepted the result of their labor terming it well-done and thanked Don Fidel and the captain. He then appointed another captain to raise the cross.

There was a little delay while they looked for this second captain, but eventually several danzantes escorted him to the oratory. We began to sing "María, A donde Vas?" as he started to sweep with the tiny straw broom. His manner was surly and became more so as Don Fidel and others near him angrily pointed out his blunders. He swept too fast, he gathered up too much lime at one time, and he began on the left side of the cross instead of the right.

By the time he closed the box on the lime, tissue paper, broom, holy water, and wad of cotton, the wrangling in the patio had begun again. Someone recalled in a loud voice that once at Los Remedios, the defunct had joined enemies of theirs and had refused to recognize them. Somebody else remembered that he had vacillated, undecided whether to dance or not for the político at the Fiesta of the Tree of the Sad Night. This brought a storm of denial that was drowned in a tempest of contradiction.

"Silence! Silence!" shouted the chiefs in the oratory.

"Sing!" Don Manuel ordered in an undertone.

"Sing loudly!" said Don Fidel to Nieves and me.

At the tops of our voices we sang "Ánimas en Pena" and for a time, as those in the patio shrieked and shouted, there was bedlam. Gradually they grew tired and by the time we had finished several verses there was comparative quiet.

"Ave María Purísima" — Don Manuel intoned before anybody could say anything. He closed the service without offering opportunity for announcements and we filed out of the oratory.

A group of the dissatisfied immediately surrounded Don Manuel. He announced that this was neither the time nor the place for an airing of differences of opinion and that he could not take part in further discussion. Then he called a taxi and we left.

On the way home the danzantes explained that the root of the matter lay in the fact that there was some doubt as to who would get the estate of Don Manuel Cortés. Apparently there was, in addition to the house, a considerable sum of money in the bank, perhaps as much as five thousand pesos. His first wife having died, Manuel Cortés, in his later years, had married a second time. For some reason the second marriage had been by civil ceremony only and, since the church ceremony is the only one recognized in some quarters, there were those who held that the wife should not inherit.

"For many years, señora," explained Fidel, "the defunct lived in peace and happiness with the companion of his years and his godson. We thought there were no other relatives. Certainly none arrived to make his old age happier."

"Then he has this illness and he dies," Miguel Luna broke in, "and this woman whom you saw tonight, señora, the one who was rude to you, she arrives calling him her dear uncle!"

"Dear uncle!" snorted Fidel. "She is not even his niece. She is only the daughter of a distant cousin."

"Do you think she will manage to inherit?" I asked.

"As you could see there tonight," Fidel pointed out, "she has the approval of many danzantes. Those who made the disorder are siding with her against the widow and the godson."

"And she has employed a lawyer," added Miguel. "If they can prove that she is the only living blood relation of Don Manuel Cortés, it will make difficulty for the señora and the godson."

"Something will happen before the so-called niece gets her hands on the property," prophesied Don Manuel who had been silent until now. "Something will happen to prevent it."

A few weeks later I met Don Manuel at a fiesta at Tlaltelolco.

"Did the niece get the property of Don Manuel Cortés?" I asked, as soon as I had greeted him.

"No, señora," he beamed. "An agent of the government investigated and found that the taxes had not been paid, or at least the widow and the godson failed to produce any tax receipts. After the government deducted taxes for many years, there was nothing left."

"¡Ay, Don Manuel!"

"The so-called niece had no money to pay her lawyer and he threatened to make trouble for her, so she left here. Oh, she was very angry, but she left without delay — thanks to God!"

Then he faced the open door of the church, glanced at the santo on the altar, and crossed himself.

Reception of Members – Ahuixotla

AFTER ANDANDO CON LOS DANZANTES for nearly ten years, I still had not attended the ceremony for reception of members into the dance. Both José Celis and Don Pancho had described it to me but I wanted to see it myself. In 1949 when Don Manuel invited me to a *recibimiento* at Santiago de Ahuixotla he was surprised at the enthusiasm of my acceptance.

About nine o'clock that October night Nieves and I took a taxi to the police *caseta* (guard house) just beyond Tacuba where fifteen danzantes had gathered. An hour later, led by a boy with an oil lantern, we hiked down a muddy trail to the railroad where Don Fidel Morales and his personnel were sitting on crossties singing alabanzas as they waited for us. When we were on our way again, strung out along the railway, I found Don Manuel beside me.

"Let me get this straight, Don Manuel," I said. "We are going to a recibimiento of the Rayados, is that right?"

"That is right, Señora Marta."

"And the Rayados are *contradanzas?*"

"They are contradanzas — sí señora."

"But the recibimiento is the same as the recibimiento of the Concheros?"

"Absolutely the same!"

"Then what is the difference between the danza and the contradanza?"

"The contradanza has no ritual, señora. And those of the contradanza do not dance under a flag — only under a banner."

When we arrived at the brickyard on the edge of the village of Santiago, we climbed down from the railroad, crossed a ditch and zigzagged between lines of adobe bricks drying in rectangular stacks. It had begun to rain, a sudden brisk shower, and the night was dark.

"Here we are," Don Manuel suddenly announced, and led us to a low adobe hut that I had thought was another pile of brick. Capitana María whom I had known at many fiestas, stood by the door to give us an abrazo or embrace, and to take our wet things. We saw them no more until we were ready to leave, when she handed them to us smooth and dry.

The altar was against the back wall in the corner opposite the door. A long narrow bench extended from it to the door, and similar benches were placed against the other two walls. Don Manuel seated us on the first bench, just in front of the altar, which was different from most dance altars. It was formed of four wide steps, and was filled with santos, candles, and flowers. Santiago was depicted in two large, framed pictures at the top. Other santos, especially the Baby Jesus, appeared more than once. Two or three images had a surprisingly human appearance, rather like rancheros or bandidos of the nineteenth century. In addition to holding the images the altar was profusely decorated with flowers, largely marigolds — the "flowers of the dead" — and daisies.

About half the crowd sat on improvised benches on the porch, while the others were squeezed inside, most of them sitting cross-legged on the packed mud floor. For nearly an hour we sang alabanzas, including some that I had not heard before. Those on the porch would sing while we inside listened quietly. As soon as they finished the last verse which, according to danzante custom, they sang slowly to measured beat, we made ready to sing one while they listened.

At twelve o'clock the ceremony began. Don Manuel announced that as Capitán General he recognized the Rayados of Santiago Ahuixotla, and asked the candidates for membership to come forward. Eight boys, a man, and a woman stood up.

"There are too many to receive at one time," said Don Manuel. "We will receive these six younger boys and then the others."

Meanwhile a clean rush mat had been spread in front of the altar; the six boys, each holding a tall white candle with a few white flowers of uneven lengths, now knelt on the mat in two rows of three each. Two alféreces marched to the corner beside the altar and took up their banners. They then stood beside the kneeling boys, one on each side of them, and slowly and deliberately removed the banners from their poles. Then they carefully spread the banners across the heads of the kneeling boys, one banner to a row, or three heads to a banner. The alféreces remained stationed there throughout the ceremony and were careful to keep the banners touching the heads of the boys until they were removed when "cleansing" with the flowers began.

Don Manuel now announced that he would request the General Fidel Morales to take charge at this point. Don Fidel accepted the honor with pleasure, bustling to the front of the room and facing the crowd.

"Clearly, these boys are very young," he said. "I should like to hear from their parents. Where are their fathers? Let them come forward."

There was a short delay while the danzantes located the fathers and brought them in. One boy had no father — only a mother who answered all questions in the affirmative, speaking so softly that we could hardly hear her. Two of the boys were brothers and Don Fidel insisted that their father be brought in, although someone volunteered the information that he did not wish to be questioned.

"Are you conforme to your sons becoming danzantes?" Fidel demanded when the man finally appeared in the doorway.

"What difference does that make?" retorted the father. "It is they who become danzantes, not I. Ask your questions of them."

"But they are very young," Don Fidel pointed out, "and the way of a danzante is often difficult. Can we be assured that they will comply with their obligations?"

"They are here to be received," stated the father, "that would indicate that they intend to comply."

Finally Don Manuel asked, "¿Estaís conformes, compadritos?"

And the danzantes replied, "¡El es Dios!"

While we sang, "Cada Santa Mesa Tiene Su Bastón" ("Each Holy Table Has Its Mace"), Don Fidel, Don Pedro Martínez, the president of our association, and Don Manuel proceeded with the ceremony. First, Don Manuel took two bunches of flowers and cleansed each candidate, sweeping the flowers up and down and around the head, making the sign of the cross above the head, sweeping down and around again and again. This he did to each boy, one at a time, the perspiration glistening on his face by the time he had finished with the sixth. Then Pedro Martínez took a bastón from the altar and went through similar motions over and around each boy. Don Fidel took the banner of Santiago in his hand. He showed it to the candidates, making a little speech, then he rolled it like a scroll, and went through the sweeping, mystic motions over, above, and around each boy several times. Don Manuel took the smoking incense burner on the altar and gave each boy an abrazo, his right arm across the boy's left shoulder, and his left arm under the boy's right arm. Each new member made the sign of the cross three times three. Then Capitán Narciso extended his hand and helped each to his feet. They repeated the same ceremony with the other candidates, taking more than two hours, with everybody sweating profusely before it was over.

From time to time during the ceremony, Manuel and Fidel made speeches emphasizing their rules: that those now being received should strive always to be good soldiers of the Conquest; that they should seek and heed the counsel of those whose obligation it was to command them; that they should uphold the dignity of the dance at all times; that they should be careful to guard their silence and respect in the chapel and in the circle, and, also, when they entered a sanctuary to give thanks, and at rehearsals and in velaciones; that they should remember well one of the Ten Commandments, "Do not take the name of God in vain"; that when they said "El es Dios," let it be with reverence and respect, since it is the oath of these obligations; and to always remember that they might be pardoned an offense once, or even twice, but the third time they would be "executed" in the very same oratory to which they pertained; and so on.

Fidel warned the capitanes of Ahuixotla to be more circumspect in their behavior. One of them, he said, had offered him a drink of pulque at a certain fiesta. He told the new members that Chalma was the most difficult of the marches they made, and he tried to impress them with the fact that they derived great honor from being under the orders of those generals who pertained to Tlaltelolco.

"It is the very matrix of our tradition," he said. "I want to tell you how our own jefe, Capitán General Manuel Luna went in company with the señora gringa, who is here present tonight with her husband, to Tlaxcala seeking the origin of the dance. They did not find it! And afterwards the padre of Santiago de Tlaltelolco called a conference of jefes and I was there. And that night he told us the history of Tlaltelolco. He told us of the conquistadores. He showed us pictures of them. He showed us the proofs that Tlaltelolco is the matrix of the dance."

Don Manuel stressed the benefits that the new members might expect: the glory of a campaign well fought in the battle of the Conquest; the aid their brothers would give them when they were sick or in trouble; the wisdom of the counsel of their superiors which would be theirs at all times; and the happiness it gave him personally to welcome them into the dance.

Once during the ceremony, Fidel stood in front of me, idle for a moment. "Señora, you have never seen these ceremonies we do here tonight, have you?"

"No, Don Fidel, I have not."

"And what do you think of them?"

"Very serious, very impressive, and very beautiful."

He was pleased.

Later during the reception of the elderly candidates, he stood there again.

"Are you going to return to your country?" he wanted to know.

"Not soon. I hope to go back for a visit next year."

"He means are you going back there to live?" whispered Nieves.

"Some day, perhaps," I told him. "My husband wants to live there when he retires. Perhaps. . . ."

"Ay, señora," he interrupted. "Do not go back. You fit so well with the Mexican Indians. You like us, no? And the Inditos are muy fina gente. Live here always, señora!"

I was touched. At the same time I wondered if he were making amends for having publicly mentioned our fruitless trip to Tlaxcala.

During the discussion at the end of the recibimiento, one of the danzantes of Ahuixotla said he wanted his group to carry the Mexican flag at a fiesta the following Sunday.

"No," ruled Don Manuel. "Los Rayados is a contradanza and contradanzas do not have the flag, only banners."

Don Fidel asked that each captain present place a quota on his personnel for Captain General Manuel Luna, who had promised the padre at San Simón that they would donate a salvo (salute) of fireworks for the fiesta there on October 27. It was five o'clock in the morning when Don Manuel, Nieves, and I finally went home.

I have attended a number of recibimientos, all more or less the same, since that night in Ahuixotla. Outstanding in my memory is the one in which my friend Juana (one of several of that name) and her husband were received at Don Manuel's oratory.

I had known attractive, good-hearted Juana and her dour husband from various fiestas, and had thought them full-fledged danzantes until this particular midnight when they came forward at Don Manuel's invitation to "Those who wish to be received." I had a seat at one corner of the altar and could see them clearly. The husband did the talking, I remember. Juana fixed her large, expressive eyes on the Señor of Chalma, the life-sized image of Christ on the altar, and seemed to forget everything else.[1]

"I will if I can," the husband answered to most of the questions, instead of the usual, "I will."

Once he said, "If I cannot, the companion of my years will do so," turning to Juana, "Is it not so?"

Slowly she turned her head and looked at him. Then she nodded and murmured, "Sí."

"I am only a poor workman," the husband said in reply to a question by Don Manuel. "I shall attend velaciones and fiestas when I can, but, as all the world knows, the Mexican worker is not free to do as he wishes, even when it is what he should do. He has to eat, and to eat he has to work. And he has to work when he is told to do so. He is not his own boss."

Juana sank to her knees on the mud-packed floor, and I saw that she was crying. Her lips quivered as the tears coursed down her cheeks, but her gaze held fast to the Christ. She was a humbled and defenseless figure in her cotton dress and dark rebozo, her beautiful pale-gold face streaked with tears that glistened in the flickering candlelight.

When the questioning was finished, Don Manuel said, "For my part, I think that our companions are not ready, but that is for you to say." He paused thoughtfully before putting the question, "¿Estáis conformes, compadritos?"

Juana was popular among the danzantes.

"¡El es Dios!" they responded heartily.

Fiesta at Acapilco, and Planting the Cross

ACAPILCO IS NEAR THE CAPITAL. The annual fiesta there, with Concheros, Arrieros, and various other groups, is always interesting, and the one in March of 1948 was no exception. It was well under way when I arrived with friends, for after my experience at San Miguel de Ameyalco, Bill insisted that I be accompanied by friends or members of the family when I went to fiestas. Inside the church, Mass was being said, while outside the publico crowded around, getting in the way of the dancers, forming unwieldy little groups as friends met and stopped to chat, or carrying on brisk bargaining with vendors who peddled their wares through the throng. An elderly man decorating the big green cross in the middle of the churchyard informed us that there would be no Concheros at the fiesta that day, but as soon as he had finished and walked away, a young man standing near said softly, "Señora, the Concheros are coming up the street on the other side."

We rushed to the east gate. The Concheros in full uniform were dancing over the hump of the hill, seeming to pour forth from the earth below. I knew nobody in the first group, and a brisk wind together with the bobbing motion as the alféreces marched, made it impossible to read the inscription on the banner. One man in the second group was a friend, since he bowed and greeted me as señora, but I could not recognize him. The third and last group was the one to which I pertained. I recognized Francisco and Longina Martínez first. He shook hands, and she gave me an abrazo. She carried her beribboned altar bell, as did Francisca Reyes (called Panchita), who came next in her rose-colored uniform of artificial silk. Captain General Manuel Luna was near the end of the line, marching beside fourteen-year-old Conchita Martínez, who beamed with pride at the honor. He gave me an abrazo and was charming to my friends, explaining that he had left the capital before daylight to go over the mountains from village to village throughout the sierra, because the Concheros were dancing in many places on that day. His sparse black beard was an inch long, and he looked as if he had not slept for a long time.

My friends sought the shade of the chapel opposite the church as the three groups of Concheros formed their circles, taking up most of the atrio, except for the space occupied by the Arrieros by each gate. In the center of the atrio, with dance circles on three sides, I had a few minutes private conversation with Captain General Manuel Luna, while the fiesta boiled and bubbled around us.

"I have much to tell you, Señora Marta. Not only has Tello, jefe of the contradanza, Los Rayados, passed his limits, but José Cortés, jefe of the mesa at Huitzilapan of which you, señora, are godmother, committed an error on the same occasion."

Conchita Martínez had already told me about Tello when she came over the day before to teach me alabanzas, but the error of José Cortés was news.

"Do you remember the fiesta at Santa Inez three weeks ago, Señora Marta?"

I did. The danzantes had invited me to go with them, but when I learned that they planned to travel an hour and a half standing up in an open truck, I declined.

"Tello, following the instructions he had received, waited for the truck with all his personnel in front of his house in San Simón where, you remember, the oratory of Los Rayados is located. After they had waited an hour or more, a messenger came to notify them that the truck would not enter San Simón, but would await them on the highway north of the city. You see, señora, the truck did not have the proper license to permit it to enter San Simón."

"Did not the messenger explain that to Señor Tello, Don Manuel?"

"It is not sure, Señora Marta, but it is known that Tello replied to the messenger that the truck would come to San Simón or the Rayados would not go to Santa Inez. It was a real disgusto, and much was said by all concerned. Finally several of the capitanía went to Tello's house and made him and his personnel conform.

"Tello was not pleased, señora, and he showed his displeasure throughout the march, which was more difficult than usual because I was unable to go, and my son, Tiburcio, had to take my place. And the next morning while they were dancing in the atrio, a bundle of cohetes exploded near the circle and two soldiers had their uniforms blown from their bodies, completely blown off them, señora! My son Tiburcio and several others were badly burned. And the concha of my comadre Natalia Hidalgo, the defunct, — the *concha* that Tiburcio was playing at the time, señora, — was blown to little splinters! You should have seen it, señora! It just burst! — in little slivers."

Apparently the padre at Santa Inez had wrapped the injured in blankets, put them in his car and started to the capital, but when they learned that he was taking them to a hospital, they insisted on being set down on the outskirts of the city and then made their way to their homes by bus. This part I had learned almost immediately after it occurred, for Longina had come to my house weeping because her Pedro was badly burned.

"¡Ay, señora!" she had sobbed. "We have been talking about it and we think that you are under the protection of some particular santo, for this is the second time that you have escaped harm because in the final moment you did not go. First San Juan de los Lagos, and now Santa Inez. Ay, señora, it was horrible! Two danzantes had all their clothes blown off them and they were terribly burned. And the concha of my dear comadre was blown to bits!"

I had given Longina bandages and medicines and she had thanked me profusely, but she had been too distraught to think of Tello and his quarrel. But not Tiburcio, Manuel Luna's son. Though badly burned he had attended a special velación and had preferred charges against Señor Tello. Captain General Manuel Luna had ruled that Tello had passed his limits and should submit to the Disciplina. Tello refused. His alternative was to withdraw from the group.

"And imagine, señora," Don Manuel grew excited as he told me the final details, "Tello says that he will have his retirement velación on a date which he himself will set, and when he is asked to name that date, he replies that he will announce it."

"¡Qué lástima, Don Manuel!"

"Not only that, señora, but it is reported that José Cortés on that same trip was — " Don Manuel flipped his fist upward with the thumb and little finger extended, a gesture that in Mexico means drinking.

"What can I do?" I asked.

"With Tello the matter is not yet settled. He vacillates. He may accept the Disciplina, or he may retire. You can advise him on the matter, señora."

I nodded. "I will talk to him. And the other?"

"Ay, señora. The other will be more difficult, perhaps. We will do nothing at present."

"Is there anything else you want to tell me, Don Manuel?"

"Sí, señora. I want to invite you and your friends to the fiesta at Texijique next week. They are going to plant the cross on the mountain and you have not seen that yet. Will you come?"

"With pleasure, Don Manuel."

"¡Ay, qué bueno! And now I must leave you for I have to go to San Miguel de Ameyalco. My son Tiburcio will look after you and your friends, señora."

Tiburcio looked after us well. At noon he came to us and said that the local capitán, Genaro García, invited me and my friends to his humble home for dinner. The name Genaro Garciá sounded familiar, but I had not met the small, efficient captain before. Then I remembered. This was the name José Celis had given as his own when I met him at Acapilco in 1939!

We joined the procession and marched down the cobblestone street to the captain's house. We went through a gate in an adobe wall and across a courtyard to the oratory where most of the danzantes ate. A table had been set for us at one end of a room behind the oratory, where the women of the family served us a delicious meal.

Afterward, while the danzantes were singing in the oratory, I stood at the door near an amiable old man I had known at other fiestas in Acapilco. We sang an alabanza, the planta of which was:

Rezemos a tu nombre	Let us pray in thy name
Rezemos en tu canto	Let us pray in thy song,
Seguimos la paloma	We follow the dove
Que es El Espíritu Santo.	That is the Holy Spirit.

"Do you understand what that means, señora?" he asked. "That refers to the dove of the Puerto del Aire that flew around the Valley of Mexico."

Several years would pass before I knew what he was talking about.

We marched back to the church with the danzantes and, as soon as they were dancing again, we went home.

When we arrived in Texijique the following Sunday morning we had no trouble finding the freshly whitewashed church with its yellow dome. It stood in the middle of the village, surrounded by a high white wall. Inside the atrio was a circle of Concheros, their feather headdresses bobbing rhythmically above the crowd that had gathered to watch them. I wormed my way to the edge of the circle. Don Manuel, in the center, was conferring with a tall slender jefe in a red satin cape.

"Don Manuel," I called, but he did not hear me.

The *conchas* began to strum and the *danzantes* to sing

"Don Manuel," still he did not hear.

"*Tata* Manuel," in a high-pitched nasal tone.

Manuel looked up and his face shone with pleasure.

"¡Señora Marta!" he exclaimed, as he crossed the circle to give me an abrazo.

"Don Manuel, we have our cameras in the car and they are at your service when you want to have us use them."

He thanked me and suggested that we "take a little turn" about the village as it was very pretty. Later on, he said, they were going to take out "the sacred wood," meaning the cross, from the church and then he would like for us to photograph it. After that they would bear the sacred wood to the top of the *cerro* (hill) where they would plant it with ceremony. Perhaps we would like to photograph the whole group there.

We strolled about the town and chatted with the vendors at the fair. When we consulted Don Manuel again, we learned that they would take the cross from the church at three o'clock. We had an early lunch in the car and sat and talked while the whole town drowsed in siesta. Then Don Manuel came looking for us.

"As soon as Mass is over we are going to take out the cross," he said. "Señora Marta, would you do me the favor to place yourself on the walk in front of the church to take a picture when we come through the door? When we arrive at the spot where the sun reaches it, I have told my compadres to incline the sacred wood so that you may get its full outline in the photograph. Will you take several photographs, señora, so that we can give some to the several chiefs?"

I took my place on the paved walk from the church to the gate, while Don Manuel bustled about the atrio, speaking to this capitán and that before disappearing inside the door. The atrio was hushed in expectancy. The twitter of quarrelsome sparrows in the trees by the road was the only sound. Then a danzante appeared in the door, motioning that the procession was on the way out. We could see the gently waving headdresses approaching through the dimness of the nave. The crowd around us pressed forward to see what was coming. Don Manuel and the tall jefe in the red cape, Capitán Jesús from Tenango del Río, appeared in the doorway carrying the foot of the white cross. Behind them came the danzantes, some merely touching it "to give spirit," some only marching beside it, and others lending full strength to bear it along. When they came into the sunshine they stopped and slowly tilted the cross forward until the sun shone fully upon it. We clicked our cameras rapidly. Then they gently lowered the head and raised the foot until the cross was again in a horizontal position, and continued down the walk. The conchas began to strum and the danzantes to sing. As they passed we fell in line near the end of the procession and joined in the singing. Through the gate we marched, skirting the fair, down the dusty road to the long, sloping trail that led up the fat, lopsided mountain. We marched in three lines with the ends constantly shifting as stragglers dropped behind when the going was rough.

The man on my left began to talk to me, which was unusual. This was one of the occasions when the danzantes should keep silent. I was unable to hear him, but I smiled and murmured, "¡De Veras!" every time he paused. Finally he slowed his pace and turned to face me.

"Look! I am a capitán."

"¿De veras?"

"That is why I have the authority to tell you you cannot take photographs."

I stared at him.

"We do not want pictures of us going away from here par' allá," gesturing toward the horizon. "We are only humble ones and you, you have never been humble, so. . . ."

"What do you say?" I interrupted.

"You have never been humble so you do not know . . . ."

"Look!" I told him, "I am humble. Does not the Bible state that the humble shall enter the Kingdom of Heaven? Of course I am humble!"

He laughed. "But you are not humble as we are humble, señora. And, though I am very sorry to tell you, you cannot take any more photographs!"

Don Manuel scrambled down the rocky hillside above the trail.

"Señora Marta!" he called. "Come forward. Go on ahead by this shortcut and take a picture of the whole group as we go around the curve in the trail."

Obediently, I struggled up the side of the cut to the level above the trail, and, with the sun pounding between my shoulders, trudged across the rocky mountainside until I reached the trail ahead of the procession. The vivid silken banners fluttering in the breeze formed great blobs of color above the flowing headdresses of ostrich plumes and the more traditional multicolored chilillos. The silk and satin uniforms, spangled with sequins and beads, mingled with the clean blue overalls and pastel shirts of the half-uniformed and the un-uniformed. In the center, halfway between the tops of the banners and the bobbing headdresses, the horizontal cross, decorated with its broad white band studded with big paper rosettes in four colors, sailed along majestically as on a quiet steady stream.

I took a picture as the cross rounded the trail between two trees, and another a minute later against the background of the valley in the distance. Then I rejoined the procession as it passed, and found myself in front of Don Manuel and the objecting captain, whom he introduced as Capitán Filiseo. A sharp uneasiness settled over me when I realized that they were deep in earnest argument, the capitán bluntly determined that the foreign woman should take no more photographs, and Don Manuel, diplomatic and persuasive, no less determined that she should when ordered to do so by him.

I tried not to listen to them; it made me nervous. I knew that we were off the beaten track in Otomí country where there was neither telegraph nor telephone. Was the capitán alone at the fiesta, or did he have numerous personnel with him? Did the other danzantes there share his opinion of foreigners and photographs? The Concheros of Texijique had only recently placed themselves under Don Manuel's orders. Could he control them? I hoped that I would not become involved in a test of his influence over them, or of their understanding of their obligation to him as chief and to the dance in general.

Finally we arrived at the jumbled, broken top of the mountain. We sat on boulders to rest while the danzantes gathered on the highest

The cross rounded the trail between two trees

Danzantes gathered on the highest point
of the jumbled, broken top of the mountain

point around the concrete base of the cross. This base was about three feet high and had been made in two sections, so that a portion of it at the back could be removed. In the center was a rectangular slot exactly the size of the end of the foot of the cross, the removable back section forming one side of the slot. This back section had been loosened when the danzantes took the cross down to repaint and redecorate it, before leaving it in the church "to hear Mass." Now they slid it back and lifted the cross in place over the slot, but before allowing it to slide all the way down, they passed a hat for money. Only coins were acceptable, and there was a flurry of bill-changing among us as we collected four silver pesos. Don Manuel called me to the center of the crowd around the base and I handed him the four pesos. Then he made a speech ending with, "The señora Marta has been andando con los danzantes for many years. She attends our ceremonies and she and the señor her husband often go on marches with me. The señora has studied the history of our country, including the ancient books, and she understands the customs left us by our ancestors better than some of us do. As you can see," holding up the pesos, "the señora Marta wishes to give four silver pesos as an offering to the Most Holy Cross. ¿Estáis conformes, compadritos?"

"¡El es Dios!" shouted the danzantes.

With a flourish Don Manuel placed the coins that had been collected in the hat in the hollow slot and the danzantes lowered the cross upon them. Then the danzantes began to replace the back section.

"Capitán General Manuel Luna," came the voice of Capitán Filiseo from somewhere below us — and I shivered — "You are the sun and the moon in the heavens and I am a tiny, flickering star. It is not proper that I should have an opinion contrary to yours and I shall never raise my voice against you." He went on to explain his loyalty to his general and his eagerness to obey orders, and ended with, "May our ancient religion endure, as it has from the beginning, to the end of all things!"

As the years went by I learned more about the crosses on the mountaintops. The ancient Mexicans worshipped the mountains and placed altars on them, especially where trails crossed. The early friars tore down each altar, buried the idol, and placed a Christian cross over it. Now the danzantes are patrons of most of the crosses on mountains; tending them, scrubbing, repainting, and replacing them when they are worn out.

Among the ceremonies of the danzantes is a watch service with a cross the night before they plant it. Years after the trip to Texijique Bill and I went to the velación of the large green cross Don Manuel's group had inherited at the death of Capitán Miguel Herrera, who had been under the orders of Capitán General Manuel Luna. This was at San Bartolo Naucalpan at the foot of the hill of the famous church of Los Remedios during the annual fiesta in October.

There were three different groups gathered under the portales of San Bartolo when we arrived, each crowded around a huge green cross extended on the sidewalk. When we found Don Manuel and his personnel, he immediately named me among the malinches who had the honor of "dressing the cross"; attaching the colored rosettes to the wide band of white cotton material draped around the cross beams and across the trunk. This we did by means of thin wire and a few safety pins. Meanwhile the rest of the danzantes played conchas and sang alabanzas. By midnight we had finished, and the capitanas placed lighted candles along the cross, as on an altar. Then the danzantes began to sing mañanitas, or songs of morning. Hours later several danzantes reverently raised the cross from the sidewalk and marched to the middle of the street with it. The others, including the alféreces with their banners, formed lines behind them and the procession moved slowly up the hill to Los Remedios. When we drew near the church, a group of danzantes came to meet us and the two groups merged with the same ceremony that takes place when a mesa arrives at an oratory. Then we marched to the church. The danzantes laid the cross flat on the ground outside the door of the church in order for it to "hear Mass," for it was too large to pass through the door. Then they formed their circle around the cross and began to dance.

We walked to the edge of the atrio on the side overlooking the city and watched the daybreak. As the sky grew lighter, a thick mist billowed up from the valley to hover in a white cloud around the foot of the enormous statue of Christ, that towers at the edge of the churchyard like a sentinel above the capital. As we stood there, light broke through the rose-colored sky, and a snow-white, fairy city drifted up through the thinning mist.

Blessing
the Oratory
and
the Banner

BILL AND I HAD TAKEN PART in several dance ceremonies in the hinterland as we went about with the Concheros, but at danzante affairs
in the capital we had been nothing more than observers. Shortly after
the organization of the association at the Church of Tlaltelolco, however, we were asked to take part in two baptisms in Mexico City within
a few weeks time of Don Manuel's oratory and the association banner.

Tlaltelolco had become a dance center — second only, perhaps, to
the Villa de Guadalupe (Villa de Madero) in the Federal District.
Eventually the government placed a stone wall between the customs
buildings and the church, thus reducing the dance space by half, but
the Indians continued to come there to dance at fiesta-time. Almost
always there were two or three circles in the long, narrow space beside
the church; a group or two on the concrete platform that ran the length
of the building, and another before the door at the back. Filling in the
spaces between the Conchero circles were the contradanzas — Los
Rayados, Las Pastorcitas, Los Broncos, Los Romanos, and others.

The first priest in charge of Santiago de Tlaltelolco after the government returned the church proper to the Catholic Church called certain
danzantes together and proposed an organization of dancers. Thus
was born the Association of Religious Dancers that Pertains to the
Church of Santiago de Tlaltelolco. Captains General Manuel Luna,
Guadalupe Alvarez, and Fidel Morales, and all the dance groups under
their orders, composed the association. The three generals shared authority equally, and proudly boasted that all three were conforme to everything done in the name of the association. They accepted the padre's offer
of the use of the church as the cuartel general of the capitanía, consisting
of the three captains general and the captains who were under their
orders. The capitanía usually worked in cooperation with the priest at
fiestas. The Church of Tlaltelolco often received invitations for dancers

from other churches. They turned them over to the capitanía which acted as a clearing house on these occasions.

Each member of the capitanía headed a mesa, or oratory. These oratories, some in existence for many years, were scattered about the outlying districts and slums of the capital; near the dance chief's house if possible, or wherever they could get a vacant room or shed near an outside area suitable for their dance rehearsals.

The oratory of our mesa was in Don Manuel's yard. Several years ago he bought a lot, thirty by fifty-five feet, in an inexpensive neighborhood. He and his sons built his house; two bedrooms across the back and a narrow ell in front of one bedroom for a kitchen. Then, bit by bit, they and the danzantes raised the walls of the oratory, a long, narrow room between the kitchen and the street. The space between the other bedroom and the street served as an open patio. The oratory roof became a problem. The Concheros could spare no more from their meager earnings. They donated labor, but materials they could not buy. Finally, through the assistance of friends, the roof was finished. The patio was large enough for dance rehearsals and the rest adequate.

Then they moved the santos from San Simón to the new altar — Jesus the Nazarene, the Savior Jesus, and "the Lord of Chalma"; a large painting of the Virgin of Guadalupe, and images and paintings of various other saints. Don Manuel asked the Tata Archbishop's permission for the priest at Magdalena to bless the oratory at eight o'clock on a certain morning, and invited me to be the one godmother, explaining that there would be two godfathers, the first and the second captains of San Miguel de Ameyalco.

Josefina, who took Brigida's place as cook, went with me to the velación the night before the ceremony. When it ended the next morning, she handed me the two enormous unlighted candles that had been on the altar all night, and we were ready for the blessing.

We waited. No priest.

At 9:30 a.m., Don Manuel sent his sons to Magdalena with a polite note. They were gone nearly an hour. When they came back they said that they had had to wait because the padre was busy, but that he had promised to come to the oratory at 11 o'clock. It was already past time for the danzantes to go to their work, but Doña Ester invited them to breakfast. About forty accepted her hospitality, saying that they would take sick leave from their jobs.

Eleven o'clock. No priest.

At noon Don Manuel sent his sons to Magdalena again. This time they were gone only a short time. They reported that the priest ordered them out, saying that he had important business to attend to and could not spend his time playing with the Indians. Don Manuel then sent a delegation to consult a kind priest who formerly had been at Tlaltelolco. Doña Ester served luncheon to forty.

At two o'clock a priest arrived to bless the oratory.

Smothered by incense and the strong odor of burning wax, we watched him sprinkle holy water on the altar, murmuring in Latin as he did so. He lavishly sprinkled the huge bunches of baby's breath in the corners at each end of the altar; over the disciplina, or lash of maguey rope with four arms that was hanging from the center of the altar; and over the godfather on my left, and the standard-bearer on my right. Somehow he missed me.

He started out the door but Don Manuel detained him to make a gracious little speech. He thanked the padre for his kindness, he thanked the capitanes and their personnel for their patience and consideration, and in closing he mentioned me. "I am disgracefully proud that the señora Marta Estony has been *andando* with us for many years. She is always with us and is always helping us. It was due to her kindness that we were able to finish this oratory, and we give her our most infinite thanks."

A few mornings later Don Manuel appeared at our house.

"I have come, señora, to ask a favor of you and the señor. If you say yes, you will be doing great honor to me and to all the danzantes who pertain to the Church of Tlaltelolco. It is this, señora: that you present us with a banner."

"A banner?"

"Sí, Señora Marta. A banner for the association. The various mesas all have their banners, but as yet there is no banner for our association. Do you think the señor would like to present us with one, señora?"

It cost about fifty dollars and was made, according to Dan Manuel's specifications, of red satin with Santiago on his white horse painted in the center. Heavy gold ropes wound around the edges and hung below on each side ending in long gold tassels. The staff was of polished brass. In big gold letters on the blue satin back, it read (translated into English), "Memento of the Stone Family to Sr. Manuel Luna."

Don Manuel was anxious that the banner be finished and baptized in time to be used at the annual fiesta on the Day of Santiago in July. Under his supervision Nieves hurried about the city buying materials and prodding the sluggish painter while Don Manuel himself conferred with the other chiefs and the priests at Tlaltelolco, trying to arrange a date for the baptism.

On the morning finally agreed upon we went to the church, Bill and I as the donors, and our friend, Luisa Alvarez, and Nieves as the godmothers. When we formed the procession Bill carried the banner and Godmother Luisa marched beside him on his left, holding the long gold tassel, while Nieves at his right held the tassel on that side. I walked on the other side of Nieves and held nothing but my notebook and pencil — as inconspicuously as possible. Behind us came the danzantes strumming their conchas and singing alabanzas.

We slowly marched through the door down the center aisle the length of the church to the altar. After a song or two the danzantes stood silent as Father Domingo Guadalupe Díaz came down to the front of the altar to sprinkle the banner. He was a young man with a warm personality, and one of the few priests I had met who seemed to have a real compassion for the danzantes. He explained their need for the banner, mentioned us as donors, congratulating them on having such friends, and urged them to continue to dance as an expression of religious feeling, but to remember that to dance was not enough, and so on. When he had finished he disappeared through a door near the side of the altar.

Softly at first, and then more loudly the danzantes strummed their conchas, then sang alabanzas. The capitanas rang their bells and swung their incense burners, while all the capitanía, capitanes and capitanas, one by one passed in front of us, knelt before the banner, and presented his or her concha or bell or incense burner to the Four Winds and to the banner. Then each reverently lifted the edge of the banner and kissed it. When the capitanía had finished, still playing and singing, with bells ringing and surrounded by a cloud of incense, the whole group, including the donors and the godmothers, backed slowly out of the church.

The Concheros stayed to dance in the atrio but, after promising to attend a velación in Don Manuel's oratory the next week, we went home.

Velación at the Oratory

THE EVENING OF THE VELACIÓN my daughter and I took a taxi to Don Manuel's house. He, his sons, and several danzantes were beside the car to welcome us before it stopped. First we went back to the kitchen to greet Doña Ester, whom we found tending large ollas of black coffee and of orange leaf tea, then we joined the danzantes in the oratory. Men in work clothes and women in cotton dresses and rebozos sat on the long benches along the walls or on rush mats on the floor. Near the altar two chairs with their seats of hand twisted maguey cord were reserved for us.

Sargento Chucho stood at the left of the altar and Capitana Panchita at the right. A capitán stepped forward and knelt in front of Chucho to present his candles and red carnations and white daisies to the Four Winds. First, Chucho swept the incense burner above and around the flowers, ending in the sign of the cross; then he held the incense burner toward the capitán who reverently kissed the lower rim before taking it from him. The capitán held the flowers and candles horizontally in his left hand and set the incense burner on top of them, his right thumb under the bundle of flowers and candles, the fingers of his right hand steadying the incense burner. He raised them toward the altar, holding them high for a moment, then brought them down near his knees, making the sign of the cross. As he knelt facing the altar, he did this three times. Still on his knees, he turned to face each of the cardinal points, making the sign of the cross three times to each. When he turned on his knees, the danzantes, including the standard-bearers with the banners, turned with him, remaining standing, however, and singing, "María, Recibe las Flores (Mary, Receive the Flowers)." From time to time Panchita rang her bell.

As the capitán went through the ceremony, his lips moved, silently forming the words of the prayer for this rite. Facing the altar, "Father mine, Lord of Chalma, light my understanding that my soul may be saved." In the opposite direction, "Father mine, Lord of the Sacred Mount of Amecameca, Messenger of the Four Winds." To his right,

"Father mine, Lord of the Conquest, conquer all the spirits that are against me." In the opposite direction, "Mother mine of Los Remedios, remedy all our needs that we may not lack the bread for each day."

Then the capitán remained kneeling beside Chucho, turning with him, while Chucho presented the flowers to the Four Winds in the same manner. The danzantes, standing, turned with them and sang, "¡Viva María! ¡Viva Jesús! ¡Viva las Ánimas Conquistadores de los Cuatro Vientos!" ("Long Live Mary! Long Live Jesus! Long Live the Conquering Spirits of the Four Winds!")

When they had finished, the capitán and Chucho rose to their feet, and Chucho handed the flowers and candles to Panchita, who with the help of the other capitanas arranged the flowers in large tin cans on the altar. They lighted one of the candles and put it in an empty soft-drink bottle. Most of these flowers would be used later to dress the Xuchil. Don Manuel had specified red carnations and white daisies when I had consulted him that morning. On the night of November 2 (All Souls), which is one of the two main velaciones for the dressing of the Xuchil, marigolds are always used, the "flower of the dead"; while on Easter, the other velación, any spring flower of pastel shade may be used, with a circular band of purple flowers halfway between the outer edge and the center. The oratory is hung with mourning from the Day of the Dead until Easter.

After all the flowers had been presented the danzantes sang alabanzas while the capitanas, with the help of the malinches in training to be future capitanas, finished dressing the altar. At the end of one song a danzante informed Don Manuel that the personnel of the mesa of Peña Pobre were approaching. Immediately Tiburcio, Miguel, Panchita, Chucho, and other danzantes, all carrying lighted candles, marched out to meet them, accompanied by the standard-bearer with the banner. We followed them.

Down the unpaved street, with the lighted candles and fluttering banners, wound the procession of danzantes, playing and singing as they came. Here and there a flashlight blinked, and near the center, a gasoline lantern lighted the red and green silk banner. The primer capitán and a capitana marched in front carrying Santiago in a blue painted wooden nicho. As they drew near, our group greeted them with cohetes, and when we met, our group knelt before the santo. Slowly the others knelt too, and together we repeated a litany. Then the two groups merged and marched into the oratory.

As they came through Don Manuel's gate the leader of the newly arrived group recognized me standing by the door to the oratory.

"Ay, Señora Marta," he greeted me, "we have been on a pilgrimage with my father, Santiago. We have been far, as far as Ajusco, and we have carried him all the way."

They entered the oratory and sang a song I had not heard — perhaps it was composed for the occasion — that told the story of the pilgrimage.

> And Santiago is very tired
> Because the way was very hard.

Susana, wife of Capitán Benjamín was standing beside me. "Now how can he be so tired, if they carried him all the way?" she wanted to know.

During the evening three other groups arrived in the same way. The last was the personnel of the contradanza, Los Rayados, whose chief was Señor Tello. They made their slow, impressive entrada carrying the image of the Baby Jesus and slowly singing in harmony, which is rare among the danzantes.

When all had arrived and presented their flowers and candles — and coffee and sugar, in some cases — Don Manuel took his place in front of the altar. He threw back his head and closed his eyes and began, "Ave María Purísima —" and the danzantes responded.

Then he "asked permission," addressing the altar: "In the name of God, firstly of God; of my father, the Lord of Chalma; of my father Jesús Nazareno; of my father Jesús Salvador; of my mother, the Lady of Guadalupe; of the Baby Jesus; of my father, Santiago; of the Four Winds; and of the Conquering Spirits, who left us as remembrances these teachings and obligations of the sainted religion; we ask permission to do these exercises and ceremonies left us by our ancestors."

He then requested Josefina to read the rosary.

The standard-bearers presented their banners to the Four Winds.

All this left only a little more than an hour for the danzantes to sing alabanzas before the main ceremony would begin.

At exactly midnight Don Manuel named Capitán Benjamín and two other capitanes "to work the flower," as well as the malinches who, with Capitana Panchita, would break the stems below the blossoms at whatever length the capitanes should decide.

"Three fingers," announced Don Benjamín.

"Three fingers," repeated Panchita, nodding to the malinches.

Panchita took a folded white cloth from the altar and handed it to Benjamín. He and the capitán who was to assist him carefully spread it so that it formed a square white carpet in front of the altar. Don Manuel lifted the Xuchil, or crude *Custódia* (monstrance, in which the Host is elevated) from the altar and handed it to Benjamín who placed

The Oratory at Easter

it in the middle of the edge of the white cloth nearest the altar. Then they put the two bastones, or wooden rods, on either side of the Xuchil, leaning them against it.

Panchita took a pair of black incense burners from the altar and placed them on either side of the Xuchil. Copal burned in these throughout the ceremony, for the moment that smoke ceased to swirl above one, the capitana would drop more copal into it with a live coal upon which she would blow. At the foot of the incense burner she placed a white saucer containing little hunks of copal and against it leaned a long, slim spool of cord.

Exactly in the center of the cloth they placed a white porcelain saucer upside down, and on top of it they set a small lighted candle, one of a bundle of unlighted little tallow candles that had been on the altar all evening. A little distance to the right and to the left of this central saucer they placed small white square tiles upon which they set similar small lighted candles. The same distance below it, in a line with the saucer and the Xuchil, they placed another tile and candle.

"Each candle," whispered an old man beside me, "represents an ánima."

Meanwhile the malinches had been breaking the stems of the flowers at the desired length. Then they placed them in small bunches of all one color, end on end in a large circle near the edge of the cloth. The two captains slowly and reverently began to "work the flowers." They took a little bunch of white flowers from the circle and fashioned a tiny white cross, flat on the cloth between the Xuchil and the overturned saucer, extending toward the saucer. Don Benjamín made the top, or head, and the right arm, while the other capitán made the left arm and a bit of the body. It was the same size as the little cross that topped the Xuchil. Then they slowly circled the saucer, laying the flowers with great care so that the short stems were hidden and only the blossoms could be seen.

After the circles around the saucer, they laid flowers to form the twelve rays of the Xuchil; for the flower arrangement flat on the cloth-covered floor was a flower representation of the Xuchil, with the overturned saucer and lighted candle in the center instead of the gleaming mirror.

After the capitanes had begun to "work the flower," Don Manuel made another announcement. "The group from Querétaro will now sing," he said proudly. He then explained to me in an undertone, "This style of singing is called coro [chorus] señora. It is the custom in the Bajío to sing in this style. You know, do you not, that Señor Tello is from Querétaro?"

I had known Señor Tello in the capital for at least ten years, but Querétaro was his tierra and I was not surprised that he had introduced some of its customs into his dance group in the capital. Later I learned that the members of Los Rayados, the contradanza of which he was the leader, were all from Querétaro, too.

The singers stood in a tight little circle in the back of the room, their faces blank, completely silent for half a minute or more. Then Tello opened his mouth to produce a deep, rising note and the others joined the upward flight. Señor Tello had a deep bass voice and the others sang either high or low. After the first moment or two I stopped trying to distinguish the words for I realized that to the singers the important thing was tone production. Each phrase was followed by a long blank pause. At any rate, *coro, estilo del Bajío* was definitely something different than coro among the danzantes of the capital.

While they were singing Don Manuel leaned over and whispered, "Señora, have you noticed? I bought a new mirror for the center of the Xuchil. See, it is not dull and discolored like the old one. It cost a lot of money but it is worth it, is it not?"

When Señor Tello and his friends had finished, the danzantes began to strum their conchas and sing alabanzas. From time to time, one or two would leave the oratory to join Doña Ester in the kitchen, to get a drink of water, or to sit on the backless bench by the well and gossip a little. The devout frowned upon this last and, after a warning from their capitán, the gossips went back into the oratory.

Inside the oratory the working of the flowers progressed while the danzantes sang alabanzas. When a complete representation of the Xuchil lay on the floor, Don Manuel inspected it and found it lacking in symmetry. Furthermore Don Benjamín had left out a ray on his side of the flower Xuchil. He would have to remedy that.

"What do the twelve rays of the Xuchil mean?" I asked a capitán who sat beside me.

"The twelve rays of the sun, or the twelve disciples of Christ, as you please, señora."

"And the mirror in the center of the Xuchil?" — delighted that he would answer questions.

"The all-seeing powers of Tezcat, a god of our ancestors, or the all-seeing powers of the ánimas benditas, señora, as you please."

Don Benjamín corrected his mistake, receiving whispered advice from those near him as he did so. Then Don Manuel announced that Capitán Benjamín "had the word." Don Benjamín made a speech, saying that the work was now finished and asking the compadritos to accept it "be it good or bad."

"¿Estaís conformes, compadritos?" asked Don Manuel.

"El es Dios," voted the danzantes.

Don Manuel took the wooden Xuchil from the foot of the altar and handed it to Benjamín. A capitana handed him the spool of cord. I saw that Benjamín and the other capitán were going to complete the working of the flowers. Usually four people do this, two laying the Xuchil out on the floor and the other two tying the flowers to the wooden frame.

Then they began to "raise the Xuchil," transferring the flower Xuchil on the floor to the wooden Xuchil. Benjamín and his companion each broke off a long length of cord and set to work. Starting with the tiny cross on top, each used the same flowers he had put on the floor to cover the corresponding part of the Xuchil. They worked silently and rapidly, taking care that the stems were hidden and only the blossoms could be seen.

"This work is also called a rose, Señora Marta," Don Manuel explained. "That is what our ancestors called it, una rosa."

As soon as they could see that there were more than twice as many flowers in the circle on the floor as would be needed to cover the Xuchil, the capitanas began to "dress the bastones." With long lengths of cord from the spool they attached flowers, selected at random as to color, around and around the rods, hiding the stems and fluffing the blossoms until the bastones took on the appearance of variegated feather dusters.

Most of the danzantes had worked hard all day and were accustomed to retire early. Now that the hour was late, heads began to droop, the music grew subdued, and now and then, a gentle snore could be heard. The broad-shouldered capitán from Peña Pobre quickly made the rounds. Moving silently he would come upon the offender without warning and jerk him wide awake with a resounding thump on the head. His fat thumb and pudgy forefinger had an expertness that indicated practice. Even a capitana was thumped before the Xuchil was completely raised. Only small children were exempt. The four-year-old "guardian of a bell," in training as a future capitana, who had been proudly introduced to the Capitán General earlier in the evening, now stretched out on a rush mat. Her baby brother also slept undisturbed in his mother's arms.

When the Xuchil was almost dressed, Juana and Luz, who had been helping Doña Ester in the kitchen, began to bring in huge cups of steaming black coffee spiced with cinnamon and piping hot tea brewed of orange leaves. The cups were of brightly colored pottery made in Oaxaca and held at least a pint. The first two, one of coffee, the other of tea, they passed to Capitana Panchita who placed them on the altar.

Then, while Luz served danzantes, my friend Juana served Martita and me, but not with coffee, for Doña Ester knew that we did not like it heavy with cinnamon, nor with tea, for orange leaf tea is thought to be a lowly drink and not fit to serve honored guests. Our cups contained foaming hot chocolate.

With the last of the coffee and tea they brought in baskets of *bolillos;* the delicious, unsweetened rolls shaped like spindles full of thread with which, it is said, the Spanish nuns in the sixteenth-century convents taught Mexican women to make bolillo lace. I knew that the Preconquest fast consisted in abstinence from salt, chiles, and tortillas with lime. Could the bolillo be the modern substitute for the tortilla without lime?

As soon as the flower Xuchil from the floor had been raised to the wooden frame — as soon as the Xuchil had been dressed — a silence fell on the group. Then Tiburcio began to strum his concha and the danzantes sang "Santa Rosita."

Santa Rosita	Santa Rosita	*Vamos cantando*	We go singing
Es mi remedio	Is my remedy	*Y vamos rezando*	We go praying
Vamos cantando	We go singing	*Y vamos diciendo*	We go saying
¡El es — !	He is — !	*¡ — Que lindo es Dios!*	— How lovely is God!

"Santa Rosita" apparently refers to the Xuchil, the wooden frame covered with flowers. "We go singing, He is —" refers to the statement "He is God." When they use it as an affirmative vote, they usually complete the statement. When they use it in the dance circle at the beginning or completion of "marking the steps," however, very often they yell, "He is — ," without repeating the word "God."

"Where does "El es Dios" come from?" I whispered to Don Manuel, who was standing beside me watching his sons lead the singing.

"In the first days of the Conquest, Señora Marta, one of the friars — I forget his name — went through Mexico converting the Indians. He carried a Cristo in his hands and when he came upon Indians worshipping idols he pointed to Our Lord on the Cross and called out, 'El es Dios.' He conquered many of our ancestors, the chiefs as well as the priests, just as the soldiers of Cortés conquered the soldiers of the Mexicans."

There are many verses to "Santa Rosita," all just alike except the first line, which in the first is "Santa Rosita." It changes to include *Flor de Amapola, gardenia, azucena Castilla, margarita, carrizo, hilo, Xuchil, bastón,* and others, to end with Santa Rosita again. Since most of the plants mentioned in the versions I heard at different velaciones were, according to Professor Martínez, used in the cures of the ancient Mexicans — and some by the Indians in modern times — it is possible that the ceremony at one time had to do with cures.[1]

When the song had ended Don Benjamín presented the Santa Xuchil to the Four Winds, and then to Don Manuel. Don Manuel presented it to the Four Winds and placed it at the foot of the altar.

"This velación is often called a watch service for the Xuchil señora," whispered Tiburcio Luna.

Holding the bastones by their short handles, Don Manuel now crossed them and held the incense burner with the one in his right hand. He presented them to the Four Winds and faced the congregation. He nodded to Benjamín, who stepped forward and knelt at his feet. High above Benjamín's head Don Manuel held the bastones with their fragrant, feathery covering of flowers. Quickly he brought them down and in a little jabbing motion made the sign of the cross. He then uncrossed the bastones and swished the right one across Benjamín's left shoulder as he knelt facing him, then the left across his right shoulder — up, down, and all around until I lost the pattern of movement and the count of the crosses. Finally he presented the lower rim of the incense burner for Benjamín to kiss.

"El es Dios," murmured the danzantes as Benjamín rose to his feet.

"Señora Marta," said Don Manuel, and I stepped forward to kneel in front of him, noticing my daughter's round-eyed amazement as I went. Don Manuel repeated the gestures he had just used above and around Benjamín. Then I kissed the incense burner and went back to my chair while the danzantes murmured, "El es Dios." This was the "little cleansing" I had first seen in the cave at Guanajuato.

Don Manuel singled out capitanes, capitanas, alféreces, and devoted danzantes who regularly attended velaciones and ensayos. One by one they knelt in front of him to receive the cleansing. All the while the danzantes sang songs of praise. When the cleansing was finished Don Manuel presented the bastones to the Four Winds and placed them on either side of the Xuchil at the foot of the altar.

The alféreces now came forward to take their banners from the corners near the altar and present them to the Four Winds. As they finished they took their places among the rest of the danzantes, standing and singing near the altar in front of the crowd. As they sang they gently waved their banners from side to side. If one forgot and held his banner still, one of the capitanes was sure to frown at him and gesture to him to motion.

Don Manuel began his closing remarks by giving his thanks to those of much faith who had attended this ceremony which was a custom left them by their ancestors.

"Some of you," he said, "have come at great sacrifice, coming from far away and by hard roads. Most of you have come here humbly, some even *pobrecitamente* . . . ."

I lost track of what he was saying in admiration for this new word. *Pobrecito,* meaning "poor little one," is common enough in Mexico. Don Manuel had added the adverb-ending *mente* to coin an expressive term, "like a poor little one."

When I came back to his speech he was emphasizing the importance of the velación, pointing out that each detail had a significant meaning. "I would recommend to Capitán Benjamín that he think on these things so that he will come to consider them worthwhile and be able to do them without mistakes."

He then led a litany with the danzantes responding. Then they sang, "Adiós, Reina del Cielo" — "Farewell, Queen of Heaven."

The capitanas and the malinches who helped them had been quietly tearing to bits the blossoms left after the dressing of the Xuchil and the bastones. They now tossed the bits out over the crowd until we were covered with the fragrant confetti.

When the velación had ended most of the danzantes lingered in the oratory to discuss affairs of the dance, but we decided to go home and get some sleep. We stepped through the door into the pale gray light of a new day and heard music coming from the house; not the danzante music we had been listening to for hours, but the throbbing, sophisticated rhythms of modern Latin American dance music.

In the bedroom behind the kitchen, a man called "the professor" sat by a bed in the corner and played an intricate melody on a guitar. Beside him another man played an accompaniment, also on a guitar. In the middle of the room, Chato, first bugle of one of the mesas, shook a painted gourd in each hand, twisting, humping, and wriggling like a member of a rumba orchestra. In the corner by the door Tiburcio hunched over the wooden seat of a handmade chair, slapping and banging it as if it were a drum. Once in a while he leaned down and spanked the soles of his shoes. On the bed a few-months-old baby stared at them unblinkingly from large dark eyes. Three other babies on the bed slept soundly. Rumbas, tangos, and congas flowed from the room. The two older men played with solemn concentration. Chato and Tiburcio, smiling blissfully, gave body and soul over to rhythm. It was eight o'clock when we finally left.

Velación and Fiesta at Tlaltelolco

THE DAY BEFORE THE ANNUAL FIESTA at Tlaltelolco D'on Manuel and his sons, Tiburcio and Miguel, paid me a visit.

"Ay, Señora Marta, we have many *molestias*," was Manuel's greeting.

"What has happened?" I asked.

"The priest in charge of Tlaltelolco has been changed again."

"Again?"

"Sí, Señora Marta, and the one there now seems set against the *danza*."

Apparently the priest had told the three generals, Guadalupe Alvarez, Fidel Morales, and Don Manuel, that they should turn over to him the three hundred pesos that they had collected for fireworks, so that he could use it for church repairs. Manuel had explained that the fireworks had already been ordered and presumably were almost finished. The priest then said that they would have to shoot them all Saturday night as he forbade them to fire them Sunday during the fiesta. Also, that the dancing would have to cease for the duration of every Mass throughout the day. There the danzantes rebelled. They would call a recess during the High Mass at twelve o'clock, but the rest of the day they would dance. At this, the priest said that they could come back when they were in their right senses.

Manuel sought Father Domingo Díaz who had blessed the association banner, and this priest had cautioned him to be careful of the present priest at Tlaltelolco for he was muy índio and muy mexicano.

"If you want a Mass in Otomí or in Nahuatl, he can say it for you, but he does not understand about the danzantes. Go back," counselled the kind priest, "and explain to him, as only you can."

Don Manuel had returned to Tlaltelolco and tried to explain the danzantes in a favorable light, but obtained doubtful results. "The new priest at Tlaltelolco seems to think he does us a great favor to permit us to use the church for the velación Saturday night. Fidel told him that it is our custom, that we have our velación there every year, but he paid no attention. So, Señora Marta, we shall see, we shall see!" Don Manuel sighed.

We sat in silence for a moment, then Manuel spoke again. "There are also other molestias, Señora Marta!" From his doleful tone I knew this would be the worst of all. "I have been given a magazine, señora, by whom, I shall not say, which shows a photograph of Manuel Pinedo in the uniform of the Concheros, dancing with that Argentine movie actress who acts in our movies now. The girl Lupe is in the same photograph. She is in uniform, too, and is standing at one side looking at the other two. It seems all three are appearing in a movie and, of course, they are being paid money for doing so."

I was properly shocked.

"I shall take this magazine to the junta Sunday night, Señora Marta. If it is as I think it is, I shall demand that they accept the Disciplina. Those two have passed their limits, Señora. They have passed their limits."

Capitán Manuel Pinedo was under the orders of Captáin General Guadalupe Alvarez and the girl Lupe was *andando* with Capitán Pinedo. Evidently Don Guadalupe, taking the part of his personnel, advocated leniency while Don Manuel urged the Disciplina. Don Fidel, it seemed, was vacilating. At least I knew which side to be on at the junta.

Nieves, Josefina, and I went to the Church of Tlaltelolco Sunday night about 9 p.m. From the street it was completely dark. When we went around to the entrance opposite the altar, however, we found that the church was feebly lighted by one electric bulb swinging at the end of a long cord hanging near the altar — the only light, said the danzantes, that they had been permitted to use.

The church was half-filled with danzantes, each capitán surrounded by his personnel, not mingling with the others as usual. At the back near the door, several of Don Manuel's personnel, including his son Miguel, were working on the portal, the decorative border that would frame the doorway tomorrow. It was of floral design and, except for the wooden frame that held it, was made of dried beans in three colors; white, brown, and black. Nearby, Tiburcio, Don Manuel's eldest son, was supervising the making of the cucharillo, the traditional Otomí decoration made by weaving the green spikes of spoon cactus into round disks so that the "spoons" stand out around the green woven centers like the petals of large green and white sunflowers. The portal for the other door would be of cucharillo.

Florentino greeted us and seated us on the two front benches on the left. Then Sargento Chucho wandered by and whispered that Don Manuel wished to speak to me in the Room of the Third Order.

About halfway between the church and the Room of the Third Order, Don Manuel stood talking to a group of jefes from the Toluca valley whom he introduced with a flourish.

"The Señora Marta stands with us against the world," he proclaimed. "She stands with us against Cecilio Morales and Miguel Morales and Guadalupe Alvarez and Fidel Morales and —" A burst of laughter interrupted him. "If the Señora Marta ever turns her back on us," he finished, "we will execute her."

This was the best joke of all and they bent double with laughter; but it was no laughing matter to me. Before it came to that, I resolved, I would retire myself across the border and stay there.

Finally Don Manuel said, "It is time for the entrada," and we made our way to the Room of the Third Order. When our lines were formed we danced out into the atrio, kneeling on the wet ground halfway to the church door while Don Manuel led the "Ave María." Then we marched into the church where the danzantes knelt again in the aisle as they approached the altar. I went on ahead so as to take pictures when they marched up the aisle.

After the entrance I found a seat near friends and the exercises began. Tiburcio, as first bugle, bowed and smiled along the aisles, from row to row, indicating the group who would sing the next alabanza. He would stand beside them and sing with them. Then as they finished, he would bow and smile and signal the first bugle of another mesa. Meanwhile, Miguel Luna supervised the arrangement of banners along the altar railing across the front of the church. The one of red satin showing Santiago on his white horse — the association banner — dominated the others.

A rare atmosphere pervaded the old church that night. The enormous space loomed dim, despite glowing candles. The odor of burning candle wax and copal, and the fitful sheen of the colorful banners lighted by the lone electric bulb swinging in the great dome, stirred the imagination to keen expectancy. Men in overalls with faded, patched shirts or threadbare sweaters, and women in cotton dresses and rebozos sat patiently on the black benches. Those who were singing lifted enraptured faces, while those who were not sat as still as Aztec images until their turn. The music of the conchas rose and fell in the background, broken now and then by a tuneless tinkle.

Capitán General Guadalupe Alvarez and his danzantes marched in and took seats on the right side of the church where they remained the rest of the night.

Don Fidel and his personnel made a dramatic entrance. First we heard their conchas outside the church. Then they began to sing and a red glow filled the doorway. Thick, black smoke bulged in. It formed a heavy cloud through which the danzantes marched. Instead of lighted candles, the first few rows carried red flares like those used by railroads, from which the black smoke streamed as they came. They marched to the front of the church where Don Fidel and his officers collected the flares and put them out. One by one capitanes from the Bajío under Fidel's orders came to the altar rail and offered flowers and candles to the Four Winds.

Three of the capitanes from the hinterland made speeches. The first two were much the same, eulogizing the dance, but the third held a surprise. "We are today the greatest force in the Catholic Church. We are its greatest force against its enemies. We are its greatest force against the Jews. We are its greatest force against the Communists. We are its greatest force against the Protestants." My danzante friends studiously looked away from me. "We will fight. . . ."

Don Fidel, in front of the altar rail, coughed and interrupted "If we take time for each capitán to make a speech we will not finish tonight. Let us now form the procession."

Don Manuel and Fidel stood side by side in front of the altar facing the congregation. Tiburcio, Miguel, and Florentino hurried about on little errands, getting ready for the procession. Capitán General Guadalupe Alvarez was silent as he sat on the right side of the church surrounded by an equally silent personnel. Capitán Manuel Pinedo and the girl Lupe were absent.

Don Manuel mounted the step to the altar and chanted, "Ave María Purísima —" and the danzantes responded. Then four danzantes carried the large image of Santiago on his white horse mounted on an *andas,* a table with handles, down the right aisle to the front of the church while the rest of the danzantes sang an alabanza about the saint. Don Manuel announced that it was now nearly twelve o'clock, and that exactly at twelve we would bear the Little Saint Santiago in a procession around the inside of the church, a procession that he hoped everybody present would join.

"¿Estaís conformes, compadritos?" he asked.

"El es Dios," responded the danzantes.

Don Florentino came up with an armload of candles and distributed them among the crowd. Don Manuel gave an order and when we had formed lines, we slowly marched down the long church, while the danzantes sang another alabanza to Santiago. As we neared the back of the church everyone knelt and Don Manuel recited, "Ave María Purísima —" with the danzantes responding. We repeated this at each aisle across the back of the church. Then the procession moved up the right aisle and across the front of the church to the other side where they left Santiago.

"Let us disarm the señora Marta and the señoritas," said Don Florentino as he collected our candles and ushered us to our seats.

Don Manuel made a little speech, mentioning the harmony among the danzantes and the cooperation of the different communities. "And now," he announced, "we will have some fireworks, not many, because the master cohuetero [maker of fireworks] has not quite finished the two largest castillos, but since we are not going to be able to shoot our cohuetes tomorrow, as you all know, we will have to shoot them tonight. Because we have no public tonight, I am asking all of you to go outside and help us do honor to our little father, Santiago. This terminates our little devotions."

Most of the crowd filed out into the atrio where some of the young men were waiting impatiently to touch off the fireworks. The velvety star-studded sky made an effective background for the "bombs"; some of them the type that soared upward to burst with a tremendous roar, others that burst with a muted boom, scattering balls of colored fire in all directions and lighting up the darkness till we could see each other clearly. One man operated a toro, or fireworks bull on wheels with a hollow space inside for the operator. As he chased the young people about the churchyard they squealed in frightened glee, for the bull exploded sparks in every direction. This was the last of the fireworks and the crowd drifted back into the church.

"When will we have the junta?" I asked Don Manuel.

"Tomorrow," he replied, which meant that we could now go home.

After a few hours sleep, we went again to Tlaltelolco. The side door was open now and we passed through it to sit with some of Don Manuel's personnel. To the traditional birthday greeting tune of Mexico they were singing "Las Mañanitas" to Santiago.

Despierta, Señor, despierta   Wake up, Lord, wake up.

Presently the priest walked down the aisle seemingly paying no attention to the danzantes. We finished singing and withdrew to seats along the aisle. After a few moments Don Fidel stood up and gave a signal. We formed lines and slowly backed from the church, singing a mañanita to Santiago as we went. When we reached the atrio the danzantes in uniform formed a double circle at one side and began to dance.

Longina Martínez, who had not yet put on her dance regalia, invited me to go with her to dress. We strolled over to the Room of the Third Order at the edge of the churchyard. Above the door was a newly painted sign, "Salon for Breakfasts of Children." Inside the danzantes were dressing — some on the stage and some in the spaces between the three long tables down the length of the room. A middle-aged woman was briskly setting the tables with an aluminum plate and cup at each place.

"Do children have their breakfast here?" I asked.

"Sí," she replied. "Three-hundred and twenty-five of them every morning — gratis!"

"How wonderful! Who does this work, the government or the church?"

"The government. The church gives the place. The government does the rest."

"And you? Are you with the church or . . ."

"I work for the government," she said proudly.

As the danzantes came in she directed them to put their belongings on the stage behind the curtain. "There is a gathering of the Third Order here on this date every month. It lasts from 9 o'clock in the morning until 2 in the afternoon. After 2 you may use the whole room. Until then you must keep your things behind the curtain."

A danzante came to tell me that the ladder was ready. Rather puzzled, I followed him into the atrio. Leaning against the main building was a long ladder.

"Tata Manuel said you would be able to take better pictures if you were above the publico," he said.

I climbed the rickety ladder and surveyed the atrio. It was a cold, misty morning. Members of danzante families stood around and shivered. Several boys came by, arms loaded with homemade fireworks, taking them into the church to be blessed.

"Are those our fireworks they are taking into the church?" I asked Don Manuel, who was crossing the atrio.

"Sí, señora," he replied.

"Will they let us shoot them?"

"Sí, Señora Marta."

"But I thought the priest said we had to shoot them all last night."

"He said that, señora, because some ladies of the church are having a kermess and were planning to have fireworks, too. The padre gave them permission to shoot their fireworks today. That was why he said we must shoot ours last night."

"Yes, I know. But why did he change his mind?"

"Because, Señora Marta, the maestro cohuetero was unable to finish the fireworks of the ladies and so now they are happy to have us shoot ours."

His eyes twinkled merrily under his old straw hat, as he hurried off on danzante business.

Nieves, Josefina, and I went home for breakfast, accompanied by two danzantas we had met the night before who delayed us until 10:30. When we again arrived at the church the fiesta was in full swing. The sidewalk from the entrance of the military prison next door to the church gate, was strewn with merchandise. The enterprising vendors hawked their wares in loud harsh voices. The less aggressive nodded in the sunshine or quietly gossiped. Straw toys, pumpkin seeds, both toasted and salted, tropical fruits, chewing gum, and whistles were offered for sale. In sidewalk eating-booths charcoal fires were glowing, and odors of frying food filled the air. Several women edged along through the crowd selling church emblems with a tiny picture of the Virgin of Guadalupe at the top.

Inside the atrio the commercial booths continued even on the long platform porch of the church itself. The fumes from tubs of piping hot cracklings were instantly noticeable. Stretched from the church wall about half-way down the platform was a small rectangle of weather-beaten canvas giving shelter to a blind organ-grinder who squatted underneath, grinding out a gay Spanish tune.

The door on the side of the church was flung wide. On the andas just inside was Santiago on his white horse. Now he was decorated with flowers, spilling across the andas, flung high behind his shield, and thrown across the front of his saddle.

We stopped at the back end of the platform and looked out over the churchyard. From the front fence to the back, it was a mass of color and movement. One dance circle after another whirled and bowed and tiptoed to several rhythms.

A service had just ended and another was due to begin. The atrio was now jammed. Inside the church, young men in the brown robes of the Franciscans herded the congregation toward the side door that was used as the exit, while outside other young men in brown robes waved the newcomers to the back door. The faithful paused on the way to gape at the danzantes, some of whom were already dancing while others were making final preparations before forming their circles. The girl Lupe, in a uniform of gold silk with bands of red appliqué in fretted design, shook a painted gourd rattle as she danced. In another group the first bugle went about the serious business of tuning conchas, while the chief objected to the huaraches of a soldier, demanding that he change them or quit the circle. Many costumes included an elegant silk or velvet cape, over which streamed ribbons of different colors falling from a band around the bewigged head, under the crown holding the feathers.

At the corner of the church I almost bumped into Don Manuel, who was clearly upset. "Imagine, Señora Marta! The segundo of Capitán Manuel Pinedo, who is under the orders of Guadalupe Alvarez, wants to dance without a sweat shirt! And when I said that I would speak to Manuel about it, he said, 'And so do I.' Imagine! Both he and his segundo wish to dance with the upper parts of their bodies bare!"

"Did you speak to Manuel Pinedo about it?"

"And do you know what he said to me, as if I were ignorant and he knew everything?"

"What did he say?" I prompted.

"He told me that our ancestors danced with their upper bodies bare. Imagine!"

"And what did you say to that?"

" 'Certainly,' " I replied, " 'Certainly our ancestors danced like that, but our ancestors were savages and we — we are civilized people.' I told him frankly that he will put on a sweat shirt or he will not dance."

"Good! Don Manuel, that should stop him."

"We shall see, Señora Marta. I go now to talk with Fidel about it. We shall see."

Near the trees beside the Salon of the Third Order, the Rayados danced their drama of the Chichimecs and the French. They were spic and span in new uniforms and none too happy about it. Tello had finally accepted the Disciplina, and Don Manuel had ruled that as punishment the whole group should appear at this fiesta in new uniforms. The cost of a new uniform is from two hundred to four hundred pesos. It was no light sentence.

"Why are you called 'Rayados,' " I asked one of the danzantes.

"Because of the custom of the Chichimecs to paint their faces in stripes, señora. Rayados means striped ones."

"¡De Veras! And why are there Frenchmen in the danza?"

"Contradanza, señora," he corrected. "Because the first Mexicans to clash with the French soldiers in the last unpleasantness were the Chichimec miners of the Puebla Sierras."

In addition to Chichimecs and Frenchmen there were also red devils, two of them. Both Chichimecs and French danced "on the march," the devils dogging their steps. They fought, both in single combat and the whole group together. When a Chichimec fell the devils went through the motions of carving him. When a Frenchman fell they argued heatedly in pantomine.

"Why do they argue?" I asked.

"Each claims the soul of the Frenchman, señora."

At twelve o'clock, true to the promise the chiefs had made the priest, the danzantes stacked their arms in the center of their circles and broke formation to eat. While they lunched in the shade we strolled through the atrio. Some offered us tacos of small fish and others apologized for not offering us tortillas, because they were made without lime.

"Do the danzantes observe the ancient fast of tortillas without lime, sauces without chili, and no salt?" I asked Don Manuel.

"Some from the far villages do, Señora Marta. Most of those from the city do not observe the fast at all. Some eat fish and eggs instead of meat. Each does according to his custom and his teaching."

Suddenly there was general movement as the danzantes began to put on their headdresses and take up their arms.

"Señora Marta! Señora Marta!" someone called.

I turned and saw Refugio Pinedo hurrying toward me.

"Refugio! What a miracle!" I exclaimed. "I have been looking everywhere for you! I went to the States and when I came back, your letter with the black border was waiting for me. Oh Refugio, I am so sorry about María. I wish I had been here to help you."

"¡Ay, señora!" he sobbed into a red bandana handkerchief. "She is gone! The companion of my years is gone! And she called for you, señora."

"¡Ay, Refugio!"

"In her last days, she called for you. She kept asking, 'Has the señora Marta come back from her tierra?'"

"I wish I had been here, Refugio!"

"¡Ay, señora! The day before she went she called me. She was very weak. She said, 'Old One, I want you to promise something. I want you to see that I am buried with the beautiful coat that the señora Marta gave me.' ¡Ay, señora!"

I could only pat the old man's shoulder and murmur "¡Pobrecito! ¡Pobrecito!"

"So, señora, I put the black coat and all the other little things you had given her into the casket with her just before we shut it for the last time."

He had to leave the fiesta because he had promised to be with a group that was dancing in Tlalpan for their *despedidas,* or farewells.

"But I shall come to your house soon, Señora Marta, for I have much to tell you."

He trudged off, a pathetic figure in his ragged sweater. He and María had been my friends for years and I, too, would miss the warm-hearted old woman who sold tortillas beside the trail at big fiestas.

In midafternoon I strolled around the church to Don Manuel's circle. The crowd had thinned now, for the fiesta was waning. Don Manuel leaned against the ladder and watched his dancers. I stood beside him and we talked.

"Why do some of the danzantes wear false hair, Don Manuel, while others do not?"

"That was a custom of our ancestors, Señora Marta. All danzantes should wear long false hair."

I thought of Diego Duran having written that the dancers of ancient Mexico wore false hair. Also, Codex Borbonicus shows the dance goddess wearing a wig.

"Some say that they wear long hair because the Chichimecs had long hair and the dance originated with them."

"That is not certain, Señora Marta. Of course our ancestors did have long hair. There were no barbershops on every corner in those times and it was the custom to wear long hair. Even so, our grand-fathers wore long false hair over their own when they danced."

"Is it true, Don Manuel, that 'the Four Winds' means the Apostles Matthew, Mark, Luke, and John?"

"Pues, in front of a church — yes."

Since we were in front of a church I dropped the matter.

Don Manuel shifted his position and sighed. "I am worried, Señora Marta. I hear disturbing rumors from San Miguel. It appears that Los Morales have departed from the rules of the danza."

"How is that?"

"They permitted twenty Americans to enter the circle and dance."

"Oh, no!"

"Furthermore they are introducing original dances of the imagina-tion which have their roots in the theater of the United States, and are not from the dances of our ancestors, which are religious dances."

"Yes," I agreed, "the dances of ancient Mexico were religious."

"They were simple dances, señora, the dances of our ancestors. Some were very difficult but only a few could dance them, so they were not often danced. Mostly the steps were simple, as they are now, because everybody danced them, young and old. And, too, they were danced for many days continuously, so they had of a necessity to be dances that did not tire the dancers."

"Yes, of course."

"But these dances that they do in San Miguel de Allende now — poof! They have nothing to do with our ancestors, they have nothing to do with religion, they have nothing to do with Mexico!"

"¡Qué lástima, Don Manuel!"

For a while we stood in silence, looking out over the churchyard at the various groups of dancers.

"Don Manuel, why is it that you so seldom wear a uniform at a fiesta? I know that you have two beautiful uniforms that Doña Ester made for you. Why do you not use them?"

"Señora Marta, I will tell you something that few know. In the old days everybody wore uniforms at the fiesta except the *cacique* [chief]."

"Is that so?"

"It is the truth. Did you ever see Ruperto Granados of San Miguel de Allende dressed in a uniform for the dance?"

"No — now that I think of it, no."

"That is why, señora."

Now was the time, I thought, to ask him something I had wanted to know for a long time.

"Don Manuel, what is the significance of those things in the center of the circle? The two bells of the capitanas, the two incense burners, and the concha, all placed on a large handkerchief spread out in a square?"

"Those are arms of the Conquest and the very basis of the dance."

"I thought they were important because they are always in the center of the dance circle at a fiesta."

"They refer to the ancient execution and the present-day Disciplina. The ancient priest performed a rite at a square in front of the altar on the pyramid. He did this before the other four priests came forward to assist him in taking out the heart of the sacrificed one. The handkerchief is used, not because it is a handkerchief, but because it is square."

"Do you mean that the Disciplina relates to the taking out of the heart in the ancient sacrifice?"

"It is the substitution for it."

"How interesting!"

"Now the things in the center have changed and are Christian because the execution has changed. The *macana,* the knife with which they formerly cut out the heart, has been replaced by the concha, and the ancient incense burner by the one of today. The big handkerchief in a square, the two bells, the two incense burners and the concha all refer to the Disciplina; that is to say, to the present-day execution."

The shadows lengthened across the churchyard. Commerce in the kermess was almost at a standstill. An Indian baby, snug in its mother's rebozo, whimpered softly. The fiesta was drawing to a close.

The danzantes in the outer circle of Don Manuel's group began to strum a march. Two capitanes placed themselves side by side in the outer circle.

"¡El es Dios!" shouted one.

"¡El es Dios!" cried the other, as they bowed and passed each other, dancing in opposite directions, each followed by the danzantes behind him; a maneuver that divided the outer circle into halves and left a gap on the opposite side that widened as the dancers progressed. Meanwhile those in the smaller, inner circle danced, one behind the other, around the circle and back to the gap so that the circles dissolved through the gap into three lines of dancers — or rather, a line of dancers, dancing three abreast toward the church door. As they passed us Don Manuel and I fell in line behind the leaders.

We stood in front of the church door and sang a despedida. As we began a second, we slowly marched in and down the center aisle to the altar, singing all the while. After two or three despedidas the danzantes knelt and Don Manuel began "Ave María Purísima —." Then we rose and, as we backed slowly out of the church, sang again.

When we were outside the door the danzantes knelt singing, and offered their conchas to the Four Winds. Don Manuel chanted again, "Ave María Purísima —."

Danzantes crowded around to bid us good-bye. Several from out of town were going to Don Manuel's house to sleep in the oratory before taking the early bus the next morning.

"When will we have the junta?" I asked Don Manuel.

"It has been postponed — probably next Sunday."

"Don Manuel," I asked, "what happened to the other castillo, the large one you were going to raise on a pole?"

"We are leaving that for the ladies of the kermess. As I told you, their fireworks were not finished and so they have not fired any today. Only ours were fired. Since they need one for later we have agreed to let them have the castillo."

"Did they pay for it?"

"Sí, Señora Marta."

The danzantes had won in the matter of fireworks and, perhaps, had made money besides. It had been a good fiesta.

The
Disciplina

IT IS INTERESTING HOW ONE THING LEADS TO ANOTHER and events build
to a peak. For years I had been trying to see the Disciplina and had just
missed it so many times that I had almost given up hope of ever seeing
it. Certainly nothing was farther from my mind one Sunday afternoon
in March when Nieves and I went to the junta that Don Manuel had
been talking about for months. It was held in the Room of the Third
Order at Tlaltelolco and failed to come up to our expectations. A priest
read the new rules of the capitanía, naming Don Manuel and Don Fidel
as principal generals, and the danzantes voted them in. There was no
mention of Capitán Manuel Pinedo, the girl Lupe, or sweat shirts. Then
another priest gave a discourse that sounded like a sermon, and that
was all.

As we were leaving, Don Manuel invited us to an *ensayo general*.
Since I had never heard of a general rehearsal, I asked what it was.

"An ensayo general," he explained, "is when all the soldados and
malinches pass in review before their chief. It is like inspection in the
army. All the uniforms have to be complete and clean. It will be held
two months from now in the month of May. I hope that you can come,
Señora Marta."

In the meantime I continued my inquiries about the Disciplina.
Long ago Don Manuel had given me a standing invitation to come to
his oratory whenever he was going to execute a danzante, but I had
insisted, "Provided the danzante to be executed wants me to see it."

How foolish! Of course nobody wanted me to see him ceremoniously
whipped.

The other chiefs disapproved of Don Manuel's invitation to me.
The Disciplina was secret, they held, for danzantes only, and no outsiders should be permitted to attend it. Don Manuel replied that in
order to write a true history of the dance, I should attend the various
ceremonies, including the Disciplina, which was one of the most important and one that all danzantes should be proud to have known.

About this time one of the other chiefs and his right arm, Capitana

María, came to call on me. As we sat in the living room drinking coffee with hot milk, he suddenly said, "I have a little plan to propose to you, señora, about your problem of the Disciplina." He glanced at María sipping with gusto. "How would it be if María should kneel on a clean petate in front of an altar and I should raise the disciplina as if to strike her; how would it be if you took a picture of us then, señora, for your book — standing behind us, of course, so that the face of María would not show."

Obviously, he had failed to talk his proposition over with María. She stared at him in consternation. "P-pues, que p-pues . . .," she almost strangled, "the señora Marta does not want lies in her book!"

And she was right.

Shortly afterward I went with Don Manuel to a group of adobe cottages perched helter-skelter along the rim of a sand mine on the outskirts of the capital. There was a dance oratory there and the mesa was under his orders. He was going to "hurl charges" at its personnel. After voting "¡El es Dios!" to dance at Tlaltelolco, they had allowed themselves to be persuaded by friends in a rival camp to dance at another fiesta instead. Don Manuel read the rules and lectured them; with the result being that the mesa voted "¡El es Dios!" to a proposal that the little jefe and his segundo present themselves at Don Manuel's oratory two weeks hence to be executed.

Two Sundays later, after the regular rehearsal at Don Manuel's oratory, they were tried by their fellows, two danzantes speaking against them and two in their behalf. The latter spoke so well that the danzantes voted "¡El es Dios!" to a proposal to pardon them.

I was ashamed of my disappointment.

The following Sunday the same mesa committed the same error. Again Don Manuel notified them to report to general headquarters the next Sunday, but not one appeared.

Then came the general rehearsal at Don Manuel's oratory. Since it fell on May 10, which in Mexico is Mother's Day ("when every man wants to be with his mother," as the danzantes explained at the April velación) Don Manuel decided to have it "in the style of the Bajío," at night, and announced it for May 9. The first part of any rehearsal is like a velación. In Preconquest times the danzantes asked permission of a dance god before they danced. Now they ask permission of a saint — or at least, the conservatives do.

I arrived early to find the altar decorated with *pastle*, a tiny moss which is a tree parasite, and spring flowers, and the oratory, as usual, scrupulously clean. The few danzantes there were dressed in ordinary clothes, but under benches and in corners were largish bundles and the long tin cylinders like quivers, in which the danzantes carry the feathers for their headdresses. As members of the various mesas arrived, Don Manuel took the chiefs around the room and introduced them. He paid special attention to one couple, a thick, squat man past middle age and his plump, elderly wife.

"He is a new jefe who has joined with us, señora," whispered Miguel Luna. "He is very well known and this is the first time that he has come here."

After the opening ceremony, a young man whom I had not noticed before, a member of the mesa by the sand mines whom I knew as Chico, "asked for the word" and Don Manuel recognized him.

"In the name of God, firstly of God," Chico began in a voice that trembled but grew stronger as he continued, "I have come to pay for my shortcomings." Taking a step forward, "I accept the Disciplina."

Don Manuel said softly, "Later, my son, after the obligation."

Chico stepped back and the danzantes began an alabanza.

The Disciplina! Would I be able to see it? I realized that in spite of his mesa's decision to ignore the second summons, Chico had chosen to remain under Don Manuel's orders and had come tonight to be executed. Would he want me to leave? If so, Don Manuel would give me a signal, or would send one of his sons to tell me. Frozen with excitement, I sat silent and watchful through the interminable exercises.

Finally, as midnight approached, the danzantes who had not already done so put on their uniforms. In the corner near me a man named Pedro put on his black stockings, dark gray raincoat, black sash, insipid mask, and wig of long white hair; for he was to play the part of La Vieja, or The Old Woman. Even Don Manuel was in uniform, wearing the one of orange silk with the headdress of black and orange chachalaca feathers.[1]

At midnight Don Manuel took his place, in front of the altar facing us. The danzantes, led by their captains, formed two parallel lines in the center of the room, extending from the altar toward the back, and, playing a paso de camino, danced in pairs toward him. As each pair reached Don Manuel, they paused in front of him for a beat or two, then abruptly divided, one dancing to one side and the other to the opposite side, then down the sides toward the back. One line danced out the side door, while the other danced across the back and out. This, I gathered, was "passing in review." When the last of the lines disappeared, I followed them out.

One electric light hung from an extension cord at the outer corner of the house, and a gasoline lantern hung in the corner formed by the kitchen and bedroom. The moon was low and bright. In this triple lighting the patio presented a bizarre picture as the bright costumes flickered and flashed in the dance circles. Each step was complicated and difficult. As each ended, La Vieja, burlesquing just outside the circle, would droop and sigh noisily. All the danzantes, spick and span in freshly cleaned or new uniforms, danced well, but none with greater fervor than Chico.

Tiburcio brought my chair from the oratory and we chatted for a few minutes, before he returned to the circles.

"Tiburcio, perhaps you can tell me, do the danzantes play the conchas in just one key, or can they play in the various keys?"

"They can play in all keys, señora, but usually they play in only two, G Major and D Major. When all are accustomed to these two keys, it is easier to tune the conchas quickly."

After an hour or more the danzantes came out of the circles in three parallel lines and danced back into the oratory. Since the one electric bulb remained hanging in the patio, the only light inside was from the altar. It was bright with dozens of candles of many sizes, but when the danzantes with their tall, sweeping headdresses had crowded inside, those near the altar cut off the light and the oratory was in semi-darkness.

Chico, in faded denim shirt and blue jeans, knelt before the altar. Head up, shoulders back, and spine straight, he did not move until after the execution. His staunch, dark silhouette against the flaming candles keyed the whole scene.

While I hesitated at the door, Don Manuel appeared by my side and escorted me to my chair which was now against the wall by the altar. Then he crossed to Chico's side and faced the danzantes.

"The alféreces will arm themselves," he ordered.

The standard-bearers raised their banners from the corners by the altar and, stationing themselves near the front, stood waving them continuously throughout the ceremony. Don Manuel took a roll of papers from inside his shirt and read:

"Article 3: All the community ought to remember one of the Ten Commandments which says, 'Take not the name of God in vain.' Thus, is the phrase 'He is God' respected, because it is the sign of these obligations."

"Article 14: To all capitanes, or personnel in general, it remains strictly forbidden to make obligations or lend their services to outside communities, or to those of the same union, without first asking permission of their jefes. The person who commits this fault will be punished in accordance with the Law of the Conquest."

He tilted his head back and closed his eyes. "These are laws of this cuartel general. I name Capitanas Gregoria and Luz to speak at the trial of our brother. Capitana Gregoria will speak against him and Capitana Luz will speak for him. ¡El es Dios!"

For a moment the swish of the banners was the only sound, then Gregoria stepped forward and spoke. "It is my opinion that the only way we can preserve the customs left us by our ancestors is to follow the Law of the Conquest and obey our jefes. Chico — [giving his full name] — voted 'El es Dios' to dance at Tlalpan in accordance with the plans of our capitán general, Manuel Luna. Then, instead of fulfilling his obligation, he danced at another place. Therefore, in my opinion, he should be executed for taking the name of God in vain. ¡El es Dios!"

"¡El es Dios!" echoed the danzantes.

"And what is your opinion, Capitana Luz?" asked Don Manuel.

Luz smiled sweetly. "Those are my opinions, too," she said.

Don Manuel stated that each member of the mesa was entitled to an opinion and urged those present to express themselves. "I will now call on Capitán Maximino Márquez, heir of Vicente Márquez, founder of the Cooperación de Concheros."

Capitán Maximino addressed the altar and said he was in favor of execution. "I myself have been executed. General Perez once gave me six lashes. I accepted the Disciplina and then retired myself from the dance. That is what I did. But God punished me. I lost my father! My beloved father died. So I returned to the dance and have been a danzante ever since. And if in the future I commit an error, I shall accept the Disciplina. I shall be executed! ¡El es Dios!"

One by one veterans of the dance spoke in favor of execution. Finally the elderly "new chief" stepped forward. By now several of the women were quietly weeping, and as he finished the tears were raining down his leathery cheeks.

"All the chiefs have been executed," he said. "They would not be chiefs if they had not. Those who accomplish much are the ones who make the mistakes, who forget the rules, and who, therefore, have to be punished. Those who do nothing commit no errors, but neither do they accomplish great things. We chiefs have all had the Disciplina. I remember well the occasion when I was executed the first time. Had I retired myself from the dance then, I would never have done anything of merit. My life would have been very different. My life. . . ." the tears had crept into his voice, "¡El es Dios!" he choked.

"¡El es Dios!" murmured the danzantes.

"It is impossible to say too much about the importance of obeying the rules," said Don Manuel quietly. "This is the only way we can continue to carry on our devotions. Behavior such as the capitana Gregoria has described to you will destroy the Conquista. Laxness toward disobedience caused us to lose three communities last year. As my compadre has said, we have all been executed. Capitana Francisca, who is a veteran in the dance, has had the Disciplina three times in her life, as have I myself. Only by strict obedience to the rules and punishment of those who break them, can we hope to preserve the customs left us by our ancestors. ¡El es Dios, compadritos!"

When the question of the sentence arose everybody talked at once. Even the women who were crying expressed opinions in tearful undertones to those who were near them. Finally Tiburcio mounted the bench along the side of the room and, bracing his back against the wall, addressed the danzantes.

"It is said of the Disciplina, that for the first time the sentence may be three lashes, for the second, six lashes or half an arroba, and for the third, twelve lashes or one arroba. This is for a first time. Therefore, I propose three lashes or a quarter arroba."

"¿Estaís conformes, compadritos?" asked Don Manuel.

"¡El es Dios!" shouted the danzantes.

"Señor Sargento," said Don Manuel.

"¡El es Dios!" answered the sargento, stepping forward.

"You will carry out the sentence!"

"¡El es Dios!" said the sargento.

"¡El es Dios!" murmured the danzantes, beginning to strum their conchas.

The sargento took his place in the front row just behind Chico. The danzantes began to sing "Alabado," and at intervals, while most of the women and some of the men wiped their eyes, the timeworn, discolored, enormous disciplina snaked out at the end of the sargento's muscular arm to land between the slender shoulders of Chico. He did not flinch. Though the rope with four arms probably removed the skin along his backbone, he did not move. I was too wrought up to try to get the words of the song, or to figure the intervals at which the sargento struck. I was thinking of Chico. It took stamina to carry this off as he was doing!

The odor of burning candle wax and copal was overpowering. This, added to the movement of plumes and feathers and the relentless beat of the strumming of conchas, made me a little dizzy. Though there were several verses after the last lash, the song finally ended. For a moment there was only the sputter of a huge candle with a faulty wick, the swish-swish of the banners, and the still figure before the altar. Then Don Manuel stepped to the center again.

"Capitanas Gregoria and Luz," he called.

"¡El es Dios!" they replied.

The two young capitanas went to Chico, and, one on either side, put their hands under his arms and helped him to his feet. Then they turned him to face us. Don Manuel made an announcement about an embrace of pardon, but I did not get the exact words. I was watching Chico's sensitive face with its taut half smile.

We sang "Penitencia, Penitencia" while first the chiefs and then the rest of the danzantes came up to give Chico the double embrace, most of them murmuring to him as they did so. He was silent, except for a "gracias" now and then.

When I gave him the embrace, I said, "Many congratulations!"

"¡Gracias!" he replied.

He was trembling!

After the closing ceremony, Tiburcio walked with me to the highway three blocks away where I would get a bus.

"Will Chico dance with us now?" I asked.

"He will probably become a member of the Peña Pobre mesa."

"What will happen to the little jefe of the sand mines and his personnel, those who did not accept the Disciplina?"

"We will never recognize them again, Señora Marta. For us they do not exist."

I was sorry. They had been my friends and I would miss them at future fiestas.

A few weeks later Don Manuel came to see us. As we sat in the living room nibbling tacos and drinking coffee, he suddenly asked, "Has the señorita Frances come yet?"

Our friend, Professor Frances Gillmor of the University of Arizona, had been spending her vacations in Mexico to do research for a biography of Nezahualcoyotl, *Flute of the Smoking Mirror*, and had been overdue for several days.

"Yes," I told him, "she arrived last night."

"We are going to have the disciplina again next Sunday, Señora Marta, and I have been thinking that perhaps the señorita Frances would like to see it, too. Will you come, Señora Marta, and will you bring the señorita Frances with you?"

I was delighted and puzzled. It had taken me years to see the Disciplina and then I had seen it by accident. Now I was invited to see it again and to bring a friend. I wondered why.

Frances and I went to Don Manuel's oratory to an ensayo, rehearsal, the following Sunday and witnessed the Disciplina as applied to one of the Rayados, who was retiring from that group and wanted to pertain to Don Manuel's mesa. He stated that he wanted to come to this mesa with his conscience clean and that, although he was retiring, he would accept the Disciplina of the Rayados. The trial was much like that of Chico and, since that particular group of Rayados was under Don Manuel's orders, the same sargento executed the Rayado.

"What did you think of it?" I asked Frances on the way home.

"Oh, Martha! The dignity of it, the tremendous dignity of it! To think that human dignity can rise to such heights!"

Months later Don Manuel explained our invitation.

"After we executed Chico, Señora Marta, a commission of dance jefes called on me. And they were very angry with me."

"Why was that, Don Manuel?"

"Because I permitted you to see the Disciplina. They said that they were going to begin now to tell the reporters and the writers that the Disciplina does not exist, that it was a custom of our ancestors, but that it has not existed for many years."

"But that would not be true, Don Manuel."

"They also said that if, when your book is published, it contains any mention of the execution of Chico, they will tell all the newspapers that it is all lies, all lies."

"Oh, Don Manuel, do you think that they will?"

"You have told me, Señora Marta, that the señorita Frances has written five books. If these lying individuals carry out their present intention, the señorita Frances can write another book and say that your book is all true, because now she, too, has seen the Disciplina."

I know of no other non-danzantes who have witnessed this important ceremony.

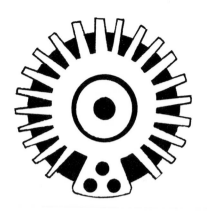

According to Danzantes, Books and Records

AFTER MORE THAN TWENTY YEARS' acquaintance with the religious dancers of Mexico, I feel sure that at some time within the first two centuries after the Conquest, the Spaniards superimposed upon the Mexicans a well-defined substitute for the pagan dance cult. In the turbulent centuries since, the dance disappeared during wars to reappear in the lulls between them: dance chiefs perished and their documents were lost. New chiefs then guided the danzantes from memory or by hearsay, and half-forgotten ancient practices were revived — or perhaps had been permitted to endure by the Spaniards in the first place. These circumstances, together with the secrecy and the double meaning that have always been within the dance cult, make it almost impossible for the danzantes to agree on its basic characteristics now.

The Preconquest religion had more than a little in common with the Christian: for example, baptism, confession, incense, fasting, and communion, though it is true all were somewhat different from the Christian practices. At the baptism, there was perhaps more oratory and the midwife played the leading role; confession was permitted only once in a lifetime with immunity from temporal punishment for anything confessed; incense was used constantly not only for religious purposes, but as a courtesy to persons of high rank. Fasting meant eating only once a day of tortillas without lime or chile or any other seasoning, and abstinence from meat, wine, and sexual intercourse; communion varied as to the special food pertaining to the worship of the particular god. In the sixth month (May 23–June 11) one dish was similar to succotash, the long bones of the human sacrifice stewed with corn and beans and eaten in honor of the god.[1] That there was a Preconquest Xuchil similar to that of the dance cult of today, and that it held a mirror in its center is almost certain; for I have a Preconquest seal of baked clay, three centimeters high, that looks quite like a custodia, with the round indentation in the center, like that of today's danzante

Xuchil. Very likely this seal is a miniature of a larger Xuchil which carried in its center an obsidian mirror, the symbol of Tezcatlipoca who was the sun god,[2] and who is also indicated by rays shooting outward to form the perimeter; just as rays surround the center of both the danzante Xuchil and the Catholic Church custodia, or ostensorium, which "has the form of the sun because Jesus Christ is a sun."[3] Ancestor worship has a kinship of sorts with praying for souls in purgatory, and no great imagination is needed to associate "human sacrifice" with "living sacrifice," a term often applied to Christ on the cross. The sign of midnight is depicted more than once in Codex Borbonicus, and various chronicles of the Conquest describe native Mexican ceremonies at midnight, rites at stated intervals of time, the practice of discipline, and of silence. What effective preparation were these for the Indians' acceptance of the recently established reforms of the Franciscans; the midnight service, prayers at stated hours, discipline, and silence![4]

Some of the features of ancient times found in the dance cult of today remain largely as they were before the Conquest. Others have changed almost beyond recognition. Most are attached, however slightly, to Christian beliefs. For example, the bastón, symbol of authority and depicted in the dance god's hands on sheet 88 of Codex Vaticanus 3773, is carried in a shortened version by all capitanas de mesa and by most dance chiefs. It is referred to as the Santo Bastón, or Holy Rod, and figures importantly in alabanzas and dance rules.[5] The ribbon streamers down the back of the dance uniform, the wide collar and cuffs, the necklace, the sandals, the cape, even the warrior's loin cloth, all depicted in the codices, appear in traditional dance uniforms of today practically unchanged. Don Cecilio Morales' dance documents, handed down for generations, stipulated that the capes of the dance chiefs of the Bajío have velvet collars and so they have, even now. Copal, which was used as incense before the Conquest, still is used as incense throughout Mexico. Though they used other formations also, the ancients appear most often in the codices dancing in circles. This is the usual formation today.

Don Manuel tells me that the term Los Concheros was the name the Spaniards gave to Los Apaches; that Los Concheros is their Spanish name and Los Apaches is their Mexican or Nahuatl name. The chances are that he is right, for outside Mexico City they are generally known as Los Apaches, even in the village of Magdalena de Petlacalco, less than twenty miles from the capital.

"Are there any danzantes in Petlacalco?" I asked a brick mason working on the American Legion school building there.[6]

"Sí, señora."

"Are there danzantes of Los Concheros?"

"No, señora."

"What danzantes are there here?"

"Only Los Apaches, señora."

I inquired of several there, but none knew of Los Concheros. Most knew of Los Apaches.

Apache may be a combination of the Nahuatl verb *a*, used in the sense of moving an object to a particular place,[7] and the noun *pachtli*, now corrupted to pastle, a tiny green moss that clings to certain trees, particularly to the ahuehuete.[8] The ancients used it to decorate the temples and to crown the priests and the idols. The warrior dancers were important in religious affairs as well as in the military. It seems reasonable to suppose that to them was delegated the work of decorating the temples and the honor of crowning the priests and the idols. Pastle is still used in Mexico to decorate churches. The Concheros use it to decorate their altars and the Xuchil, and to test a danzante as to his knowledge of dance ritual. It is entirely possible that Apaches originally meant "Those who place the pachtli."

In connection with dancing, the codices depict persons rubbing turtle shells with a bone, a deer horn, or a skull, obviously to produce rhythm. In a private archaeological collection in Mexico City, I saw a Tarascan figurine of a seated person holding an armadillo shell to his shoulder in violin fashion and rubbing a large seashell across it. The Spaniards had only to turn the armadillo shell over, and give it a neck, pegs, and strings to form the concha.[9]

It is doubtful that Preconquest music is used in the dance cult now, though the words of some of the songs are sung to extraordinarily ill-fitting tunes, but the uses of music then and now are similar. Duran said of the ancients,

> They sought permission from the dance gods before they danced . . . . For many days before a fiesta they had rehearsals of songs and dances . . . . Singers composed for them songs of the greatness of their ancestors . . . . Other singers composed divine songs in praise of the greatness of their gods . . . . For new songs, they have new adornments of capes and feathers, and false hair, and masks.[10]

According to Mendieta,

> When they had a victory in war, or elevated a new lord, or married a principal señora, or for any novelty, the music masters composed a new song, besides the usual ones which they had in the fiestas of the devil, and of the heroic feats of the ancient ones, and of the lords of the past.[11]

Today the conservative Concheros sing before an altar to obtain the permission of the saint before making him an offering of their dance. For many days before an important fiesta they have rehearsals of dances and songs. They sing of the greatness of God, of the Christ, of the Virgin, of the saints, and of their ancestors. They have songs of praise, morning songs, and songs of farewell. They have marches for processions, "steps of the road" when they dance from one place to another, and a variety of dance tunes that synchronize rhythmically with the various dance steps at a fiesta. They have ballads "for any novelty," like "The Señor of Villaseca" and "The Alabanza of Cazadero," and a special song for each sequence of a velación. When a danzante refuses to accept the Disciplina and retires from a dance group, the danzantes produce cacophony instead of music. When a danzante has served as the leader of a contradanza for the time pledged in a promesa, he "retires himself" in a decorated oratory to tuneful music of farewell.

The Mexicans had a solar year which at the time of the Conquest was more accurate than that of the Spaniards, for the Gregorian correction was made later. The calculations of the divisions of the year, however, were different. Instead of seven day-names, the Mexicans had 20 day-signs, each easy to draw, for theirs was a picture writing. Their solar year was composed of 18 groups of the 20 day-signs, or 360, plus five additional days, making 365 days in all.[12] In addition to the solar calendar, they also had the Tonalamatl, or "The Book of Good and Evil Days." Here the 20 day-signs were arranged in 20 groups of 13 day-signs each, or 260 days in all, with each group called by the interpreters a "week." The days of each week were numbered in continuous series and a day-sign was not complete without its number. In this way each had a number that did not recur in connection with that particular day-sign for the space of 260 days. The initial day of the week gave the name to that entire week. Each day was presided over by a god who exercised special influence over it and over everybody born on it. It was the custom to name babies at the time of their birth by the name of their birthday and any other names were added later. Each week also had a patron god who presided over it.[13] In the opinion of Vaillant, "The computations that kept the solar and religious calendars in harmony with the seasons were made by the priests. The gods ruled; the priests interpreted and interposed, and the people obeyed, not the priests, but the rhythm of action whereby the gods lived."[14]

The goddess of pulque, Mayauel, presided over the eighth Tonalamatl week beginning on *ce malinalli*, which contained more evil than good days. She was also ruler of the eighth day, Tochtli, "Rabbit," in a sense the emblem of the earth, which according to the interpreters was created on the day "1 Rabbit." Above all it was the emblem of the pulque made from the sap of the agave, and of its intoxicating properties. The pulque gods were called "The Four Hundred Rabbits," and the pulque gods' chief and high priest, who was at the same time the chief of the temple music, was called "One Tochtli." The interpreter of Codex Vaticanus A, states that Mayauel was a woman with 400 breasts, and because of her fecundity the gods changed her into the agave plant that yields the raw material for pulque.

Mayauel appears to have been generally identified with Xochiquetzal, the goddess of dance and the patron of *maqui*, the female warriors who were the associates of the bachelor warriors in the dance house near the temple. The interpreters of Codex Telleriano Remensis give Cipactonal as another of Mayauel's titles, and this name is accepted as synonymous with Tonacaciuatl, goddess of procreation, hence also with Xochiquetzal, the dance goddess.[15]

Mayauel and the innumerable pulque gods were important factors in Preconquest life and religion, for generally speaking pulque was not drunk for social but for religious reasons, though at ceremonial feasts and drinking bouts the devout often expressed their devotion by drinking to the point of insensibility.[16] Each step in the cultivation of the maguey from which pulque was to be made — the transplanting of the hijos, or sons (the young plants), the cutting out of the heart, the siphoning of the sap, and the scraping of the empty center — was accompanied by its appropriate prayer.[17] When the new pulque was ready, a special invocation was made to the pulque god, Tezcatzoncatl.[18] The priests of the pulque gods were the music masters of the temple; composing the music, teaching and directing it, selecting the participants, and acting as masters of ceremonies at the fiestas there.[19] Intoxication by younger people on other than religious occasions was punishable by death.[20] Pregnant women and the very old were allowed to drink when and as much as they liked.[21] Seler states that pulque was the warriors' drink. Later he indicates that under certain religious circumstances it was believed to be an aid to procreation.[22] Spence remarks that pulque gave strength and courage to the warrior.[23] Payno says that soldiers on campaign were permitted a certain dose. In the codices, the circular symbol composed half of the sun disk and the remainder of the starry night sky, denoting sunrise or sunset (half day and half night), usually appears with the pulque gods. Among various Concheros groups today, "the hour of the sacrifice," or dance time, is usually from sunrise to sunset. Some danzantes obtain permission to drink *unos traguitos* (some little swallows) of pulque before "entering the sacrifice" at sunrise and after the dancing has ended at sunset, with the sergeant of the march counting each swallow. I have never known Don Manuel Luna's personnel to do so.

Malinche, as the ordinary woman dancer of the Concheros is called, is a name applied to a character or characters in several dance groups of Mexico. In one group that I watched in the atrio of a village not far from Mexico City, the malinche, with an oversize bust and a doll dressed like a baby, seemed to be a fertility figure. In another village where the main dance of the fiesta seemed to center around the world directions, the malinche apparently represented the West, the region of the women. The ancient Mexicans believed that the souls of the warriors who died on the sacrificial stone went to the eastern heaven; and their female counterparts, the souls of the women who died in childbirth, went to the western heaven. The souls of the warriors escorted the sun as it rose in the east to its zenith where they relinquished this honor to the souls of the women who escorted it to its setting in the west.[24] But neither of these representations of Malinche seemed to bear any relation to the malinche of the Concheros.

Since the change in the Concheros dance cult involved the superimposition of the Christian dance on the pagan, it seems quite likely that the name malinche harks back to that change. This brings us to the Indian slave who was born a *cacica* and the only heir to a *cacigazco*, but was sold into slavery while she was still a child by treacherous relatives scheming for her heritage, and remained a slave until middle age when she married a Spanish gentleman who took her to live in Spain.

After the first battle between the Spaniards and Mexicans (the battle of Cintla, about March 25, 1519) the vanquished Mexicans, as a sign of their capitulation and acceptance of the Christian religion, and of their vassalage to the King of Spain, sent their conquerors valuable tribute which included 20 women slaves, among them the slave who had been born a cacica. Cortés requested Father Olmeda to take charge of them for religious instruction and designated 20 of his officers as their future masters. The slaves accepted the Christian religion and were immediately baptized and given Christian names. The only name of the 20 to come down to us was the one bestowed on the slave who had been born a cacica, Marina.[25]

Some authorities hold that she was called Malinche because she probably was born on the day *malinalli*. To the stem *Malin,* add the suffix denoting rank, *-tzin,* and the result would be Malintzin; which to the Spaniards, who found some Nahuatl sounds impossible to achieve, likely would become Malinche.[26] This would be plausible had she been born on *ce* malinalli, for that would place her under the patronage of Mayauel who was a variant of Xochiquetzal, the dance goddess, and thus would establish a connection with the dance cult. But there is slight evidence that her birthday was ce malinalli.

Others claim that since Nahuatl has no *r* sound, and *l* is substituted in foreign words containing *r*, Marina became Malina to the Indians who added *-tzin* to the stem, *Malin,* and the result was Malintzin or Malinche.[27]

After her ability as a linguist was discovered she became the principal interpreter for the Spanish army; Cortés demanded her presence at the parleys with ambassadors from the various city states, for she was also very skillful at persuading the Mexicans to accede to the demands of the Spaniards. The result was, according to the chroniclers of the Conquest, that they often addressed Cortés as "Malinche," too. Robelo says this is a mistake, that they were saying not "Malinche," but "Malinche-e"[28] (literally, "He who has Malinche," meaning, "He whose slave Malinche is."). She and the other female slaves usually accompanied the conquistadors on their expeditions against their enemies.

It is possible that the ordinary woman dancer of the Concheros is called a malinche because an Indian slave woman of the sixteenth century accompanied the Spanish soldiers on their "marches"; sharing whatever befell them, interpreting, persuading, and negotiating for them. It is even possible that she is a malinche because this Indian aide was the archetype of the maqui, the Preconquest female warrior. It is also possible and much more probable that she is a malinche because Malinche was the first native-born Mexican of record to renounce the pagan religion and be baptized a Christian.

A little plant that grows in marshy places probably gave the name *chilillo* to the traditional feather headdress of the Concheros.[29] Señor Jesús Valencia, steeped in the knowledge of the history and folkways of his country, described it to me as a "small plant having a stem about 12 centimeters long and a rose-colored flower that grows upward on it like a little worm." The chilillo headdress is made by attaching small feathers around a slender rod about a foot and half in length, more or less as flowers on a spike.

"The chilillo is the traditional danzante headdress, Señora Marta," Don Manuel Luna explained. "Our ancestors wore chilillos. The ostrich plumes that you see today have been in use only since it became possible to obtain imported feathers. In the old days there were only the feathers of the birds of Mexico, usually of the eagle and of the turkey — especially of the white turkey, señora, of the soft breast feathers of the white turkey."

Before the Conquest, a ball of downy feathers was a symbol of the sacrifice. Captured warriors destined for the sacrificial death were decorated with bunches of feathers from the breast of the white eagle. Seler was of the opinion that since white eagle feathers were difficult to obtain, the ancients probably eked them out with the breast feathers of the white turkey.[30] The chilillo headdress is usually made of the breast feathers of a white turkey interspersed with more breast feathers of a white turkey that have been dyed in vivid colors. The Third Provincial Council, which met in New Spain in 1585, prohibited the wearing of coronas, or headdresses, by the Indians when they danced, because "by them they manifest some sort of idolatry."[31]

The *Ciuapipiltin*, phantom goddesses from the west, and the *Tzitzimime*, "Demons of Darkness," may have been the ancient forebears of the spirits, witches, and unknown terrors that, some believe, inhabit the darkness. On certain dates the Ciuapipiltin; spirits of the women who had died in childbirth, female counterparts of the slain or sacrificed warriors; came down from heaven to strike the children with epilepsy and to beguile men to lust and sin. They appear in the codices as associates of the five gods of dance, song, and sport; the torchbearers with the four balls that are symbols of the dance god depicted on their shields and banners. The Tzitzimime, spirits of certain gods who fell from heaven, according to Seler, were demons who, when a solar eclipse took place, swooped down in the form of eagles to swallow up the people.[32] In the codices they are sometimes accompanied by spiders, scorpions, shells, turtles, or bees.[33]

According to legend, the wind god, Quetzalcoatl (Feathersnake), while traveling eastward from Cholulu, shot an arrow into the air and pierced the bole of a tree in the center thus forming a cross.[34] After that he bore as a sign of his office "a mace like the cross of a bishop," and the worship of the cross was connected with him.[35] Somewhere on the east coast he immolated himself and after eight days arose from the dead to become Venus, Herald of the Sun, with a skull for a symbol. Chimalpahin describes an ancient rite of the Chichimecs in which they painted a cross on the ground and ceremoniously arranged a bow with a drawn arrow on top of the painted cross so as to cover it. Then they shot the arrow. They gained nothing by this, he says, but did it purely for witchcraft.[36] When a decorated cross, like the one the danzantes used in planting the cross, is placed on a surface flat on its back with the starched white streamer arranged in a perfect arc, it bears a striking resemblance to an enormous bow and arrow drawn in readiness for shooting.

In another legend, Tezcatlipoca let Quetzalcoatl see himself in the mirror that gave Tezcatlipoca his name. Quetzalcoatl, with his tusks and feather mask, was so shocked at his ugliness that he decreed that his image should be carried covered up forever after, and so it is.[37]

While the Aztecs were moving about from place to place looking for a home, their leader, Huitziton, grew ill and died; he left them his bones and skull so that through his skull they might communicate with him and he with them. They carried these relics with them in a bundle to Tenochtitlan, which they founded between 1312–1325.[38]

As late as 1536, an Indian named Mateo testified before the Inquisition that his father had a wrapped-up idol, very heavy, that they never untied unless they were worshipping it — due to the reverence they had for it and because they said that whoever untied it would die. His father carried this bundle to Escapuzalco (Atzcapotzalco), to the cacique there, called Ocuicin, where they kept it for a certain time, covered up, with much veneration.[39]

Flaxique is a corruption of the Nahuatl *Tlachixque*, translated by Molina as *atalaya*, "He who watches something."[40] Alemany defines atalaya as "tower in a high place, or a man who takes notes from an atalaya and announces what he has seen." In other words, "The guard in the watchtower." The Flaxique is one of the "Comic Four," any one or all of whom may act as guards at the fiesta of today. Clavijero describes a similar character in the Preconquest dance.[41] According to Don Manuel, the Comic Four are the Flaxique dressed as a devil, the Old Man, the Old Woman, and the Hermit. In recent years, I have noticed another guard at fiestas; Death. This last one wears black jersey tights on which the bones of the body are painted in heavy white lines and he uses a mask that completely covers his head in the form of a skull. At small fiestas one guard is adequate, but at larger ones more are needed. All guards are men — the Old Woman is a man dressed as a woman — and sometimes all are loosely referred to as flaxiques. They patrol the edges of the dance circles, both inside and out, burlesquing the dancers, chasing the children, and joking with the bystanders. The Devil cracks his whip, the Old Woman hurls her (his) "child,"[42] the Old Man brandishes his cane, the Hermit shakes his staff threateningly, and Death delivers resounding whacks with his scythe. Even the stoutest troublemaker in the crowd gives ground when the flaxiques, with hideous outcry, rush at top speed toward the mass of humanity closing in on the dancers. In one way or another the flaxiques maintain order and prevent the public from overrunning the dance circles. The dance chief appoints them for each fiesta, usually inviting the field sergeants of the mesas represented in the dance circles to serve.

Apparently the early friars trudged over the Americas carrying staffs with a crucifix attached to the top of each.[43] One wonders if the Indians noticed the similarity between the friar's staff and Quetzalcoatl's mace with the cross on top of it. Motolinía, in describing how the friars went about the conversion of the Indians, stated: "It is necessary to begin by explaining to them who is the living God. . . ." Perhaps the friar pointed to the crucifix on his staff and said, "El es Dios" (He is God), just as Don Manuel Luna described to me at the velación in the oratory years later.

Xuchil or xochitl *(suchil* or *suchitl)*, generally accepted as the Nahuatl term for flower, apparently had broader connotations originally. Elizabeth Andros Foster, who translated *The Indians of New Spain,* says that throughout his book Motolinía uses the word *rosas* (roses) to mean simply flowers; that sometimes the word stands alone, at other times it appears as *rosas y flores* (roses and flowers) in which the two words seem to be synonymous; and that in the sixteenth century and earlier, rosas y flores seemed to have been a set phrase meaning flower.[44] More than once I have heard danzantes, including Don Manuel Luna, refer to the decorated danzantes' Xuchil as "una rosa" (a rose or rosette).[45] The ancient Mexicans divided the day into 13 hours and the night into nine. Each hour had a sign and a lord. The sign of the third night hour was xochitl and the lord was the sun god. According to Joyce, "the perfume from the flowers carried at the banquets and ceremonial dances might only be inhaled from the edges of the bouquet, since the center belonged to the sun god, Tezcatlipoca.[46] The danzantes' Xuchil often is quite similar in appearance to a large bouquet. In the codices the xochitl, the symbol for flower, signifies the blood sacrifice.[47] Since the Preconquest peoples made war mainly to gather prisoners to sacrifice to the gods, the warrior, whose patron was Tezcatlipoca, was always a potential blood sacrifice.

The Xuchil, say the danzantes, is the *palabra de las ánimas,* the sign, or revelation of the spirits or souls. It is the sign of the sun god, of Quetzalcoatl, and of a hereafter; at the same time, of Jesus Christ, "The Light of the World"; of the custodial or ostensorium, in which the Host is elevated; of the souls in purgatory; and of heaven. According to Don Manuel, "We are going to plant the rose," or "We are going to arm the Xuchil," means that the danzantes are going to decorate the Xuchil. With reference to the dance circle, "We are going to cover the Four Winds," means that the standard-bearers are going to occupy positions in the circle that correspond to the places filled by the little tallow candles in the flower Xuchil spread on the floor of the oratory previous to the elevation of the Xuchil. This means that there will be a banner at each of the Four Winds, or the four world directions, and that the oldest, most important banner present will be in the center of the circle. This last is called the "guide" or "light," and refers to the torch in the leader's hands when the ancient tribe was "on the march" to war.

The circle of dancers in the atrio is a living representation of the Xuchil as it is spread on the floor of the oratory at a velación. The flowers are represented by the feathers, the smaller candles by the banners, and the candle in the center by the oldest banner that is present. This banner is kept waving constantly above the square handkerchief on the ground in the center of the circle, upon which rests the symbols of the Christian substitutes for the symbols of the human sacrifice in ancient times: the concha for the macana; the present-day incense burner for the ancient; the feather headdress for the downy feathers decorating the prisoner of war destined for the sacrificial block; the Holy Rod for the ancient mace like the one in Codex Vaticanus 3773; and the decorated bell possibly for the ancient war conch, though the danzantes seem uncertain about this.

Soon after the Conquest the clergy began to show concern about Indian religious dancing in New Spain. Padre Acosta, who found the Mexicans worshipping "ravines, huge stones, hills and mountaintops that they called *apachitas,* for which they had great devotion"; agreed with Pope Gregory that the fiestas and celebrations of the Indians should be done in honor of God and the saint whose feast day they were celebrating.[48] Bishop Zumarraga wrote that it was a "matter of great shame and irreverence for men wearing masks and women's clothing to go before the Sacred Host dancing with obscene and lacivious gestures making noises that interferred with the singing of hymns. . . ."[49] Duran warned his readers that should they see an Indian in better costume than the others, dancing a little apart from his companions and muttering unintelligibly, they could be sure that the Indians, while pretending to dance at the Christian fiesta, were actually honoring their pagan gods whose fiesta fell near the same date.[50]

In 1555 the First Provincial Council, meeting in Mexico City, ruled that "as the Indians are very inclined to dances, *areitos,* and other ceremonies," they should not be permitted, while dancing, to use banners or ancient masks "that cause suspicion," or to sing songs of their ancient rites or histories, unless said songs were first examined by religious persons, or persons who understood the Indian language well. The Evangelical Ministers should see that such songs did not treat of profane things, but of Christian Doctrine. Also, the Indians should not be permitted to dance before dawn, or before High Mass, and when the bell rang for vespers, they should leave off dancing and attend. Should the Indians fail to abide by these rules, the priests in charge should punish them. Furthermore, the Indians were not to be permitted to have processions on the fiesta date of their villages or their churches unless the vicar or minister were present. If such days should fall when there was no minister there, they should have it when the minister could be present.[51]

"Where did the Mexicans first dance in honor of the Christian religion?" I asked the dancers as I went to fiestas with them.

"Pues . . . probably in Tlaxcala, señora," they often replied, though almost as often they said Querétaro, or San Miguel de Allende, or simply the Bajío. All were rather vague until I asked Refugio Pinedo. Refugio had a story to tell.

Si, señora, it happened in Tlaxcala. Have you heard of the great battle when Cortés conquered Tlaxcala? Well, after this battle the Spaniards were camping just outside Tlaxcala and Cortés announced that on a certain day he would make his entrance into this city that he had conquered. Then the Tlaxcalans began to prepare for a big fiesta in his honor on that day. It was at that time, señora, that a commission of danzantes from Tlaxcala went to Cortés to ask permission to dance at this big fiesta. And Cortés gave them permission to do so, if they would dance in the honor of the Christian saints instead of in honor of their idols. And that was the first time they danced in the Christian religion. That is what they say, señora, and I believe it, because they conquered my tierra — Querétaro, that is, señora — after they conquered Tlaxcala and when they conquered my tierra there were Concheros there on the side of the converted ones. It is the truth, señora.

Have you heard about the Sangremal, señora?[52] The Sangremal was the famous battle when the Spaniards conquered Querétaro, but it was different from the Battle of Tlaxcala, señora. They did not fight to kill each other, or to capture prisoners. No, señora. You see, Querétaro was conquered for the Spaniards by a great Chichimec general. His real name was Conin, but they called him Fernando de Tapia at the time of which I tell you. Sí, señora, they had converted him to the Catholic religion and when they baptized him, they changed his name to Fernando de Tapia. But his real name was Conin.

Well, this great Chichimec general gave orders that the Spaniards and the Chichimecs could fight, but that they must fight without their arms. The Spaniards could not use their guns or their horses and the Chichimecs could not use their bows and arrows or their slings. And so they fought, señora. And they kicked and they scratched and they bit with their teeth and they pulled hair and they gouged each others' eyes out with their thumbs. And the blood flowed in a stream, señora.

And while they were fighting thus, the day became dark, almost like night,[53] and there appeared in the sky a rose-colored cross. And everybody fell on their knees to worship this cross and that is how the famous Battle of Sangremal ended.

But the whole time it was being fought, señora, the great General Conin was sitting on his horse on the mountainside watching the battle. And on the ground beside him stood a Chichimec with his bow and arrow. And in front of him stood a Conchero. Sí, señora, in front of him stood a Conchero playing his concha. It is the truth. And so, as you can see, there were Concheros then.

And when it was over, señora, the Indians asked for a cross like the one they had seen in the sky. The Spaniards gave them a cross of wood, but the Indians would not accept it. Then the Spaniards gave them a cross of iron, but in the night the Indians tore it down. Then the Spaniards saw that they could not fool the Chichimecs, señora, and they went out on the mountainside and found three great stones of *cantera*,[54] and made them into a cross for the Chichimecs. You can see it when you visit my tierra, señora. It is in the Church of the Holy Cross in Querétaro.

When I asked Don Manuel about the origin of the Christian dance, he, too, had a story to tell me.

I think that the dance in honor of the Christian saints probably did begin in Tlaxcala, Señora Marta, because many years ago there was an old chief from the Bajío who came to the capital on his way to Tlaxcala to get permission from the Palabra General[55] to raise the Palabra Segunda[56] in the Bajío. Sí, Señora Marta, it is true that they had been dancing in the Bajío for many years, but it seems they had neglected to get the permission from the Palabra General — or that is what they say. — I was very young then, or perhaps I had not been born. It was many, many years ago. Well, it was during the time of the Porfirio Diaz Government, I think. — The Old Chief came to the capital to pray in the cathedral and those of the government said that there were witch doctors in the caravan. And so they arrested the Old Chief and put him in jail. They put him in a cell all by himself in the national palace, Señora Marta, and they kept him there without anything to eat or drink for fifteen days. And for fifteen days the whole caravan waited outside the palace, for he was their chief. In the old days there was a park in the Zócalo in front of the palace. Those of the Bajío camped in the park.

At the end of fifteen days those of the government unlocked the door of the chief's cell expecting to find a dead body, for he was very old and frail, señora. But the soldiers had a great surprise. The Old Chief walked out of his cell looking better than when they had locked him in there! Those of the government could not understand it. They were very stern with him, señora. They demanded an explanation. The Old Chief told them that every morning and every night a señora dressed in black had entered his cell and had given him food and drink. Imagine, señora! He had rested and had grown fat.

After this miracle — Sí, Señora Marta, it was a miracle, for the señora in black was none other than the Virgencita herself. That is what they say. Of course, I was not there. It was before my time. But I have heard many people talk about it for many years. — After this miracle those of the government freed him and, more than that, they gave him money to help him on his way to Tlaxcala. And so, as you can see, the Palabra General was in Tlaxcala.

The last stanza of a song of praise, very popular with the danzantes goes:

Pueblito de Tlaxcala,	Little town of Tlaxcala,
No te puedo olvidar,	I cannot forget you,
Porque alli esta fundada	Because was founded there
La Palabra General.	The Palabra General.

Even so the Concheros, or Apaches, are generally referred to as Las Danzas Chichimecas and the Bajío as the place of the origin of their dance. In the sixteenth century the Bajío was populated mainly by Otomies and Chichimecs (many writers make little distinction between the two), seminomadic and bellicose peoples who were unconquered and unconverted. In 1529 Nuño de Guzman, Governor of Pánuco, in search of riches and fame, took an army through the Bajío and the regions to the north and to the west. He inflicted useless and sadistic cruelties on the Indians, decimating a population of 2 million. Those Chichimecs who survived fled to the mountains. Eventually Nuño de Guzman was recalled to Spain, but when the Chichimecs moved down from the mountains they were even less inclined to submission and conversion. By 1550 the famous silver mines of Zacatecas had been discovered, but the land of the fierce Chichimecs lay between the stronghold of the Spaniards and these riches.[57] In 1560, because of the depredations of the Chichimecs along the road from the City of New Spain to Zacatecas, the Spaniards attempted to establish a colony of Tlaxcalans in the Bajío, in the hope that the Chichimecs would emulate their new neighbors and settle into a sedentary life conducive to peace and conversion to the Catholic faith. The attempt failed and as late as 1576 the Chichimecs still took "a high toll of Spanish blood" along the Zacatecas road.[58] It was not until 1591 that 401 Tlaxcalan taxpayers under the patronage of Viceroy Luis de Velasco succeeded in colonizing there and opening the way for the friars. These Tlaxcalan colonists probably brought to the Bajío the custom of dancing in honor of the Christian saints that, according to Refugio Pinedo and Don Manuel Luna, was already established in Tlaxcala. It is possible that the Chichimecs did emulate their Tlaxcalan neighbors who had put away their idols only fifty years before. Perhaps they, like the older Tlaxcalan colonists, in the beginning only mixed the new with the old; for Motolinía wrote that when the friars were destroying a pagan temple in Tlaxcala (about 1526), they found the images of the Christ and of the Virgin that they had given to the Indians among the idols on the altar.[59] The period of mixtures seems to have lasted longer in some regions than in others.

A casual remark by Don Manuel sent me looking through Inquisition material where I found several items of particular interest. In 1536 an Indian charged with idolatry and witchcraft was accused of giving "some Suchiles" to two other Indians and urging them to use them as offerings to Our Lord, because they were of their ancient gods.[60] In a collection of documents relating to the trial of Don Carlos Ometochtzin (renamed Mendoza?), cacique of Texcoco, charged with idolatry and concubinage, the Governor of Texcoco testified that travelers from Huejotzingo said that they had seen smoke coming from Tlaloc Mountain and had found incinias[61] (used exactly as Don Pancho used that word) of sacrifice there.[62] Another Indian of Texcoco swore that he heard that those of Huejotzingo practiced *limpiar,* or cleansing, and that they cleansed their roadways as in ancient times they used to cleanse the houses of the devil (pagan temples).[63] The expression, "We are all equal and conforming," appears several times in the collection. The danzantes use it today. In the preface by Don Luis Gonzales Obregón, it is made clear that what Don Carlos was suspected of was the practice of human sacrifice. He was condemned and was burned in the plaza of Mexico City. Opinions still differ as to the degree of his guilt and to the punishment he deserved. Don Luis points out that idolatry did not end with Don Carlos, and recalls that "not very long ago" (about 1907) there was brought to Archbishop Alarcon an idol in the form of "a precious eagle head" (symbol of Tezcatlipoca), that Indians in the State of Morelos had been worshipping.

Without doubt conversion was a strong motive behind the Conquest. The dedicated friars were capable of creating, as an integral part of religious practice for the stubborn Chichimecs, a new dance cult with the more appealing features of the old, but with a new "execution."

Perhaps something of the sort is the reason behind the general term, Las Danzas Chichimecas. Nearly always there is a reason behind the reason, and sometimes even a further reason behind that, for in Mexico history telescopes upon itself. At any rate, it seems fairly certain that at some time after the Conquest there was superimposed upon the Preconquest dance cult a complicated, well-planned substitute with both Christian and pagan elements, excluding human sacrifice.

La Cosa

THE CONCHEROS, notwithstanding their tenacious adherence to an ancient custom, adopted practices from various periods of history, weaving the new into the old to weather the storms of change. Perhaps the most significant periods in their past were the sixteenth century, when Christian dancing in Mexico began, and the Mexican Revolution, when it disappeared for a time.

Tales of chivalry, popular in sixteenth-century Spain, are said to have had a profound influence in New Spain. Bernal Díaz referred to Roldan, and quoted Cortés as doing so also. Knight-errantry was the order of the day and more than one journey to New Spain was motivated by it.[1] Among the Concheros, the designation of the most important banner and lesser banners, young danzantes in training, the importance of personal dignity, and the tendency to defend the weak and help those who cannot help themselves, are reminiscent of knighthood. These characteristics blend well with the compadrazco as practiced in some parts of Mexico.

Compadrazco refers to the relationship between persons who are godparents of the same person or thing. (Bill and I were made godparents of a flag.) Though a godfather is a compadre and a godmother a comadre, when spoken of together they are compadres. It is in the duty of compadres to visit one another when one is sick or in difficulty of any sort, and to help each other if possible. The duties of a dance captain to his soldiers, as described by Don Pancho, could be part of the compadrazco of the danzantes. It is similar to a blood relationship in that there can be no sexual relations or marriage between compadres — not unlike the godparents' relationship of the Catholic Church, though it probably harks back to some Preconquest custom. (I once heard Ralph Beals make a remark to that effect.)[2] I have noticed that when a married couple is received into the dance, only one of them continues to dance. Often both attend velaciones, but only the one who dances takes active part in the ceremonies.

Several years ago a group of danzantes called on me. "Señora, we have come to tell you that we will not be dancing any time soon, for a terrible thing has happened. A jefe of the Bajío and his only son have been murdered! Sí, señora. Even now the widow and mother is here conferring with the dance chiefs. We have placed ourselves in her service. We have all asked our employers for our annual vacations from work at this time. We will search for the murderers. We will collect evidence against them."

A few weeks later they were back. Eight of the criminals were in jail, they said, and the remaining two soon would be. The danzantes would be dancing the next Sunday.

The ánimas form an important part of danzante belief. The Velación of the Dead on the night of November 1 seems to center around them, and for this reason I first thought that they were connected with the souls in purgatory. Perhaps they are, but they are more than that. Apparently even the best-informed dance chief cannot explain what the belief in the ánimas stems from, what it has been substituted for, or when it became a part of the dance cult.

According to the danzantes, there are about twenty ánimas, but I have never met anybody who could, or would, name them all. Nearly every mesa has María Graciana, the Old Chief, and the Ánima Sola (the Lonely Spirit). Most mesas have at least one of the others too; constituting the Four Winds, or guardians of the mesa. An ánima is one who had sinned while alive, and had become holy after death through a miracle.

María Graciana was a married woman of the Bajío. She had a lover whom she used to meet surreptitiously. One day when they met in a cave — according to some, a cave in Culiacan Mountain — they quarreled and her lover stabbed her to death. Of course she was missed and her husband and friends searched for her. The next day her little white dog led them to her body. Though she had been dead for more than twenty-four hours, her blood was still fresh and her body had not begun to decompose. For this reason she became an ánima.

"She was a sinner in life who became sacred in death through a miracle, señora," explain the danzantes.

It is María Graciana through whom they establish contact with the rest of the ánimas. "We call on her, señora, and she calls on the others to cooperate."

Macedonia Montes was a clever, resourceful bandit. For a long time he was so successful that it was said that he could not be captured. When finally the federal soldiers caught him, they cut his body into small pieces and placed them in a large pot. His blood remained fresh and he, too, became an ánima.

Sometimes a danzante will tell this same story of Juan Mineros, but if I mention Macedonia Montes he will immediately decide it is Macedonia Montes of whom he is thinking. It seems that both were bandits and so, some say, was Benito López. All are ánimas.

Anilino Aguilar was the grandfather of a dance chief of Querétaro. Carlos Granados was the father of Don Ruperto Granados, the fine old man who was kind to us in San Miguel de Allende. (Don Ruperto passed away the year following our visit there, and perhaps is himself an ánima now.) Fernando de Tapia, the Chichimec chief who accomplished the conquest of Querétaro for the Spaniards, is another ánima popular in the Bajío.

Felipe Aranda was the beloved jefe of José Celis and of Fidel Morales. He came to the capital by invitation of Capitán General Felipe Hernandez and was killed at the corner of Tlaxpana, near Melchior O'Campo and San Cosme streets, in a collision between a bus and a streetcar. He is an ánima, too, and figures in alabanzas.

Abraham Perez was another dance general, jefe of Don Guadalupe Alvarez, and at one time of José Celis, too. Jesús Caballero was a dance chief of Charmacuero. Juan Gutiérrez and Manuel Luna are two of the ánimas about whom I have been unable to learn anything except that they were from the Bajío. Don Manuel Luna says that he has tried without success to learn the history of the latter because they have the same name, though they are not of the same family.

A famous bandit of Querétaro was captured and killed on the mountainside. After eight days the blood that covered the ground where his body had fallen was as fresh as if it had just been shed. The Indians planted a cross in the blood, according to the danzantes, and the cross rather than the bandit became an ánima. Legends cluster around the Santa Cruz de la Justicia, or the Holy Cross of Justice, as it is called. Perhaps the one most often told is the one about the woman who wanted to confess to the priest who refused to listen to her.

There was a woman who was very good at the laying on of spells, señora. When she was getting old she decided that she would withdraw from that life, and so she went to the priest to confess. When she started her confession, he interrupted her. He was very angry, señora. He told her, "There is not one word of truth in that, I refuse to listen!"

She insisted on confessing, señora. She wanted to withdraw from that life. But the priest kept telling her that what she was saying was lies, all lies!

"I will believe you when something like that happens to me!" he said.

"It is well, Padre," she answered, and she went away, señora.

The following Sunday the sacristan arrived and rang the bells to call the people to Mass. Then he tapped at the door of the priest's apartment.

"Come in," the padre called, and his voice was very weak, señora.

The sacristan opened the door and saw the padre lying on his bed. Imagine, señora, his stomach was swollen to large proportions! His serapes stood high on his bed like a tent.

"¡Ay, Padre! What happened?"

"My son, I am in great pain."

"Ay, Padre, what shall I do? I have rung the bells and the people will be coming to the Mass!"

"You see my condition, my son. I cannot put my foot to the floor."

"What shall we do, Padre? Everything is ready for the Mass."

"Do you remember the woman who was here yesterday?"

"Sí, Padre."

"Look for her, and bring her here."

"Sí, Padre."

Then the sacristan hurried out and went searching for the woman who was very good at the laying on of spells. He found her, señora. And he brought her to the padre's apartment.

The padre looked at her, "So you wish to be confessed?"

"Sí, Padre."

"It is well. Relieve me of my condition so that I may say the Mass."

"Sí, Padre."

And the woman stuck her finger in her mouth and made a cross with her saliva on the padre's stomach. That is what they say, señora!

Then the padre's stomach slowly began to decrease underneath his serapes. After a few minutes he was able to raise himself from his bed. Then he began to get ready for the Mass.

"Come back at three o'clock this afternoon," he told the woman, "and I will confess you."

"Sí, Padre. But there is one thing that you must do before then, Padre," she replied. "As soon as the Mass is over you must take a candle of tallow to the Cross of Justice and burn it there."

The padre did as she said, señora. As soon as the Mass was over he took a tallow candle and set off on his mule for the mountain where the Cross of Justice is located. When he arrived at the foot of the cross he had a great surprise. The earth all around it was covered with tallow candles, señora. Imagine! There were hundreds of them, and they were all lighted. The padre stood and looked at them. Each one had been put there in recognition of, and in thanks for, a spell, señora! The padre added his to the others.

I went looking for the Chapel of the Cross of Justice and finally found it on the outskirts of a mountain village in the state of Querétaro. Those in charge told me that the chapel had been robbed of the "five-foot cross of solid silver." They were very sorry, but the "pilgrim" was all that remained.[3] Would I care to see the "pilgrim"? They showed me a silver cross about a foot high, covered with little metal *milagros,* symbols of miracles.

"It is muy milagrosa," they said.

When I went back to the capital and told my danzante friends what had happened, they were skeptical.

"Do not believe it, señora," said one. "It is because the priests found the drippings of too many tallow candles! They knew the Indians were practicing witchcraft there and they took the cross away. That is what really happened, I think!"

Another ánima is the Old Chief. According to Don Manuel Luna, it was "a little print" that the Church issued in the early nineteenth century. It now looks like a blur — almost black. One oratory I know has this framed with an electric-blue tinfoil mat in a gold-leaf frame. At night with a lighted candle under it, it gives a weird effect.

The Ánima Sola, say the danzantes, is an orphan girl in Purgatory. Since she has no family on earth to pray for her, the danzantes have undertaken to do so. I think there may be more to the Ánima Sola than this, but I have been unable to learn it.

Padre Jorge, whose photograph Don Cecilio's group took to the cave in Bufa Mountain, Guanajuato, is an ánima too. He was the priest who started the ceremonies in the cave there. As Don Cecilio said, he was the Indian's friend, and the danzantes say that both his photograph and his tomb are "muy milagrosas."

Vicente Márquez, the dance jefe who founded the Cooperación de Concheros, and Capitana Natalia Hidalgo are ánimas, too.

Padre Pro — R. P. Miguel Augustin Pro, S. J. — friend of the suffering Mexicans during the troublesome time of the religious persecution, was shot by government officers on November 23, 1927. A heroic figure in his country's history, his memory is dear to countless Mexicans besides the danzantes. In 1952, the twenty-fifth anniversary of his death, the Sacred Congregation of Rites approved the preliminary documents of his beatification. Perhaps the danzantes were ahead of their time in this case. Padre Pro's photograph often stood among the saints on danzantes altars, as an ánima and a *mártir* (martyr) even before that date.

The mártires puzzled me for a long time. For one thing, they were so similar to the ánimas. Finally I came to the conclusion that all martyrs are ánimas, though not all ánimas are martyrs.

"Suppose a man is killed down here on the corner, señora, and I am present," said a danzante in reply to my questions. "I will proclaim his ánima and I will pray for his well-being. I will intercede for him before Our Lord, and when I am in trouble, I will call on his ánima for aid. We will help each other, you see."

Because the danzantes are reluctant to talk about the ánimas, I learned all this little by little over a period of years. When I would ask if I might put what they were telling me in the book, they would become thoughtful. Finally they would consent for me to mention the ánimas, provided I did not name them as my sources.

About this time, in a similar connection, I heard about *puertos*. At first I thought the danzantes were talking about ports, as that is the usual translation of the word. Gradually it dawned on me, however, that the things they were saying about puertos could not apply to ports.

"What is a puerto?" I asked an old friend.

"Señora a puerto means to us a place where our ancestors went to make their requests and to perform their ceremonies. We go there now to say our prayers. A puerto is an enchanted place, a place where there is power. We call Las Cruces a puerto. It is where Padre Hidalgo fought his great battle for our independence. Many soldiers fell there and many of them were danzantes. It is a place of great power, Señora Marta."

Belief in the *bruja*, or witch, and her daughter, as manifested by red and blue balls of fire, is not confined to the danzantes. It is fairly general among the Mexicans who live close to nature, as is the belief in the special significance of balls of fire in various parts of the world.

Then there is the matter of evil spells and similar practices. Some seem to think that the danzantes have to do with these. Once a danzante presented me with a tiny pamphlet.

"Here, señora, is a little prayer that we love to pray. I hope it brings you happiness."

On the cover was printed, "To the Holy Death," with the picture of a skull and crossbones underneath. Inside was a curse for one's enemies. When I showed this to Don Manuel, he was upset.

"This is not of the dance, señora! Who could have given you such a thing? Throw it away! Destroy it! It has nothing to do with the dance!"

Another thing that puzzled me for a long time was the meaning of the word *Conquista*, as the danzantes' use of the term in Danzas de la Conquista, or Dances of the Conquest.

"Don Manuel," I asked, "is your oldest banner, your reliquia general, of the Conquista?"

"Sí, Señora Marta."

"What does that mean?"

"It means the dance before the Revolution, señora. Before the Revolution there was only the Danza de la Conquista. After the Revolution there was the Cooperación de Concheros, too. The Cooperación is new. It did not exist before the Revolution. And they of the Cooperación de Concheros have San Miguel Archangel as patron, while we of the Conquista have the Christ. And they call each other compañeros, while we are compadres." Compañeros means companions, and was the familiar term between soldiers during the Revolution.

"How old is your banner, Don Manuel?"

"Very old, Señora Marta. Maximino Téllez, the grandfather of Ester my wife, raised it in 1883.[4] That makes it more than seventy years old, does it not? Sí, señora, he raised it over here in Mina Street; this was a little village in those days. The grandfather of my wife was a great dance chief. When he died, Ignacio Becerra, the father of Ester, became jefe. As he had no son, señora, and Ester was his oldest daughter, I became jefe after he died."

"And, since the grandfather of Doña Ester raised his banner before the Revolution, the patron is Christ and it is a Danza de la Conquista. Is that correct?"

"Perfectly correct, Señora Marta. And the Conquista — have I told you? — it had three basic objects: to honor the prince, to announce battles, and to represent the conversion of the ancient priests by the friars. And during the Conquista — before the Revolution, that is — the boundaries of the dance were strictly observed. A dance captain from the Bajío could not cross into Tenochtitlan, and a captain from here could not go into the Bajío, without special permission. When a strange captain arrived in any section the jefe would say, 'El es Diós, señor. Permit me to examine your documents.' "

"I had no idea that they were so strict!"

"Sí, Señora Marta. Many times in the old days, a fight ended in a death!"

"¡Qué lástima! And the other old banner, the one that Ignacio Gutiérrez has, it was raised after the grandfather of Doña Ester raised yours, was it not?"

"Sí, señora! Jesús Gutiérrez broke the rule of the boundaries when he came conquering from San Miguel de Allende to the Federal District. His nephew, Ignacio Gutiérrez has that banner now. Jesús Gutiérrez raised it here in 1887. That was four years after Maximino Téllez, the grandfather of Ester raised his banner. Because Jesús Gutiérrez broke the rule of the boundaries, I do not ask permission of the chiefs of the Bajío before I make conquests in Acambaro and Aarón. And I like to go into the Bajío and talk to those jefes there! I go there and defend myself; that is what we call it, señora — I say to them, 'Yes, of course, "El es Dios" is from the Bajío. But it comes from a Spanish friar and not from our ancestors!' That is the way I talk to the capitanes and sooner or later I conquer them." Meaning that they accept him as captain general, place themselves under his orders, and will follow his ritual at velaciones.

"Does that not make the other chiefs of the Bajío mad?"

"Sometimes. But what can they say? Jesús Gutiérrez came conquering from the Bajío to the Federal District first."

"And his dance was of the Conquista, too?"

"Sí, Señora Marta. But the Cooperación de Concheros is not. It was formed after the Revolution. Vicente Márquez, the uncle of jefe Maximino Márquez who is now andando with me, raised that banner in 1922. Vicente Márquez called together all those who had been capitanes before the Revolution, and with them he formed the Cooperación de Concheros."

"So that is the difference between the Danza de la Conquista and the Cooperación de Concheros!"

"The real difference, Señora Marta, is the Revolution! During the Revolution, oratories were destroyed, santos and the arms of the danzantes were stolen or burned, and danzantes were killed. But the worst of all was that so many of the old jefes perished in one way or another. The dance was lost during the Revolution, Señora Marta. It disappeared completely! With this result; after the Revolution, ignorant and uninformed persons were able to rise to high positions in the dance."

Perhaps this is why the dance chief of today guards his rules with great care. They are the measure of his knowledge of the dance cult. By experience and observation in strange oratories, as he goes about on conquering expeditions, he can add to this knowledge. Hence, the alert dance chief is constantly revising his rules, even though he has inherited those of well-informed ancestors. Probably because, as Don Manuel said, the dance was lost during the Revolution and ignorant persons filled high positions after its revival, the danzantes have tests by which they gauge the knowledge of strangers.

"Señora," Refugio Pinedo told me, "if anybody ever asks you what lies in the very center of the cross, you can know that he is testing you. Sí, señora. That is one of the main questions that is asked for a test. And you must answer, 'The heart of Jesus.' Just that and no more. Then he will not doubt that you are andando con los danzantes."

A dance jefe told me how he tested a captain who was retiring from his orders.

I had thought that he was a promising young capitán when he began to andar with me, Señora Marta, but I soon saw that he loved to make people think that he knew much, when in reality he knew very little. Finally I could stand it no longer, and I arranged it so that he would leave my orders. And at his retirement velación, señora, I made a little test. He failed, señora. He failed my test!

This is the test I made. I took a tray and I crossed four little candles on it — in the form of a cross, señora — and I put the censer in the center of the cross. Then I surrounded the tray with pastle, which is an herb that we have. — Sí, señora, it is something like moss only it is green. — When this capitán came to "render arms," he knew enough to present his concha at the altar, but he presented it with the armadillo part up, and that is wrong. He should have presented it with the strings up. And he did nothing to the tray and the things in it and around it. Nothing at all!

Why, Señora Marta, had he known as much as he tried to make people think, he would have taken the tray off the altar with the censer still in the center of it. Then he would have removed the circle of pastle from the altar, and with it he would have made a cross on the floor beside the tray. Then he would have lighted the four little candles and placed them at the four points of the pastle cross. That is what he would have done, Señora Marta, had he known much instead of little!

The grouping of candles, censer, and pastle on the tray in this test is similar to the arrangement of the maguey spikes, eye, and pastle of the sign of midnight on sheet four of Codex Borbonicus.

Most of the disgustos, or quarrels, among the danzantes arise from differences of opinion about dance customs. Dance jefes and mesas vary as to these. Some jefes are like one I know who has no oratory of his own, but presides over that of one of his personnel. Others build up power through danzante politics and watch for a chance to take over an oratory when some chief dies. (I know two *generalas,* or women generals, who were oldest daughters of sonless generals. Neither is married, and each, in order to keep the chieftainship in her family, is presiding over her personnel until she marries a consort.) Some, I am told, do not dress the Xuchil. Others do not sing "Santa Rosita" when the Xuchil is dressed. The number of candles burned in the ceremonies varies and so does the order in which they are lighted.

The most serious difference of opinion in recent years was over whether the dance, with its religious character, should become a part of a government section called "National Dances." This grew to great proportions and shook the Concharía, as the danzantes sometimes call the danzante world. For a while I remained neutral in the midst of the various factions. I was the friend of all danzantes. It was during this time that Don Pancho came, straight from the Turkish Bath and dressed in his best, to withdraw himself from friendship with our house.

"I have just learned, señora, that my worst enemies receive the same welcome here that I do!"

We talked it over and were still friends when he left, but he came no more to teach me. (Later when he married a young woman from Texcoco he invited us to the wedding.) But whatever their particular beliefs and practices, the danzantes put aside their differences of opinion at fiesta-time, contributing to what Frances Gillmor calls the "togetherness" of a fiesta.[5]

I must confess that after all these years of "andando con los danzantes," I am uncertain as to what part of the Church is in the dance cult, or what part of the dance cult is in the Church.

"We are Christians, Señora Marta," Don Manuel assured me. "We are good Catholics. These ceremonies honoring our ancestors that you have observed in the oratories, they are like a parenthesis, only a parenthesis!"

Perhaps the dance cult has always been surrounded by an aura of mystery. Certainly after the Conquest it was clothed with secrecy and double meaning. Mystification with a guileless sort of deception is general among the danzantes of today.

"The ancient priest did not reveal all that he knew to the common people," one jefe told me. "In the same way we jefes have our secrets, señora. I have told you more than I have told anyone, except my son who will inherit my position."

The danzantes often perform bits of dance practice in such a casual, offhand manner that even a keen observer would fail to note them; like playing the invocation to the ánimas in the presence of the unsuspecting malinches and soldados.

A jefe from the Bajío told me about a collector of music who visited his group.

He said that those of the government were making a book of Mexican music, señora. He said that he wanted some of our music because it was truly Mexican, and so we invited him to a velación for a short time. And, señora, the music he liked was "The Ánima of Manuel de la Carrera." Sí, señora, Manuel de la Carrera is a chord of the ánimas that we play during the invocation of the spirits at a velación. And that was the music that this composer wrote down. It is probably in a book now because he said it would be published in 1940. Of course, nobody will understand what it means but a dance jefe!

I venture no statement as to the number of danzantes in Mexico or even in the Federal District. Estimates range from about 50,000 Concheros in the Federal District and the states of Guanajuato, Querétaro, Tlaxcala, and Hidalgo, to not more than 10,000 in all the Republic! Whether these include those who "andan par' alla," or have nothing to do with priests, I do not know.

Even those taking part in a ceremony may not know what they are doing. For years I sang "María, A donde Vas?" at the raising of the cross, thinking that it referred to the Virgin Mary. It was not until we went to the Old One's saint's day celebration that I learned that this was not the case.

The Old One, several times a grandfather and a respected dance chief, came one day to invite us to his saint's day party. As we sat talking, I showed him Duran's calendar and he was so interested that I brought out the Codex Borbonicus and showed him the dance god's sheet. He was delighted with the first sheet (sheet 4), pointing out dance features and commenting on the ancient Mexicans. When I showed him the other sheet (sheet 19), however, a wary expression crept over his face and he asked, "Where did you get this book, señora?"

I explained that the manuscript was a copy, the original of which was in Paris. Then I traced its probable history from áncient Mexico to France.

"Who made the first book, the one from which this was copied?" he asked sternly.

"One of your ancestors," I answered. "His name is not known, but he lived before the Spaniards came."

"Do you understand what these pictures mean?"

"Oh, yes," I assured him.

He stared at the page, then he folded the sheets together without comment and laid them on the table.

When Nieves and I went to the party on his saint's day, we found him dozing in the patio of the new three-room house that his sons had recently built for him. We apologized for arriving early and he apologized for being asleep. He had had a busy day. At dawn a group of young "soldiers of the Conquest" had huddled beneath the one window of the new house to serenade him. First, they had sung the "Mañanitas" — the traditional birthday song of Mexico. Then they had sung alabanzas of the danzantes, corridos (ballads) of his tierra (Guanajuato), marches of the Revolution, and a few modern songs to make him feel that he was in step with the times.

"They remained the day, señora, and after dinner they went to sleep on the rush mats that my sons had bought for that purpose. They will be getting up soon, for they will play and sing again this afternoon."

Other guests began to arrive, among them the jefe of the sindicato where the Old One's grandson worked. He was a chunky mestizo in his late forties with a condescending manner toward his host.

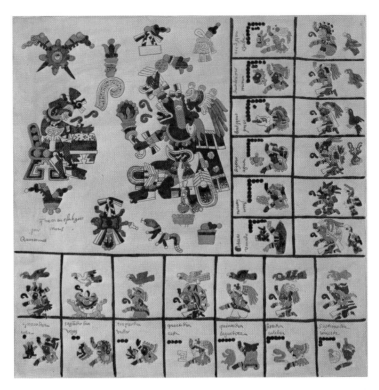

Codex Borbonicus (handpainted reproduction of sheet 4)

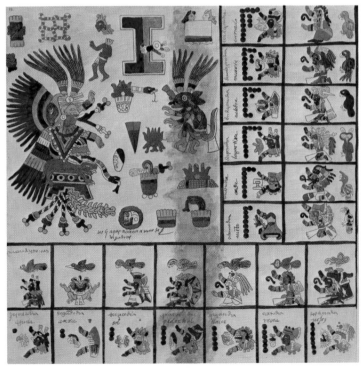

Codex Borbonicus (handpainted reproduction of sheet 19)

"I never drink pulque," he shuddered, when the Old One announced that his compadres had presented him with a barrel of Ayotuzco pulque. "I drink only wine," eyeing the bottles Nieves and I had brought.

Throughout the afternoon the soldados played their instruments and sang, with long rest periods when the grandsons operated a borrowed record player. The younger people danced on the hard-packed earthen floor of the patio, while the oldsters sat on benches or mats and smoked or drank.

In the midst of the festivities, the Old One whispered, "Señora, would you like to see the altar?"

He led me through one bedroom into the other with its two beds and a wooden floor. Across the corner, about five feet from the floor, was a triangular shelf, the dance chief's altar. At the back, in the corner, was the blurred little print of the Old Dance Chief. In front of this were two small images; one with a black beard, the other of two of the ánimas (Macedonia Montes and Benito López, I think.) In front of these was a bundle about the size of a football wrapped in gray flannel.

"This is the Old Chief," he began. "He is at the back of the altar because that is the principal place. It is the most holy. And these two are benditas ánimas, señora."

Then slowly and carefully, he unfolded the gray flannel. For seventeen years I had been trying to find out what was in The Bundle. Now that it lay open before me I could only stand and gasp.

The Old One looked at me in surprise. "Why, señora, you know all about it. You showed it to me in the ancient book that is in your house, the one that you said my ancestors painted."

"W-why, so I did!" I stammered.

"This is the *mera matriz de la danza*, señora. You must not put it in your book."

How could I write a book about the dance and leave out the very matrix?

"Let me say in the book that I have seen it, Tata Jefe. I will not say what it is. I will call it, La Cosa. But let me mention it, for I want the whole world to know that I have seen the mera matriz of the dance!"

He stood silent and thoughtful while I held my breath.

"You are right, señora," he finally said. "To write the history of the dance you must mention it. Do not say what it is, for it is very secret. Call it La Cosa in your book, señora."

There was the sound of voices in argument in the next room and the Old One quickly covered it up again.

"The light in front of it is never allowed to go out," he told me. "It is the symbol of María Graciana, she to whom we sing, 'María Adonde Vas?' "

"But I thought we sang that to the Virgencita!"

"We sing it to María Graciana, señora. Though every cuartel has one of these bundles, few know her. I will show this to my sons and they will show it to their sons. But not to the captains! We will not show it to the captains."

"Why not?"

"Because of the disgustos that are in the dance, señora. For example, Trinidad. You have heard that he has refused to accept the Disciplina and will retire himself, have you not? Suppose he had been told all that I have just told you? What would happen then?"

The curtain across the door was swept aside and the jefe of the sindicato stamped in.

"Now I am going!" he snapped, putting out his hand to shake hands with the Old One. "You are so busy with the foreign woman that you have no time for the jefe of the sindicato of your grandson. And so I am going!"

This particular grandson was the highest wage earner in the Old One's family. The old man was aghast at what he had done.

"Do not go," he begged. "The señora has been my friend for a long time. She is the friend of all the danzantes — it is better said that she is the friend of the Mexicans. It is true she is a foreigner but she is a muy fina persona and a friend of my family. And the señor her husband, though it is incredible, he is finer still!"

The jefe of the sindicato made a flowery speech of apology and invited me to join him in a glass of wine. I left mine unfinished for I had to rush home to look at the Codex Borbonicus again.

I could see what the Old One meant. Now that I knew what to look for, La Cosa was there in plain view.

The Conquest

THE CONQUEST was another ceremony that the chiefs, including Don Manuel, seemed reluctant to have me attend, though they readily described it. "First there are the juntas, sometimes one, but more often several; then they draw up a treaty and the conquerors and the conquered sign it, with witnesses for both sides. All this is in confidence among the jefes, Señora Marta. The danzantes do not know the terms of the treaty, which depend on what the conquerors demand and what the conquered are willing to surrender."

The more I heard about it, the more I wanted to see it, even incompletely. Then, in the fall of 1948, Don Manuel invited Nieves and me to the annual fiesta at the Church of the Holy Cross in Querétaro, remarking casually, "The jefes of Mexico City are going to conquer a jefe of Querétaro. Fidel will be there, and perhaps some of the chiefs of the Bajío. I shall do the best that I can for you, Señora Marta."

The danzantes planned to leave on a midnight bus because some of them would work late Friday night in order to have Saturday free, but Nieves and I decided to leave on the afternoon train so as to have several hours' sleep before the fiesta began. We arrived in Querétaro about ten o'clock in the evening, hired a *cargador*, or carrier, for our luggage, and set out to find the Church of the Holy Cross and the dance chief to whom Don Manuel had referred us.

The air was fresh and pleasant after the stuffy train. The streets were fairly well lighted and a hazy moonlight softened the shadows. Querétaro had gone to bed, though dim light shone through a scattering of windows along the way. Here and there a dog barked, and once a gray cat streaked across the road in front of us. Finally we turned down a jog in the street, and faced a hill topped by a massive church from whose dome a lighted cross stood against the sky.

"¡Ay, qué bonita [How beautiful]!" we exclaimed together.

"That is the Church of the Holy Cross," the cargador informed us. "It is on the top of the hill; we will go slowly."

"We would not call this much of a hill in Guanajuato," Nieves whispered to me.

Apparently the church faced a square. We could see the fires of the stalls and sidewalk cafes that outlined it. Suddenly the throng in front of the church opened and a line of dancers appeared. The bright plumage of their headdresses, the brilliant banners, and the colorful uniforms made a definite pattern in the night light. Quickly they wound around the square to a side street at our right.

"Those are the people we must talk to," I exclaimed, beginning to run. Nieves ran with me while the cargador clumped along behind us with the luggage. Finally we reached the end of the line of dancers.

"Pardon me," I called. "Can anyone tell me where to find Don Margarito Aguilar?"

"We are going to his house now," said an alférez.

Immediately a young man fell in step beside us and began to question me.

"We come from Capitán General Manuel Luna," I told him. "We are from the Association of Religious Dancers That Pertains to the Church of Tlaltelolco in the capital. For many years I have heard of Querétaro as the cradle of the dance and I have wanted to come here, but have not had an opportunity to do so until now."

He burst into a eulogy of the dance and Querétaro, ending with a recital of their problems. "Do you know what happened only recently, señora? An article appeared in a magazine and with it pictures of our personnel. And underneath those pictures it stated that we were danzantes from San Miguel de Allende! Imagine! But we are not! We are from here. And Querétaro is the most historic place pertaining to the dance."

This gave me opportunity to mention my plan to write a book giving a clear picture of the true dance. By the time we reached the doorway where we seemed to be going, the danzantes had disappeared, but we had quite a retinue of interested listeners, among them the cargador with my suitcase on his back and our lunch basket in his hand.

"Come in! Come in!" invited the young man.

We went through the doorway of a typical Mexican house; a square hall between two front rooms with the street door at the front and an open patio at the back. Someone brought chairs and after we had paid the cargador, we sat in the hall answering questions about where we had been with the danzantes.

"Do you know Los Remedios?" somebody in the crowd wanted to know.

"We were there last month."

"Have you been to Chalma?"

"Yes, we have, by the Ocuila Trail."

"The señora plays the concha divinely," Nieves volunteered.

"Oh, no!" I protested. "I play it only a little and very badly."

As if by magic, a concha appeared in the young man's hands. His name was José Martínez Aguilar, he said, as he carefully tuned it. Margarito Aguilar was his uncle and would be home soon. Then he handed the concha to me.

I played an alabanza and some dance tunes. José said that I had an excellent sense of time, but that I should practice more. Practice, he said, was the secret of playing well.

While we were talking a fat man with wide, black moustaches came through the street door, followed by several danzantes in uniform. The fat man strode toward me.

"This is my uncle," said José stepping back.

"Don Margarito Aguilar?" I asked.

"I am," he grimly replied.

"I have some letters I should like to show you —" handing him the one from the canon at the Basilica and another from the priest at Tlaltelolco. He immediately passed these to the elegantly uniformed danzante beside him, who read them in a low voice.

When he had finished the fat man said in an undertone, "You tell her!"

"No," refused the other, "you have the word. This is your jurisdiction. I can say nothing."

The fat man turned back to me, hitched his trousers, bent over, and thrusting his chin forward, demanded, "Why have you come here?"

"Oh, no-no-no!" groaned the elegant danzante, clutching at the back of the fat man's shirt. "You do not understand!"

He whispered something to him, then formally asked for the word. The fat man bowed his consent.

"We are a little confused," said the elegant one, "because there is another mesa here and we have heard that a paisana [person from one's own country] of yours is andando with them. They are not our friends and when we heard that a foreign woman was here looking for Don Margarito Aguilar, we thought it was this countrywoman of yours who is andando with these others."

"May I have the word?" asked Nieves.

Again Don Margarito bowed ceremoniously.

"We have come here," she said oratorically, "because we have been instructed to do so by the jefe under whose orders we are. Capitán General Manuel Luna gave us this address and told us to come here. Had he told us to go elsewhere we would not be here. The señora is a member of the Association of Religious Dancers Pertaining to the Church of Santiago de Tlaltelolco."

"As the letter clearly states," added the elegant danzante.

Don Margarito bowed, then straightened up and made a flowery, though somewhat belated, speech of welcome. Then he introduced the danzantes. The elegant one was Natividad Reina of San Francisco del Rincón. I had seen him at San Juan de los Lagos and we had just missed him at the Anthill in Guanajuato.

He drew Margarito aside. "Have you a room?"

"Yes, I have a room."

"Then you will have to invite them to stay here. You can do no less."

They were hardly six feet away; of course, we could hear every word!

Don Margarito bowed again. "With your permission," — and he and Natividad Reina went into the room on the left and shut the door.

I turned toward José. "Will you do me the favor to direct me to a hotel?"

"Oh, no — please! Wait a bit. I am sure that my uncle wants you to stay here."

"We could not think of it," I assured him. "It would be too much trouble, entirely too much trouble!"

"One moment, one little moment! Wait one little moment until my uncle comes back."

Then Don Margarito opened the door to the front room and invited us in. It was a large room with an iron bed, two tables, a mirror on the wall by the street window, and a chair.

"Here you have your room," announced Margarito proudly. "Even though it is very humble, it is very poor, and it lacks many things, it is yours with all our hearts."

We praised it enthusiastically, and accepted it with many thanks. Then we sat on the side of the bed while José played the concha and various members of the family came in to make our acquaintance. Victoria, Margarito's elderly wife, made us a pretty speech of welcome and excused herself to prepare for other guests. Their only son, Sabino, still in danzante uniform, reminded me that we had met at a previous fiesta. Both tables were piled high with dance regalia, and danzantes were in and out from time to time. About midnight they bade us good-night and left us. We locked the door.

Shortly after two o'clock quick footsteps came down the cobble-stones outside our window and we heard voices.

"Don Manuel!" exclaimed Nieves, getting out of bed and running to the window. I heard her soft greeting to someone outside. Then she said that we had had a pleasant trip, too.

"Who was that?" I asked when she came back.

"It was Don Manuel, Fidel, and Lorenza, his wife; and that señora who calls herself his right arm, the Capitana María; and Don Florentino, and José Cortés."

We heard an exchange of greetings in the hall, and after a short time, the murmur of a junta that was to last until breakfast. The Conquest was on! I could hear Don Manuel in a long speech. Then somebody else would hold forth. At six o'clock Nieves, unable to sleep since the arrival of the Mexico City contingent, made coffee on the little sterno stove from our basket. Then she went to the well in the patio to wash her face, leaving our door slightly open.

I heard Don Manuel say, "Then we have lost. We cannot accept such an arrangement. As everyone knows, the true dance, following the tradition of our ancestors, is contrary to such ideas . . . ."

I smiled to myself. Don Manuel was a clever strategist.

We dressed and napped until 8 o'clock when there was à tap at the door. Nieves opened it and the danzantes swarmed in for their regalia. Altagracia, Sabino's bride, with a serious, housewifely air, pulled his sleeveless tunic over his shirt, arranged his headdress, and fastened his deep cuffs, while he, smugly satisfied, twisted and turned at her bidding. Lorenza helped Fidel; her years of practice had given a technique that required little assistance. As soon as the men left, Altagracia served us a delicious breakfast on the table by the door. Documents and photographs relating to the dance were kept there, as well as a small but powerful radio, which was turned on all day and most of the night.

Don Manuel, in dance uniform, came in. One look at his beaming face and I knew that the Conquest had been accomplished. Don Margarito came in, too, to greet us. Then, while Don Manuel, Margarito, and Natividad Reina had a special conference, Don Margarito's brother escorted Nieves and me to a house he owned in the next block. He wanted us to meet his tenant who had been in the United States during the war as a mechanic.

Come in! I am very glad to know you. Come in and have a seat. Where are you from? And where did you live in the States? That's where I learned English. Yes, I like Americans. I would rather do business with Americans than with any other nationality. I tried to remain in the United States. I liked it there. I would have stayed if I could. But the law is the law, is it not? So here I am, back in Querétaro.

You have heard that I was in Burlington during the war, have you not? I worked there. I started very low, señora. I was just a grease boy in the round house. I ended as a full-fledged mechanic with an assistant. Imagine!

While I was working as an assistant to a mechanic there, a very curious thing happened. This mechanic said to me, "I am going to recommend you for a promotion."

So he took me to the boss. "I have an assistant here who is a better mechanic than I am."

Did you ever hear of such a thing? And that is how it happened that I was promoted! That is why I ended as a full-fledged mechanic with an assistant. And I had started as a grease boy in the round house.

When we came out of his house we could see a sparkling brilliance in front of Margarito's house.

"The danzantes are in uniform!" exclaimed Nieves. "Hurry, señora!"

"He is a good man, my tenant," explained Margarito's brother as he chuffed along in our wake. "He loves Americans and likes to practice his English and so I thought that he should meet you."

The danzantes were forming lines in the hall and patio when we reached the Aguilar house.

"Where are we going?" I asked.

"To ask permission. We have just signed the treaty and now we go to ask permission at the Mesa Real which is next door." Don Manuel told me.

"Oh — !" Then noting that strange danzantes were listening, "Does that mean that Don Margarito is not jefe of the Mesa Real in Querétaro?"

"Yes. Margarito has an older sister who was his father's heir. She has the Mesa Real. It is next door."

He placed Nieves and me beside Lorenza, Fidel's wife. Then, playing conchas and singing an alabanza, we marched through the street into the house next door. It was a small oratory and was so lavishly decorated with pastle and other greenery that by the time we had crowded in, we could see practically nothing. We kept close to Lorenza; facing the Four Winds, kneeling, crossing ourselves, and singing when she did. Finally Sabino, Don Margarito's son and heir, had the danzantes immediately in front of us move so that, by leaning over and twisting our necks, we could see the space in front of the altar. Don Manuel was offering his concha to the Four Winds while the danzantes sang. Margarito received the concha and offered it to the Four Winds. After this ceremony Don Margarito announced that Natividad Reina had the word.

Natividad Reina, with bells tinkling and plumes quivering, took his place before the altar and made a speech, ending with: "You all know what happened last night. We hope that the jefes of Mexico City will govern wisely and well, giving us a Disciplina that is neither too hard nor too lax."

Then Don Margarito announced: "We now give the word to the jefes of Mexico City, or more especially, to Don Fidel Morales and to Don Manuel Luna."

Don Manuel, after addressing all the saints on the altar, the Four Winds, and the benditas ánimas, said that the jefes of Mexico City wanted to help the jefes of Querétaro in any way that they could. He asked blessings on the union thus created — the placing of Querétaro and Mexico City under the same word — and stated that this was a federation, not a cooperative. He ended by hoping that they would always be in union to help each other. Then he led a litany and the danzantes sang an alabanza.

"Will the persons who are going to carry the trees please come forward?" Don Manuel asked, raising his voice so that those at the door could hear. After a slight delay the Alféreces came forward and took up the banners. The danzantes began to play and sing and we backed out.

Nieves and I marched near the end of the lines, but when a car coming toward us in the narrow street temporarily disrupted the order, I managed to stand by Don Manuel for a few minutes.

"Don Manuel, did I understand you to call the banners 'trees'?"

"Sí, Señora Marta."

"Why?"

"Because, señora, in ancient times our ancestors made their banners out of paper or cloth that was made from the bark of trees. They beat it until it was of a sufficient thinness, then they shaped it and painted it. And that was how they made their banners. And here in the Bajío — and in other places where they follow the old customs — the banners are referred to as trees."

The car had passed, we formed lines again, and marched up the hill. When we turned the corner I saw the Xuchiles, three of them in all, in waxy loveliness at the edge of the sidewalk. They were similar to the Xuchiles of San Miguel de Allende, except that these had spots of color scattered through them. On closer examination the spots proved to be tortillas painted rose, blue, green, and yellow. Two near the top of each, had nose, eyes, and mouth drawn on them. Each Xuchil had a cross on the very top.

While our friends formed their circle in front of the church, Don Margarito's brother acted as guide, showing us the main points of interest around the old church.

"Here, señora, is your paisana," he suddenly said in a low voice.

Behind me, at one side of the square in front of the church, was a circle of dancers. Cecilio Morales was one of the jefes in the center. Near them sat a blond woman dressed in the costume María had worn at the fiesta on the Anthill in Guanajuato. She was beating out the rhythm of the dance steps on a handsome *teponaxtle,* or Preconquest drum. As we watched her, she raised lovely blue eyes in a long, sensitive face and smiled at me.

"Señora," said a voice behind me, "would you like to see the cross of cantera?"

I turned to find Sabino standing there. We then trooped around the side of the church and up some stairs to a room behind the main altar. The walls were covered with a mural depicting the Battle of the Sangremal, and on the side behind the altar was a massive cross of rose-colored stone. A beaming Sabino perched on the railing around the stairwell and told the story of the famous battle, more or less as I had heard it from many danzantes, ending with: "Once many years ago, señora, the Holy Cross began to grow, nobody knew why. The padres were very puzzled by this and they finally cut off the part at the end where it was growing. From this part that they cut off, they made some small crosses and two of them they gave to my ancestors. You will see them when you visit my father's oratory."

When we came down the stairs they took us through the ruins of the old convent with its tangled, overgrown garden.

"Come, señora," exclaimed Sabino, "and see the plant of the cross."

In the corner of the convent garden was a spreading shrub, almost a tree, that had been allowed to grow at will. The sacristan was with us now and it was he who selected the thorns and gave them to us. The perfect, or mature, thorn had five thorns attached to it. With the two medium ones on either side of the mature thorn, the shape of the Holy Cross was formed, with three tiny thorns growing on the ends, in the position of the nails that pierced Our Lord's hands and feet.

"It is the only plant in the world like this, señora," the sacristan told me. "A group of your paisanos came down from a convent in California to investigate it. We could only tell them that it has always been here in this garden. We gave them a piece of it, and they are going to try to make it grow in California."

He carefully selected a perfect thorn, broke it from its branch, and gave it to me.

When we returned to the front of the church our friends were dancing in two large concentric circles. In the inner one was José Martínez Aguilar, Don Margarito's nephew we had met the night before. Beside him danced a tiny girl, hardly more than a baby. No step was too complicated for her. Each step was dramatized; no jefe danced with a more perfect sense of rhythm.

"Ay, buenos días, señora," greeted José. "I hope you rested well. This is my little daughter. She is going to be a danzante, too."

She had just celebrated her fourth birthday.

On our way back to Margarito's house at noon, we met Cecilio Morales and María with my blond paisana. She was Alice Paul who in her youth had been a dancer with the Martha Graham group in New York. She had long since retired to bring up a family. While in San Miguel de Allende on vacation she had discovered the danzantes.

We did not tarry long. Don Cecilio was a powerful chief of the Bajío and the chiefs of Mexico were making a conquest there. After my reception the night before, I was uncertain as to the limit of "togetherness" of a Querétaro fiesta.

When we reached the house, Sabino showed me his father's oratory, which was only a little smaller than Don Manuel's in the capital. Leaning against the front of the altar were the arms of the danzantes; two conchas crossed on one side, and a bow and arrow with the bag that usually hangs from a danzante's waist on the other. On the left wall near the altar was a picture of the Señor de Esquipulas, the Black Christ of Central America. On each side of the altar, was a Xuchil decorated with cucharillo. One, I noticed, had alternating long spokes, each topped with a little round mirror. There were also several crosses, a painting of the Virgin of Guadalupe, and in a box with a glass front, two little images, one with a black beard. A slender white card attached to the glass announced that these were Anilino Aguilar and Fernando de Tapia.

"Who are they?" I asked.

"My grandfather and the Conqueror of Querétaro," answered Sabino. "They are the benditas ánimas of this oratory."

He then called my attention to the two crosses of cantera. "These are the crosses I told you about, the ones that were given to my great grandfather by the priests. They were made from the extended part of the Holy Cross that you saw in the church, on the occasion when it grew miraculously."

Late that afternoon, Don Manuel tapped at our door and asked permission to learn the hour by the radio.

"Will the danzantes dance tonight?" I asked.

"No, señora," answered Don Manuel. "They will rest for tomorrow."

Fidel and Lorenza came in with bundles of luggage.

"Is this the room for those from the Federal District?" asked Fidel.

"It is the room for those from the Federal District," Don Margarito, behind him, assured.

"Don Manuel," I whispered, "did you people from the capital have to sit up all night because I locked this door?"

"Oh, no, señora! Have no care. It was after two when we arrived because our train was late, and we had to sit up the rest of the night because we had to make the Conquest."

Nieves and I stretched out on the bed. The others spread rush mats and blankets on the floor. As is the custom at fiestas, nobody undressed, not even to the loosening of belts. Soon Fidel was asleep, but Don Manuel's work was just beginning. Danzantes arrived singly and in groups to consult with him. I had slept that afternoon and was wakeful. It was impossible not to overhear. Once I thought a danzante was telling him that he had discovered that his employer was a murderer, but I could not be sure. At any rate, Don Manuel advised him to leave his job and go elsewhere, saying that he was sorry that he could do no more than advise him at the present time. Another had a sick child and Don Manuel loaned him ten pesos. But most of them consulted him about danzante matters — rules, traditions, and jurisdictions.

When I awoke the next morning the danzantes were gone, and as soon as we had eaten we hurried to the church. The dance circles were larger than they had been the day before. In Don Margarito's, Natividad Reina and his segundo were performing the Dance of the Sun and Moon with fancy variations. Just outside the circle a priest stood watching them.

"He is a new priest, recently sent here from Spain, they say," said Don Manuel, who had come to the edge of the circle to speak to us. "He knows nothing about the danzantes or the danza."

At the dramatic end of the dance, the young priest applauded enthusiastically.

"We call that a *danza fantastica*, Padre," Don Manuel informed him. "There is a difference between danzas fantasticas and danzas tradicionales."

"¿De veras?" the priest asked doubtfully.

"De veras," Don Manuel replied firmly.

Then he came out of the circle to show us around the church.

"This is the Chapel of the Señor de Esquipulas," he informed us as we strolled into a chapel at the left of the main sanctuary. "Do you know him, Señora Marta?"

"I have heard of him. He is a santo from the village of Esquipulas in Guatemala near the borders of Honduras and El Salvador. They call him the Black Christ."

"That is the one, señora! He is dark — almost black. See! Here he is!" — stopping in front of a dark image of Christ on the cross. "He is very popular in the Bajío."

On the opposite side of the chapel was a secluded place between two columns, a sort of alcove with two altars. On one was a group of figures representing the souls in Purgatory with garish yellow flames painted around them. On the other were six images, including a man with a black beard and a woman with flowing hair. Candles were burning in front of them.

"What are these, Don Manuel?"

"Those are the souls in Purgatory, Señora Marta, and these appear to be the benditas ánimas, but I have never seen them in a church before. Con permiso, señora. I am going to find out if these are ánimas."

When we came out of the church we met him near the door.

"Come, Señora Marta. They wish to honor us. I will tell you about the ánimas later."

He led me to the center of the circle beside Don Margarito and Natividad Reina. The danzantes were dancing, but as soon as we were in our places the music changed to a paso de camino, and they wound around in a huge "S" to pass through the center of the circle and bid us farewell. As each paused in front of me he gave me a double abrazo. Then he placed the palm of his right hand, thumb down against mine, rolled it over so that the thumb was up and our hands were back to back, brought his hand to his heart, then pushed our hands until my hand was on my heart, saying "Go with God, comadrita."

"What a beautiful *despedida* [farewell]!" I exclaimed to Don Manuel on the way back to Margarito's house.

"We have been highly honored, señora — very highly honored."

It was long past noon, and our train was due to leave a little after three.

"Don Manuel, have you a return ticket for the bus?"

"Sí, Señora Marta."

"Has Don Fidel?"

"No, he thought he might ride back on a truck, but the truck will not be going to the capital today."

"Won't you give your bus ticket to Don Fidel and accept a train ticket from me? Nieves and I would like to talk over the fiesta with you. We should have much pleasure if you went back on the train with us."

And so it was arranged.

I wanted to leave some money with the Aguilares, at least as much as it would have cost to stay at a hotel.

"Do not offer it for Margarito, Señora Marta," cautioned Don Manuel. "Offer it for the ánimas of his oratory. I will tell you what to say."

He taught me a flowery and somewhat complicated speech which I did not understand but recited glibly before the family and guests. Their openmouthed surprise was gratifying. Then with many thanks and invitations to the capital, we took our leave. As we passed through a little market on our way to the station, Don Miguel stopped. "I want to get a bowl for Ester. She broke her largest one the other day."

"Oh, let me buy it," I urged. "Let it be a present for Ester from me."

When we boarded the train, Don Manuel was carrying my suitcase and Doña Ester's large bowl. He followed us into the first-class day-coach, where I stopped beside two seats facing each other.

"Let me ride backwards," said Nieves. "You and Don Manuel sit there, señora, so that he can explain the fiesta to you. Put the bowl here —," patting the seat beside her.

Just as Don Manuel was about to sit down the conductor grabbed his shoulder.

"What are you doing here, you without shame?" he snorted, "Do you not know your place? It is for such as you that we have the second-class coach. Go back to the second-class coach!"

"I have my ticket," stammered Don Manuel as the conductor shook him. The Capitán General seemed small and frail as the big man towered over him.

"Go back to the second-class car or I will put you off my train!"

The conductor snatched up the bowl from beside Nieves. "Take your trash off this seat! I am busy now. I shall attend to you later. I shall be back, you without shame!" — stalking off toward the front of the train.

"Without shame himself!" muttered Nieves.

Later the conductor passed through the car again and glared at Manuel, calling him a name as he passed him.

"Excuse me a moment," I said, getting up and following the conductor. I caught up with him in the vestibule.

"Señor," I said, handing him my foreign relations card. "If anyone has offended you, it is I. The man to whom you object is my guest. I persuaded him to give away his bus ticket and to accept a ticket from me for your train. Of course, if he leaves the coach where he is now sitting, so shall I."

The conductor stared at my card. He turned it over and stared at the other side. Then he handed it back to me.

"I have nothing to say," he told me. "Nothing to say."

I went back to my seat and opened my notebook.

"Don Manuel, did you find out about the altar? Were those the benditas ánimas on it?"

"Sí, Señora Marta. I asked several danzantes and all said that on the special occasion of this annual fiesta, six of the benditas ánimas were honored on an altar in the church."

"And which ones were they?"

"The one with the long hair was the one that is called María Graciana, Señora Marta. And the others were Macedonia Montes, Juan Mineros, Benito López, Jacinto Vargas, but I could not find out who the other image was, though some said it was Felipe Aranda."

"Felipe Aranda? The one who was Don Fidel's jefe?"

"Sí señora, but I do not think that this image was Felipe Aranda. I think it was more likely that it was one of the others — Manuel de la Carrera, perhaps. He was from the Bajío."

"And did you ask about the Black Christ?"

"The Señor de Esquipulas? Si, señora, and they told me some interesting stories about the santo."

"Tell us!" urged Nieves.

One is about a mayordomo of the Confradia. It was his obligation to care for a beautiful image of Christ on the cross. And this mayordomo fell in love with a woman and he married with her. And, imagine, señora! His wife was an atheist. And she began to talk to him and finally she converted him. And his wife said to him, "If you love me and are really converted to my religion, you will burn this foolish bit of wood, this image of the Christ that you have."

So this mayordomo of the Confradia built a great fire and placed the Cristo in the middle of it. And the fire burned down to ashes but the Cristo would not burn. It only changed to the dark color it now has.

And, of course, the mayordomo was not an atheist anymore and he abandoned his wife. He never saw her again, for soon after that she died. — Or that is what they told me, señora.

But I like better the story they told me about the sacristan. This sacristan — so they say, señora — was married, but he, too, fell in love. He had a *querida*, a mistress, in addition to his wife. And he brought his querida to live in the house with him and his wife. Then the querida began to give the wife a poison that would kill her in five or six days. The husband did not know this, and he would not believe it when his wife said that she was very ill.

So the wife appealed to her favorite santo — her favorite Cristo in the church where her husband held the position of sacristan. The worse she felt, the more fervently she prayed. She prayed that she might get well for her children's sake, señora. Soon the santo began to change to a dark color.

"¡Ay, de mi, what have I done to thee, my Lord!" exclaimed the wife.

Then she heard a voice saying, "Have no fear, my child. The poison that was given to thee hath passed into me. This day I take thy illness and thy troubles on me."

That was the Señor de Esquipulas. Qué bonita, — eh, señora? Qué bonita story!

We were silent for a moment as I sat idly turning the pages of my notebook. Then I saw the note I had made.

"Oh look, Don Manuel! Here is the name of another santo you were going to explain to me; the one we saw in Tlaxcala with the ribbon hanging down in front of him. Here is his name: San Benito de Palermo."

Nieves laughed. "Oh, San Benito!"

"But you promised!"

"So I did. This San Benito de Palermo is one of the santos to whom persons with evil intent address their prayers — for the evil people pray as well as the good, señora."

"Who prays to San Benito?"

"Many believe that when you have an enemy whom you would like to be rid of, San Benito will help you."

"Is that so? How?"

"All you have to do is catch your enemy asleep. If you can measure him from the top of his head to the end of his big toe without his knowing it, you can cut the article with which you measured him — the string, the tape, or the ribbon — at the point to which he measured and hang it in front of San Benito with a prayer. Then your enemy will die."

I paused in my writing. "Does anybody really believe that, Don Manuel?"

"¡De veras! Many people believe it! As you could see by the length of the ribbon in Tlaxcala, some evil person had prayed for the death of a child."

"That is true, señora," Nieves assured me. "I know people who believe it."

"How strange! And there is something else, Don Manuel, that I do not understand. What did you mean last night when you told the jefe named Pedro that the jefe named Juan would have to make a reverence to his Palabra General?"

"You understand, Señora Marta, that those two jefes, Pedro and Juan, had had a serious difference of opinion. Now they are conforme, so Juan, who offended Pedro, will have to enter Pedro's circle with his personnel and kneel in the center to the banner of the association. Then Pedro, if he is conforme, will kneel facing their banner. All will make reverences to the Palabra General, which means that they present arms. You have seen us do that with our conchas, presenting them to the Four Winds, have you not?"

"So I have. Thank you, Don Manuel. Now I understand."

When I had finished my notes, we settled in our seats to rest, for it had been a long fiesta and we were tired. Soon Nieves was dozing and Don Manuel, with the end of his serape over his head, was snoring. The man in the seat behind us leaned forward and touched my shoulder.

"Señora," he said in a low voice, "I just want you to know that not all Mexicans are as prejudiced and as bigoted as the man to whom you talked in the vestibule a little while ago."

"Señor, I know that!" I told him.

The train pulled into Buenavista station and Bill was waiting when we stepped off. As he was greeting us he caught sight of Manuel.

"Hombre!" he shouted, springing forward to give Manuel an abrazo. "I had hoped they would be with you. Now I know they were well taken care of."

"We all stayed at the same house for two whole days," Nieves announced happily, stealing a glance at the conductor.

Bill took the bowl from Manuel and a basket from Nieves and, chatting gaily, we turned our backs on the gaping conductor and hurried toward the exit and home.

The Hill of the Bell

For years I have been chasing a piece of paper. Sometimes I have it almost within my grasp; sometimes it seems so far away, I doubt its existence. A professor in the Institute of History and Anthropology in Mexico City is supposed to have read it to one of his classes, but nobody can remember which professor it was, and none of the professors I know can remember having read it.

It may have been written by a Franciscan friar of the sixteenth century; perhaps by Fray Andrés de Castro or by Fray Jerónimo de Mendieta. Whoever he was, the friar forbade the Indians of San Miguel de Ameyalco to perform a certain ceremony according to their custom on top of a nearby mountain. The Indians ignored the friar's orders, going about their preparations for the fiesta as usual. There is a sacristan in this document who made it his business to find out what the Indians were up to, and reported his findings to the friar. They were going to leave for the mountaintop at midnight, he said, on the last night of the year. The friar decided to follow them.

The Indians did leave at midnight and reached the mountaintop, with its Preconquest platform and altars, just before dawn. They went to the cliffs on the side of the mountain that overlooked the City of New Spain and began their rites. The friar hid behind a tree and watched. The chiefs rolled a stone away from the mouth of a vertical cave and out flew a dove with a gold bell hanging from its neck. Straight from the mountain it flew, circling the valley of the City of New Spain three times. Meanwhile the chiefs performed their rites among the rocks and put out offerings of flowers, fruit, and other foods. Should the dove peck at the food on its return, there would be a good year with plentiful rain and abundant crops.

As the dove came flying back to the mountain, a little bird with a shrill voice, perched in the shrublike tree behind which the friar was crouching, made such an outcry that the Indians discovered him. The chiefs quickly hid their priestly paraphernalia while the friar picked up a rock and threw it at the dove. The dove wailed like a child, fluttered in a circle, then zoomed dazed into the rock wall of the barranca; leaving its outline there before it fell to the bottom dead.

I hope I find that document some day. I want to see how much the story has grown by word of mouth in the 400 years since it was written, for Don Manuel had told me the story long before I heard about the document.

I have heard many stories about the dove and the fiesta of the people of Ameyalco on the Hill of the Bell. For example, several years ago, a dance chief told me about the favor he once did for a priest of Ameyalco.

I saved his life, señora. The boys from there came in and told me, "Jefe, we are going to kill the padre."

"Why are you going to do that?" I asked them, for I did not want to scold them until I knew all about the matter.

"We are going to kill him because he prohibited the fiesta of the Cerro de la Campana. He prohibited it three weeks before the fiesta because, he said, it was paganism. Then he sent the sacristan to watch to see if we would go."

"And did you go?" I asked them.

"Sí, Jefe. And the sacristan hid at La Carita and gave the padre the names of all who went and since then life has been very hard for us. The padre put terrible penances on all who went. And so we are going to kill him."

And they told me all their plans, señora, and I found fault with them all, telling them that each was impossible.

Then I said, "Boys, for a thing like this your plans should be very sure. Go back to your village and talk this over carefully. Eight days from today come back and tell me what you have thought. — Yes, come back here and tell me what you have thought. We will see, muchachos. We will see."

But as soon as they left, I hurried to a padre I know and told him what they had said. And now, señora, there is a new padre at San Miguel de Ameyalco. The one who forbade the fiesta on the Cerro has been changed to a church somewhere else. And this new padre likes the Indians. Do you know what he did, señora? He gave the money for lime and for the burros to haul it to the top of the Cerro so that they could build a chapel there. And they are going to use the stones that are already there, the stones from the platform of the Ancient Ones. Imagine, señora!

When Don Manuel conquered the Association of San Miguel de Ameyalco, I asked him to invite us to the first fiesta they had on top of the Hill of the Bell. I have been there several times now, but that first time is still outstanding.

Nieves and I went with twenty-three danzantes by bus from Mexico City to the village of Salazar just off the highway to Toluca. Don Manuel had arranged for his compadres of Ameyalco to have mules waiting for us beside the highway, but as there were neither compadres nor mules, we walked to the village.

According to the danzantes, the people of Salazar are inhospitable to outsiders, for whom the cool springs halfway between the highway and the village are a special attraction. To discourage the public, said the danzantes, those of Salazar tore out the bridge over the little stream. We walked across the beam of the framework that remained.

When we arrived in the village there were no compadres. Since it was now noon the danzantes decided to lunch, and while I ate sand-wiches from our basket, the others bought hot food from the food stalls. Within three minutes, *chicharrón*, or cracklings, had risen from $1.50 a kilo to $1.75. When my friend Juana learned that Cacahuate (Peanut), a tall, blond soldier, had paid the lower price, she protested, insisting that the vendors return twenty-five centavos to her.

"Ask the señora Marta," she told them. "Ask any of the persons here buying food!" Turning to us, "Is it not just that they return twenty-five centavos to me, my friends?"

One by one and all together, we remarked about justice, fair play, good advertising, and gallantry to ladies; but Juana received no refund.

After lunch we strolled toward the mountains beyond Salazar. "We will walk slowly," promised Don Manuel. "Surely we will meet my compadres on the way."

Soon our pace proved too slow for some of the group. Led by Eva — a well-built young woman with even, white teeth and a fixed smile — they tramped on ahead, and disappeared behind a mountain. As we walked around and between mountains the conversation turned inevitably to danzante customs and beliefs.

"Don Manuel," I asked, "do you believe that people who are dead can help you in this life?"

"Señora Marta, I do all that I possibly can to help my son now while I am alive. Will I not do all that I can to help him after I die?"

"Sí, I think you will," Nieves broke in. "Don Manuel, you are not like I had always heard the danzantes were. Imagine! I had heard that the dance jefes were brujos (witch doctors)!"

"Some are witch doctors, perhaps," he admitted. "I do not know where my powers come from, but they never fail me when I call on them properly and am myself deserving. And I know this, señora: that I have never called upon them for evil!"

"Another thing I wanted to ask you, Don Manuel: Do only dan-zantes have the raising of the cross, or do other persons have it, too?"

"All humanity, Señora Marta. All humanity!" he stopped in the narrow trail, as though startled by a sudden thought. "Do you not have it in your country too, señora?"

"No, Don Manuel. I had never seen it until Don Nicolás died."

"Then what do you do when people die?"

"Oh, we have ceremonies, sometimes in a church, sometimes in the cemetery, but we do not have the raising of the cross."

I knew that I had asked a question too many, for blankness closed over his face. I was sorry I had spoken. I did not want to emphasize the differences between our customs. Then I heard what Tiburcio and Nieves, just ahead of us, were saying: They were asking riddles.

Nieves was saying:

Soy una fruta exquisita	I am an exquisite fruit
Que causa satisfacción,	That causes satisfaction,
Y llevo en mi los colores	And I carry in me the colors
Del nacional pabellón.	Of the national flag.

After several mistakes Tiburcio guessed, "Watermelon!" Both shouted with laughter. "Now it is your turn," she said.

Fuí a la plaza,	I went to the market,
Compré bellas.	I bought beauties.
Vine a mi casa,	I came to my house,
Lloré con ellos.	I wept with them.

"I know that," Nieves cried gleefully. "I know the answer to that: onions! Now it is my turn."

Redonita, redondón,	A little circle, a big circle,
Que no tiene	That has neither
Tapa ni tapón.	Cover nor top.

Tiburcio had to work on this one, but he finally guessed the right answer: a ring.

"We have this custom in my country," I told them. "We ask riddles often."

"Ask us one, señora! Ask us one!"

Anxious to point up a mutual custom, I plunged into the first, and only, one I could think of.

> Big at the bottom,
> Little at the top.
> A little thing in the middle,
> Goes flippity-flop!

I glibly translated the first three lines before I saw what I was headed for. The answer of course, is a churn, the old-fashioned kind with a dasher, like my grandmother used. But I had never heard a Spanish word for churn, nor had I seen a churn in Mexico. Three pairs of eyes were staring at me inquiringly.

"It is a thing that makes butter," I explained.

"A cow, señora?" Nieves finally guessed.

"Oh, no, no! A thing you use in the house when you make butter out of cream."

"Oh — the electric beater!"

I repeated it, in Spanish, except, "flippity-flop," which I said loudly and distinctly in English, while moving my fists up and down in front of me as though clutching the dasher of a churn.

"Belly!" guessed Tiburcio triumphantly.

"How silly!" Nieves snorted. "A thing that makes butter?" At that moment there was a loud shout from behind the tall, craggy rocks beside the trail ahead. "Somebody is lost," she said, quickening her pace. "I will try to overtake them and tell them to wait for you."

"I will go with you," said Tiburcio, and they left us.

"Many will come to this fiesta, señora," said Don Manuel, as we followed them, "for it is very famous."

"That is why I want very much to see it, Don Manuel."

When we rounded the rocks, we saw Nieves and Tiburcio coming back. They had failed to find the others. As we joined them, another shout rang out behind us. A man I knew as Isidro and his wife came around the tall rocks we had just passed and hurried toward us.

"I was right!" the señora exclaimed breathlessly. "You see!" I was right."

"So you were," Isidro agreed.

"We saw tracks of many small feet and tracks of one pair of large feet and I said to Isidro, 'The señora is with us.' And I was right!"

"Of a truth, she was!" Isidro exclaimed.

We came out of the foothill forests to a narrow, flat strip of pasture land called Los Pastores, or the Shepherds, near the foot of the Cerro de la Campana.

"See, señora," Don Manuel pointed to the left. "La Carita lies that way. It is where the trail used by those of Ameyalco begins."

Apparently we were not going the Ameyalco way.

"No, señora. We will go by the trail that those of Salazar use whenever they have occasion to ascend. It is shorter than the other, for those of Ameyalco often bring supplies to the fiesta by animals. That is why they use the trail on the other side which is a long slope which mules and burros can climb."

We were climbing now by a wide, cleared trail so smooth that it seemed a country road.

"A car could travel here," I remarked.

"Not far," Isidro informed me.

Then the trail branched, the left fork branching again a few feet farther on.

"Wait here," ordered Don Manuel, as he trotted to the left. He studied the ground carefully at the second fork. "Yes, they took the wrong trail. They will be lost, for this fork leads to nothing but a patch of herbs that many like to cook with pork. Tiburcio, follow them and put them on the other fork."

Tiburcio handed our thermos and basket to Isidro and started up the fork of the other trail.

"You will reach the top before us," his father told him. "Pitch the tent twenty-five steps below the chapel so that the señora will be protected from the wind. A cold wind blows just before daybreak."

We rounded a curve and the trail abruptly degenerated to a narrow path through drifts and gullies made by rains.

"This must be where rain begins in these parts," Nieves observed.

"Perhaps the ancients thought so," said Don Manuel.

This was a lead worth following, but I was conserving my strength. The uneven land ahead was not encouraging. The others were silent too as we struggled over the rough terrain. Then the trail changed from scraggy earth to enormous boulders. Don Manuel would vault to the top of one, I would push on my walking stick with my right hand while he pulled on my left until I was up. Then we would climb another in the same way. Nieves scampered from one to another without even breathing heavily. Around the top of the Hill of the Bell were lumpy shafts of rock, like fattish fingers clutching at the sky. There were three breaks in these, said Don Manuel, one on the Ameyalco side and two on our side. On the highest point of the mound was the chapel. But each time we reached the top we found ourselves behind a gray lump of rock!

Then Don Manuel and Isidro disagreed as to the direction we should take.

"We are going this way," Isidro finally said, handing the thermos jug and basket to Don Manuel. Then he and his wife scrambled off toward our right. For an hour and a half we climbed up and down without finding the break in the rock. Once when we stopped to rest, Nieves pointed to the valley below.

"Look, señora! What do you see?"

The Valley of Mexico was spread before us, bathed in the mellow sunshine of late afternoon. Since we were in the shade, the whole capital, from San Angel to Tepeyca, stood out clearly. As I sat enjoying it, we heard shouts.

"The boys!" exclaimed Don Manuel.

He shouted a signal and was answered.

"They are lost!" he announced. Then he shouted a different signal.

"What are you telling them?"

"That we are lost too, Señora Marta."

As we started to climb again we heard shouts from the opposite direction. Isidro and his wife were also lost! Nieves and Don Manuel laughed heartily.

A few minutes later, Don Manuel gave a yell. He had found the break! Isidro and his wife, guided by our voices, hurried back and went through with us. Don Manuel shouted a signal but received no answer, so concluded that the boys were already in.

The top of the mountain was covered with trees and shrubs. We sniffed the pine-scented air and fought the cockleburs that plucked at our clothes from both sides of the trail. The sun had set, but it was too early for the evening chill that would surely come. We crossed a little wooded ridge, and were within a few feet of the remains of the ancient platform with the rose-colored chapel perched a couple of feet above it.

"Why did they not build it level with the platform?" I asked. "That would have been more convenient."

"Because, señora," Don Manuel explained, "the chapel covers the ancient altar. That little porch is exactly over the front of it. Look what you are passing, señora!" He pointed to a low stone cross on a stone pedestal built over and around a boulder. "That covers another ancient altar." He lowered his voice. "They say there is an idol buried there.

The padre who forbade this fiesta in the sixteenth century put six of these stone crosses over the rocks that the Indians worshipped."

"Where are the other five?"

"In the chapel," he replied, as we climbed the little incline that had once been steps to the platform. "When they finished the chapel they put the crosses. . . ."

Shouts interrupted us. The danzantes, busily pitching the tent on the other side of the chapel, had caught sight of us. Tiburcio came toward us.

"No, compadres," he called. "No keys. And the chapel is locked!"

Don Manuel hurried down to the tent. It was too close to the chapel. He had said it must be twenty-five steps below the chapel. He ordered the danzantes to move it. When they had moved it, he said, they should line it with rush mats and blankets and should build a big bonfire in front of it.

A young soldier ran down to say that a compadre had just arrived and was even now unlocking the chapel.

"I want to talk to him," said Don Manuel. "I want to ask him why they did not meet us with the mules."

Several danzantes began to talk at once. They had already asked him about the mules. He had replied that at a junta in Ameyalco last night it had been the general opinion that a foreign señora would be afraid to try to ride up a mountain on a mule, and that she would not want to spend the night on top of a mountain with the Indians, anyway. It would be foolish to provide mules for a señora who would not be there, they decided.

Don Manuel climbed to the chapel. Nieves and I followed slowly so as to give him an opportunity to talk to his compadre in private. As we went up the two steps at the end of the narrow, unenclosed railing-less porch, we saw a smoking incense burner with two lighted candles along its edge, just over the rim of the ancient altar underneath. We were to see this throughout the fiesta.

The chapel was small and crowded, with the altar taking up almost one-third of the space. The sixteenth-century stone crosses, like the one outside over the rock, were on it, as were various santos and photographs. Between the altar and the door — leaving just enough room to enter the door, to sit along the sides, and to kneel comfortably at the altar — was a round depression about six inches deep. All around it were candle-sticks with tall candles, which the compadre was lighting. Beneath the altar were two rectangular openings, one on each side. I edged forward trying to peer into one of them. I was thinking of La Cosa, the symbol of María Graciana.

"Go no closer, Señora Marta," warned Don Manuel softly.

"What is hidden there?" I whispered.

"I do not know, but whatever it is, they want no one to see it, not even me."

Reluctantly I moved away.

After supper, as we sat around an enormous bed of coals from the big bonfire that the danzantes had built in front of the chapel that afternoon, Tiburcio announced that the tent was ready.

Nieves and I went down to rest. She joined a group of young people, including Eva, around the bonfire just outside. I lay on a blanket on top of a rush mat in the tent. The only other occupant was Isidro's wife. I could see that she was exhausted. Isidro gallantly cut a small log as a pillow for her, and she wrapped herself in her blanket and went to sleep.

Outside, the young people at the bonfire sang songs, mostly popular love songs with a corrido, or an alabanza now and then. Between songs they talked. When I first began to pay attention to what they were saying, they were talking about a woman of the group who was last seen that afternoon having an attack of exhaustion.

"The señora of Isidro had an attack too," somebody said.

"But my señora wanted to sit by the fire and talk when she arrived," came Nieves' voice filled with pride.

"And she is a foreigner," said a man's voice.

"Sometimes it is impossible to tell, is it not?" murmured another.

"It is the truth," said a woman.

Presently there were footsteps running down the hill. A new voice demanded breathlessly, "Where is the flashlight?"

"In the tent," answered Nieves.

"The foreign woman has two flashlights. I saw them!" came a man's voice.

The flap of the tent flew aside and a young man's head appeared.

"Where are the flashlights, señora? We have to go to the spring for water. The jefe is sending us. The flashlights — where are they?"

"With much pleasure," I told him, taking the flashlight from the top of the basket and handing it to him. He quickly passed it to someone behind him and, picking up the second flashlight which had been beside the first, disappeared.

"Bring back a flashlight," I called, poking my head out of the tent. "You may use one, but not two."

"But we have to get the water," he protested.

"If I were not here, you would get the water in the dark. As it is, you will get the water by the light of one flashlight. That is why I have brought two, one to lend and one to keep by me all the time. Give me my flashlight!"

He hesitated, balancing himself on a boulder. I drew a deep breath. "Don Manuel," I bawled.

He leaped down and handed me the flashlight.

"It is so dark," he grumbled, "that somebody will fall down the mountainside and kill himself."

"But none of us will die in the dark," I retorted.

The others had remained silent during this exchange. I replaced the flashlight and rolled myself in my blanket again. Then came Eva's voice, raised above a normal conversational tone.

"*Todos somos iguales y conformes,*" she said. "We are all equal and conforming. On these trips we take, we all eat the same, we all drink the same. We are one for all and all for one. And we use the same things on these marches."

"Not my flashlight," I called out. "One you may use; the other stays by me."

I heard Tiburcio talking in an undertone, but whether he was scolding or explaining I could not tell. Eventually he began a song and the others joined in. They sang several songs before I heard them complaining about the fire. They had used all the dry wood and the damp refused to burn.

"Get the other flashlight and go look for some dry wood," urged Eva.

Tiburcio said firmly, "Wait until the boys come back with the water and then use that flashlight."

"But it is completely dark," complained Eva.

It was when they had just finished the next song that I heard vigorous thumps on the ground outside.

"¡Ay, señora! Señora!" called Nieves in a frightened voice. "This boy is having a fit!"

I handed her the flashlight and got up. The fire was out and it was dark. I could see the flash of the young man's white shirt in the dim light as he thrashed about on the ground. Desperately, I tried to remember first aid, but could think of nothing for epilepsy.

"What can I do?" I cried.

"Have you a handkerchief, señora?" asked Nieves. "We want to tie his tongue to prevent his chewing it."

I gave her the handkerchief and asked what else I could do.

"Nothing, señora. The boys are holding him. His brother says that is what they do when he has these attacks."

After a time the young man stopped struggling. Finally he got up and walked away.

"We were afraid he would roll down the mountain," Nieves told me. "There is a barranca just beyond that stump by the rock."

I went back to my blankets and Nieves sat in the door of the tent.

"Here comes the boys with the water," she announced.

A young man I had not met before politely returned the flashlight, while the bonfire group chattered to the water boys about the urgent need we had had for the second one during their absence.

"Tell me, señora, how did you know we were going to need it?" Nieves wanted to know.

Since I had no answer for this, I laughed and called attention to Isidro's wife who was snoring.

"She is sleeping, but I am not comfortable. The rock is too near the surface. This mat and blanket are as nothing. Nieves, let us go to the chapel and sing alabanzas."

"¡Qué bueno, señora! I was hoping you would say that."

We stumbled up to the chapel and almost walked into a "limpiadito." Don Manuel was cleansing the young man who had had the fit, using some of the flowers from the chapel. Perspiration stood on his forehead as he swished and crossed them above, below, and around the boy. Finally he made sweeping motions out the door and was finished. The danzantes strummed their conchas and started to sing.

At midnight, Nieves, Juana, and I were singing, sitting on a mat with our backs to the wall of the chapel, when someone came in the door. A whisper ran through the room, "The comadres are arriving!"

Nieves and I slipped out. There was bright moonlight now. We could see the file of black-and-white figures moving up the slope through the trees. When they reached the bonfire I saw that they were wearing the typical dress of the Toluca hill women: dark pleated wraparound skirt, white embroidered, square-neck blouse, and dark rebozo. There were seventeen of them of all ages past twenty. Later I was told that only three spoke Spanish. I could understand only one. The men of Ameyalco, though they conversed among themselves in Spanish, always spoke to the women, even those who spoke Spanish, in Nahuatl or Otomí. In a short time a low, wide white tent was spread near the bonfire. The comadres had put it up themselves without fuss or flurry. I do not know where the huge earthen pots came from — some of the men brought them on burros, I think — but soon after the arrival of the comadres they were bubbling over the coals of the enormous bonfire that had been burning since our arrival. A corps of young men kept busy bringing large cans of water from the spring half-way down the mountain. They now had a gasoline lantern to light their way.

At 1:30 a.m. the comadres served coffee and *aguitas*, "little waters," as the danzantes call orange-leaf tea. We sat on the big rocks and talked. The moon was high now and the atmosphere clear. The Nevada de Toluca, snowcap of the Toluca valley, shimmered like a white wraith in the sky opposite us.

"It seems to be at the same height we are, does it not, señora?"

"Sí, Nieves. So it does."

"Is it, señora?"

"No, I am sure the Nevada de Toluca is higher." I turned to a man from Ameyalco who had been listening, "How high is the Cerro de la Campana?"

"I do not know to tell you, señora, but it is very high. The Nevada de Toluca is a little higher, I think, because it has snow on it. But the Cerro is very high."

Later I learned that from our tent door the Hill of the Bell is 11,100 feet high. The Nevada de Toluca is 14,000 feet.

On our way back to the chapel Nieves drew me aside. "Señora, I feel so lonely up here on top of the world in the middle of the night. I wish we were both safe at home asleep in our beds!"

I knew what she meant. I, too, felt far from home and the world seemed very large.

Back in the chapel, Don Manuel was cleansing Isidro's wife.

"Ay, señora!" said a young man just inside the door. "Will you lend us your flashlight? Eva has had an attack."

"Which one is Eva?" Isidro asked.

"She with the *sonrisa Colgate* (Colgate smile)," said my friend Chato in the doorway.

Suddenly I felt quite at home "on top of the world in the middle of the night." I handed the boy the flashlight and he hurried out.

When he had gone, the rest of us settled ourselves to sing alabanzas. It was nearly 4 a.m. and many of the danzantes were sleeping.

"Señora Marta," said Don Manuel, "try to get a little sleep. You will need rest tonight for the trip down tomorrow."

Juana, Nieves and I stretched out on our rush mats and closed our eyes. They were asleep, but I was awake when a tall boy in blue jeans came in, his thin face shining in the candlelight.

"I heard them, Jefe!" he told Don Manuel. "I heard voices over by the Puerto de Agua and I slipped over there . . ."

"And who was it?" asked Chato.

". . . Voices were coming from the exact spot where our friends were struck by lightning last year, from the exact spot where they were killed!"

"Is it surprising that our companions should be with us?" asked Don Manuel, raising his voice a little. "It was their custom to attend this fiesta. They came here last year. Is it extraordinary that they should come back this year?"

The boy joined friends in the opposite corner and was soon enthusiastically describing the trail we had climbed that afternoon. The capital was now enhanced by a million twinkling lights; for the land where, according to legend, sunlight and moonlight had their beginning was now blazing a trail for the rest of the world in artistic and effective lighting.[1]

"Don Manuel," I asked, "who was killed by lightning last year?"

"A man and a woman, Señora Marta. They were climbing up the trail that passes by the Puerto del Ojo de Agua. There was a storm at this time last year just when all were climbing the mountain. Lightning struck a tree that they were under and killed them."

"Were you here," Don Manuel?"

"Sí, señora, though I had not yet conquered this association. Don Casiano had invited me. Now, Señora Marta, rest yourself and try to sleep."

Just before day he called me, "My compadres have arrived, Señora Marta. They are forming their lines to make their entrada as day is breaking. Will you come and take a picture of them now?"

On the way to the door he stooped and lifted a thick serape from sleeping danzantes. "Get up, muchachos, the jefes of the association have arrived."

He threw the serape across my shoulders.

"But I have my heavy coat!" I protested.

"You will need this, too."

He was right. A strong wind biting with cold seemed to blow through all I had on. I pulled on my gloves and, with the danzantes' help, mounted a large boulder near the sixteenth-century cross. In front of me, facing the side of the chapel, were about seventy-five men and women, assembled in an inverted "U" with their banner in the center at the back. The women wore the typical wraparound skirt and blouse or print dresses with rebozos, while the men had on blue jeans or overalls, sweaters, and bright plaid jackets or serapes. Most of the women were barefoot. Many of the men had bulky white bundles tied to their backs; material for the offerings, Don Manuel told me.[2]

As soon as I had finished taking pictures, the compadres made their entrada. Just as the first rays of sunlight touched the chapel, they formed a solid square on the ancient platform in front of it and, repeating a prayer in Nahuatl, saluted the Four Winds.

"Come, señora," said Don Manuel, as soon as they had finished. "We go now for the distribution of the offerings. The first place is the Puerto de Mexico."

I knew nothing about the distribution of offerings but I did not want to miss anything connected with the Puerto de Mexico, which was where the sixteenth-century friar had killed the dove.

We crossed the mountaintop in the direction from which we had arrived the day before, heading to the cliffs instead of veering toward the break through which we had entered. Apparently some of the lumpy crags had broken off even with the ground along the edge of the cliff, forming a pavement like oversized cobblestones. We seemed to be just above the place where we had followed the false trails the day before. Mexico City had about the same position, but instead of a pastel city below us, it was an enormous bowl, banked high with thick, constantly shifting clouds, cold and white in the first light of day.

"Look, señora!" called Don Manuel. "Here is where the ancient priests rolled the stone away."

Then I saw that there was a split in the mountain, behind the cliff where it came to a point over the valley. It was as if a broad wedge had been taken out of the side of the mountain. This was the barranca, or canyon, that the danzantes had talked about. On our side, behind the cliff, was a cavity, a sort of pocket, near the rim of the barranca. It was of oval shape bordered by a ledge on the cliff side about six feet below the level of the trail and cliff. I scrambled down inside the pocket to this ledge which had a natural railing of stone along its outer edge. I knelt and looked out over the railing. Across the pocket, several feet below us, I could see jagged rocks sticking up where the rim of the pocket had broken down. I peered downward but could not see the bottom of this vertical cave. A puff of smoke wafted up in front of us and I could smell copal.

"Where did the smoke come from?" I asked.

"Look down, señora," said Don Manuel.

Directly below us, on a circular ledge smaller than the top of a card table, a jefe was making the sign of the cross with the incense burner.

"What is he doing?" I whispered.

"You cannot see it, Señora Marta, but he is kneeling before a tiny cave. That is where our ancestors kept the dove. That little cave is connected with a hole near the side of the cliff and that is where they rolled the stone away. But down where he is kneeling is where they did their ceremonies in honor of the dove."

On the side of the pocket adjoining the mountain, which was covered with growth, was another ledge where the capitanas perched with their incense burners. Several of the danzantes, I noticed, carried long lighted candles. "The dove" was on a rock in a notch in the opposite side of the barranca. It was a natural formation that looked like a waterworn bas-relief of a dove, its wings almost folded, falling headfirst.

As soon as the ceremony before the little cave ended, the danzantes threw their offerings, trying to touch the dove. Flowers, bolillos, bananas, and tacos flew through the air. A danzante scored a direct hit with one banana.

When it was over we walked slowly back to the chapel. On the way we passed a marker placed by a club of hikers. Somebody had scratched away the date with a sharp instrument. As we drew near the chapel a group of white-calzoned jefes stopped us. They were a commission from the association of Ameyalco and they wanted to ask a favor of Don Manuel.

"Tata Manuel, will you tell us the history of this place that you have been talking to the foreign señora about?"

Don Manuel told them the story of the dove with the gold bell hanging from its neck. They were amazed! They had celebrated this fiesta all their lives only because their ancestors had celebrated it. Don Manuel told them that I was looking for a document that would tell all about the history of the fiesta.

"Señora," said their leader, "when you find that document, will you make a copy of it for us? Since it is of the history of Ameyalco, and since we are of Ameyalco, it is proper that we should have it in our archives. Will you make a copy for us, señora?"

"With much pleasure," I answered him, "if I ever find it."

They were silent for a moment. Then another spoke timidly.

"There is another reason too, señora. We of Ameyalco have always had our fiesta on top of this mountain but in recent years the people of Huixcalucan have been planting their cornfields on the slopes near the foot of it on the other side. Now they are petitioning the government to give them this mountain. If we could show this document that you mention, it would help us in this matter. You will continue to search for it, will you not, señora?"

"I shall do so," I replied. "I had lost hope and stopped looking, but then I learned that it was not called San Miguel de Ameyalco in the sixteenth century. It was Santa María Magdalena Ameyalco, so now I shall look for this story under that name."[3]

"Magdalena!" exclaimed one of them. "That was the señora's name. That is why they called it that. Because her name was Magdalena."

"What señora?" I asked.

"The widow! Magdalena was her name."

"Whose widow was she?"

"The señor who was the owner of all these lands in the first place. He died and it was while his widow was in charge that the land was distributed and all these villages formed."

"What date was this?"

"¡Ay, señora! I do not know to tell you. I only know what the old people have told me, but none of them mentioned dates. I am very sorry, señora, but I do not know anything about it." — and I had reached another dead end!

According to Don Manuel, the ceremonies at the other puertos were much the same as that at the Puerto de Mexico, except that there was no dove; so I did not attend them, but rested in the tent while the others went.

I joined Don Manuel and Nieves at the chapel. The sixteenth-century cross near the ancient altar was beautifully decorated with flowers, while on the ground at the open side of the stone table was an unusual offering of flowers, mostly calla lilies, and bolillos arranged around an egg in the center. The boulder on which I had stood to take the pictures was also elaborately decorated.

"¡Ay, Don Manuel! When I stood there this morning, did I profane something?"

"Have no care, señora. They know that you meant no offense. Come, I want you to see the chapel."

The circular depression over the ancient altar was filled with flowers, and tamales, tortillas, and other foods. In the center was a silver plate upon which was a baked chicken with its unplucked, crested head held erect. Lighted candles formed the edge of the circle and an elaborate antique candle holder, like a plate attached to chains, hung low from the ceiling above the chicken's head. I wondered how such quantities of flowers had survived the trip over the rough trail in excellent condition. They were as fresh as if they had just been cut. Outside the chapel was a new bronze church bell, a gift from hikers' club, Don Manuel said. I started forward to admire it, then remembered what the ethnologist had told Bill and me years ago and shied away.

The sixteenth-century cross near the ancient altar was beautifully decorated

After breakfast, though the compadres urged us to stay, we started home. One of them offered to let me ride his horse down the long slope that Don Manuel had pointed out as the one used by the people of Ameyalco, and I accepted with many thanks. Since there was no saddle, I sat high on a pack pad and the danzantes fashioned stirrups out of ropes of maguey fiber. Then the compadre attached a long lead rope to the bridle and led the horse down the trail toward the slope. Don Manuel, Tiburcio, Chato, Plato, and Nieves walked. The horse was also going home and we soon left them.

Shortly after we started down the slope, the trail divided and the compadre led the horse onto the less-traveled fork on the left where the grass was green and the going fairly easy. From the top of a sharp dip in the trail, which was little more than a path now, I could see a cluster of huge rocks just ahead and a small clearing beyond them. As we drew nearer I saw that a man and a woman were ceremoniously swishing long leafy branches in a "little cleansing" of the two largest rocks which were almost flat on top and stood a few feet apart, one behind the other, like parallel tables, forming the long sides of a hollow rectangle with two tall jagged rocks forming the short sides, all in natural formation. The flat rock at the back, where the woman swished and brushed, was decorated with flowers, and additional flowers spilled from a basket on the ground nearby. While the compadre shortened my constantly stretching and slipping stirrups, I watched the stout Indian woman sweep the green branches back and forth, up and down and all around, completely absorbed in what she was doing, moving her lips slightly as if in prayer. I am not sure that she knew we were there.

As we moved forward again the man, who was cleansing the flat rock in front, turned suddenly and saw us. He bounded toward us and planted himself across the path, blocking the compadre's way. In angry, excited undertones he upbraided the compadre. I could not hear what he said, but I heard the compadre's reply.

"It is not that I am guiding her through here"; he said clearly and deliberately, "it is that the jefe sends her by this path. They tell me that the señora is a capitana and a friend of the danzantes."

The man opened his mouth for another tirade, then with a gesture of exasperation stepped from the path and motioned the compadre on.

"Muchas gracias," I said politely, as the horse and I passed him. He glowered.

"They were giving a 'little cleansing' to the altars," I chattily remarked, but the compadre strode swiftly on as if he had not heard me.

"Which puerto was that?" I asked in a louder voice.

"We have to find the entrance to the main trail at this point, señora," he said. "It is very ugly and it is hidden, but it is not long. Here it is! Lean back, señora," and he coaxed and scolded the horse through a short, steep drop into the main trail below.

The long slope was rough and difficult, but not nearly so difficult as the trail that we had climbed as we went to the fiesta. It was a beautiful morning, and when we had passed La Carita and were off the mountain, I began to enjoy it. We skirted Salazar, fording the stream at a shallow point. I could see Nieves and the danzantes as they sauntered along the now familiar road near the village. When they saw us they waved and shouted greetings and we waved and shouted in return. We reached the bus stop on the highway first and, as the compadre had business elsewhere, I dismounted and sat in the shade of a telephone pole to wait for them. They strolled leisurely along the graded road, laughing and talking. When they reached the skeleton bridge, Nieves and the boys climbed down the woodwork to the stream to drink from the spring and to fill the thermos jug with cold spring water. Don Manuel came on alone.

As I watched him walking along the country road toward me, I thought of all the Concheros I had known through the years, living unencumbered by nonessentials, and filling their needs of the moment with the gifts of nature; such as collecting the cochineal insects that look like small oval pearls from the broad, flat leaves of the nopal cactus to obtain the rich red coloring that dyes the downy feathers of their chilillo headdresses. When lacking other means of transportation, they cover incredible distances, walking on their broad, short feet to the atrio, where with inherent ingenuity in contrasting and blending colors, fabrics, feathers, sequins, and beads, they give their dance circles, in the midst of the dark attire of the public, the appearance of huge variegated bouquets of tropical flowers. The simplicity of their daily living and the high degree of their devotion to the dance cult are typical of various elements in the fusion of the two widely different cultures that has produced their fascinating country. Don Manuel, now only a few feet away, straightened his shoulders and lifted a happy face to the sunlight pouring over the mountain beyond the highway behind me, a man of integrity with mission accomplished.

Notes

Notes to pages 1-22

CONCHEROS AND FIESTAS

[1] The *concha* is a musical instrument similar to the lute.

[2] Copal is the transparent resin of a native tree.

[3] The *chilillo* headdress.

[4] White cotton pants used by the Indians of Mexico.

[5] Malinche was Cortés' friend and interpreter, the Aztec princess who saved the Spanish army from annihilation at Cholulu.

FIESTA AT AMEYALCO

[1] "Well . . . " indicative of hesitation.

[2] "Truly."

[3] The literal translation of concha is "shell."

[4] A large walled courtyard, marked by prominent axial relationships, and approached by monumental arcaded gateways near the center of one or more of the surrounding walls — a form peculiar to New Spain, and only rarely imitated elsewhere. George Kubler — *Mexican Architecture of the Sixteenth Century.* New Haven: Yale University Press — 1948. Vol. II, Ch. VII, pp. 314, 315.

[5] Literally, "The Dark One."

[6] "Oh, how good of you!" Literally, "How good!"

[7] Francisco Saverio Clavijero — *Historia Antigua de México — Traducido del Italiano por* José Joaquín de Mora — *México 1826 — Tomo I Cap.* 7 pp. 358, 359, 361.

[8] *Pulque,* the fermented juice of a maguey (Agave Americana), is the mildest of the alcoholic beverages made from the various magueyes of Mexico.

JOSÉ CELIS, INSTRUCTOR

[1] This hymn, taught to the Indians by Fr. Antonio Margil de Jesús in the eighteenth century, became a kind of national anthem of Mexico. Robert Ricard, *The Spiritual Conquest of Mexico.* Leslie Byrd Simpson, tr. Berkeley & Los Angeles, The University of California Press, 1966. Ch. II, p. 185.

[2] In fact a danzante "oratory" is neither an oratory nor a chapel, but the room that contains the family altar. There, except during danzante ceremonies, the family goes about the various household chores, sewing, shelling corn, mending sandals or shoes, and in the evening spreading serapes and blankets on the floor, for the "oratory" is often used as a sleeping place. Mendieta, writing in the sixteenth century, referred to its Preconquest counterpart as a chapel (Mendieta, Jerónimo de, O. F. M. — *Historia Eclesiástica Indiana.* Ed. Joaquín Garcia Icazbalceta — México, 1870 — Lib. II, Cap. XXXI, p. 140) but in present-day Mexico one must have a dispensation for a chapel, which is considered Church property and therefore is owned by the government.

[3] This does not apply to "general marches," like those to Chalma and to the Villa, when the danzantes take their own food.

[4] The "Mananitas" is the traditional birthday song of Mexico.

[5] The *cuartel general* is the headquarters of the dance group — the oratory.

[6] This included the wooden *huaraches,* loosely woven Mexican sandals; feather headdresses, and musical instruments.

[7] *Malinche abanderada* means "malinche of the banner."

[8] The Bajío includes the states of Guanajuato, Michoacán, and Querétaro where the ancient Otomí, Tarascan, and Chichimec kingdoms were located.

[9] The jute in this case is a fiber of one of the agaves of the Teotihuacán Valley.

[10] To trample under foot; to insult with abusive language; to hurry or confuse.

[11] Spirit, soul.

[12] "What misfortune!"

[13] Similar to "Who Knows Who" and "The Song of the Kid," of the Passover Haggadah, the forerunners of most cumulative songs.

[14] The "Tree of the Sad Night" signifies an ahuehuete (cypress) tree where Cortés wept for his slain warriors (June 30, 1520) in Popotla (a section of the Federal District). — Don Fernando de Alva Ixtilxochitl — *Historia Chichimeca* — México: 1892 — Tomo II, Cap. LXXXIX, p. 399.

[15] *Codex Mendocino* shows Otontecutli, the Otomí god, represented by a bundle of sticks.

THE GENERAL OATH

[1] December 11 or 12 is widely celebrated in Mexico as the birthday of the Virgin.

FIESTA AT SAN JUAN DE LOS LAGOS

[1] This was before the Mexican Government's campaign against illiteracy.

[2] Dough.

[3] Charcoal stove.

FIESTA AT TLALTELOLCO

[1] El Padre Fray Diego Duran, *Historia de las Indias de Nueva España y Islas de Tierra Firme* (México, Atlas, 1867), Trat. 3; Lam. 1 (Escritor del Siglo XVI).

[2] Native village, literally, "earth."

[3] Now a part of The Plaza of Three Cultures: The Preconquest Ruins, partially destroyed; the colonial church; and the tall modern apartment buildings.

AFTERNOON TEA AND REHEARSAL

[1] "With what motive — " (do you seek these data)?

[2] Also Tenochtitlan.

[3] "Clear!" or "Clearly!"

[4] "Yes, of course!"

[5] "They walk toward over there," "They walk on the other side," or it could mean "They walk an alien path."

GODPARENTS OF A FLAG

[1] *Pastorcitas* are "little shepherdesses": little girls dance in and out of a circle carrying flowers; the dance ends with a Maypole. A similar ancient dance described by D. Francisco Saverio Clavijero in *Historia Antigua de México.*

VELACIÓN IN A CAVE

[1] A sweet drink made of ground corn.

[2] Corn gruel; peppery sauce of many ingredients; puree of avocados, tomatoes, chiles, and onions; rolled tortillas stuffed with meats and spices and baked in sauce; rolled tortillas stuffed with meats and spices and fried; a corn husk filled with corn dough, meat and chili sauce, closed tightly and steamed; fried tortillas piled with meats, beans, lettuce, avocado, cheese, and chiles; chicken in a sauce of ground almonds and chiles; chiles Jalisco style; and pressed guava paste with creamed cheese.

FIESTA AT SAN MIGUEL DE ALLENDE

[1] Wooden frames, about 30 feet x 5 feet, of lattice work filled with spoon cactus decoration. The spoon cactus, the *frontales*, and the Xuchiles are usually referred to as cucharillo.

RAISING THE CROSS

[1] A handful of dried straw tied tightly in the middle and clipped evenly at both ends to form a double brush — symbol of Tlazolteotl, the Earth Goddess.

RECEPTION OF MEMBERS

[1] When Don Manuel was questioned by a priest about this Cristo, he explained that it was given to him years ago by the head of a convent that was closed by the government at that time, and who told him that it had been baptized "Señor de Chalma."

VELACIÓN AT THE ORATORY

1 Maximino Martínez. *Las Plantas Medianales de México*. México, 1933.

THE DISCIPLINA

1 Chachalaca, a type of grouse. The danzantes are adept at dying and painting feathers, with the possible exception of ostrich plumes. Though evidently the colors of the feathers of the chachalaca vary in several areas, it is safe to assume that the feathers of Don Manuel's crown had been touched up to key in with his new orange silk dance uniform.

ACCORDING TO DANZANTES

1 Fray Bernadino de Sahagun, *Historia General de las Cosas de Nueva España.* México: Editorial Robredo, 1938, Tomo 2, pp. 212-217; Tomo 1, p. 321; Mendieta, *Historia Eclesiastica*, Lib. II, pp. 107-108; Eduard Seler, *Tonalamatl of Aubin Collection*. Berlin-London: 1900–1901, pp. 94, 106; *Codex Vaticanus 3773*, p. 54 (Fig. 195), Index, *Tlacatlaolli;* Bulletin 28, Smithsonian Institution, Washington, D.C.: 1904, pp. 204-206.

2 Seler, *Codex Fejérváry - Mayer.* Berlin-London: 1901–1902, p. 53.

3 Abbé Durand, *Catholic Ceremonies and Explanation of the Ecclesiastical Year.* New York: 1896, p. 167.

4 Leopoldo Von Ranke, *History of the Popes.* Translation E. Fowler, New York: P. F. Collier and Son, 1907, p. 118.

5 Probably the *maza* or mace of Preconquest and Colonial Mexico.

6 The construction and maintenance of that building was a project of Alan Seeger Post No. 2 of the American Legion of Mexico City.

7 Seler, *Codex Aubin (Tonalamatl),* London, 1901, p. 71.

8 Cecilio A. Robelo, *Diccionario de Mitología Nahuatl*, México: 1911, p. 367.

9 The concha is said to have been patterned after the *bandurria*, a Spanish stringed instrument of the lute family. Webster's *Third International Dictionary Unabridged.*

10 Duran, *Historia de las Indias,* Tomo II, pp. 227-231.

11 Mendieta, *Historica Eclesiastica.* Lib. II, pp. 140-143.

12 J. Eric Thompson, *Mexico Before Cortez.* New York: Charles Scribner's Sons, 1933, p. 39; Seler, pp. 36-71.

13 Lewis Spence, *The Gods of Mexico.* London: T. Fisher Unwin LTD., 1923, pp. 359-363, 366-368; Clavijero, *Historia Antigua de México.* Tomo I, p. 290.

14 George Vaillant. *Aztecs of Mexico.* Garden City, N.Y.: Doubleday, Doran and Company, Inc., 1941, p. 187.

15 Seler, *Tonalamatl*, pp. 68-73.

16 J. Eric Thompson, *Mexico Before Cortez,* p. 68; Thomas A. Joyce, *Mexican Archaeology*, p. 32.

17 J. Eric Thompson, *Mexico Before Cortez*, p. 68.

18 Herbert Spence, *Gods of Mexico*, pp. 288-290.

19 Clavijero, *Historia Antigua de México*, Tomo I, p. 251.

20 Thomas A. Joyce, *Mexican Archaeology*, p. 32.

21 Manuel Payno — *Memoria Sobre el Maguey Mexicana Y Sus Diversos Productos*, pp. 9, 276.

22 Seler, *Tonalamatl*, p. 89; *Zapotec Priesthood and Ceremonials.* Bulletin 28, Smithsonian Institution, p. 276; *Codex Fejérváry Mayer*, p. 187.

23 Spence, *Gods of Mexico*, p. 288.

24 Eduard Seler, *Codex Vaticanus 3773*. Berlin-London: 1902–1903, p. 306.

25 Bernel Díaz del Castillo, *The Discovery and Conquest of Mexico, 1517–1521,* Edited by Genaro García, Translated by A. P. Maudsley. Published in this series in 1928; 1933; 1936. Mexico: 1936, pp. 106-117; The *Roumagnac Dictionary*, p. 528.

26 Bernal Diaz, *Discovery and Conquest of Mexico*, pp. 112-113.

27 Miguel Trinidad Palma, *Gramatica de La Lengua Azteca O Mejicana.* Mexico: 1886, p. 15.

28 Robelo, *Aztequismos*, p. 186.

29 Professor Maximino Martínez describes the chilillo as an herb with alternate lanceolate leaves and small, rose-colored flowers on a spike. He states that it is useful in the treatment of rheumatism and skin diseases — *Las Plantas Medicinales*, p. 110.

[30] The turkey, Chalchiuhtotolin, (the jewelled bird), was a symbol of Tezcatlipoca (Smoking Mirror), patron of the warriors. Seler, *Tonalamatl (Aubin),* p. 100.

[31] *Concilio III Provincial Mexicano.* Celebrado en Mexico el Ano de 1585. Confirmado en Roma Por El Papa Sixto V, y Mandado Observar Por El Gobierno Espanol En Diversas Reales Ordenes. Publicado Con Las Licencias Necesarias Por Mariano Galvan Rivera. Primera Edición En Latin y Castellano Mexico: Eugenio Maillefert y Compañia, Editores, 1859, p. 23.

[32] Seler, *Aubin (Tonalamatl),* pp. 52-53, 78-81, 105.

[33] J. Eric Thompson, *Sky Bearers, Colors and Directions in Maya and Mexican Religion.* Washington, D.C.: 1934, Reprint from Publication No. 436 of Carnegie Institution, pp. 209-242.

[34] Sahagun, *Historia General,* Tomo I, p. 281.

[35] Daniel G. Brinton, *Myths of the New World.* New York: 1876, p. 98.

[36] Don Domingo de San Anton Muñoz Chamalpahin Quauhtlehuanitzin, *La Cuarta Relación.* Traducción y Noticia Preleminar de Silvia Rendon, Anales del Instituto Nacional de Antropología E. Historia, México: 1947–48, Tomo III, pp. 199-218.

[37] Joyce, *Mexican Archaeology,* p. 49.

[38] Spence, *Gods of Mexico,* p. 75; Joyce, *Mexican Archaeology,* pp. 55-56.

[39] Publicaciones del Archivo General de la Nación, Director Don Luis Gonzales de Obregón, *Procesos de Indios, Idolatres y Hechiceres.* México: 1912, p. 116.

[40] *Atalaya* is a Moorish word that almost supplanted the Spanish *centinela* in 16th Century Spain; Fray Alonso de Molina, a Spanish missionary, wrote the first Nahuatl dictionary, published in 1571.

[41] Clavijero, *Historia Antigua de México,* Vol. I, p. 361.

[42] A large ungainly doll.

[43] Fanchón Royer, *The Franciscans Came First,* p. 138.

[44] Motolinía, *History of the Indians of New Spain,* pp. 51, 53.

[45] Velásquez, *Spanish Dictionary,* p. 565.

[46] Joyce, *Mexican Archaeology,* p. 99.

[47] Seler, *Tonalamatl,* p. 46.

[48] Padre Joseph de Acosta, *Historia Natural Y Moral De Las Indias.* Madrid: 1792, Lib. V, p. 10.

[49] Carlos Gonzalez Peña, *History of Mexican Literature.* Translation, Gusta Barfield Nance and Florence Johnson Dunstan, Dallas: 1945, p. 75.

[50] Fr. Diago Duran, *Historia de las Indias,* p. 80.

[51] Concilios Provinciales: Primero, y Segundo, de México, Celebrados en la Ciudad de México, en 1555, y 1565; con las licencias necesarias en México, en la Imprenta de el Superior Gobierno, 1769. Today, if the fiesta day falls on a week day, the fiesta is usually changed to the nearer Sunday.

[52] Sangremal — literally "Bad Blood."

[53] The eclipse of the sun, July 25, 1531.

[54] A rose-colored building stone.

[55] The first "word of authority," meaning the first dance group.

[56] The second "word of authority," meaning the second dance group.

[57] Alberto Leduc, Luis Lara Y Prado, Y Carlos Roumagnac, *Diccionario de Geografia, Historia y Biografia Mexicanas.* Mexico: 1910, pp. 418, 419, 1078, 1079.

[58] Charles Gibson, *Tlaxcala in the 16th Century.* New Haven, Connecticut: 1952, pp. 158, 183.

[59] Motolinía, *The Indians of New Spain,* p. 49.

[60] Publicaciones del Archivo General de la Nación, Director Luis González Obregón, *III Procesos de Indios Idolatras Y Hechiceros.* Mexico, D.F.: 1912, p. 20.

[61] La Comisión Reorganizadora del Archivo General Y Público de la Nación, *Procesos Inquisitorial del Casique de Tetzcoco.* Preliminar por Luis González Obregón, Mexico: 1910, p. XI.

[62] Meaning human sacrifice, an integral part of idolatry.

[63] *Procesos Inquisitorial del Cacique de Texcoco.* p. 18.

LA COSA

[1] Irving A. Leonard, *Books of the Brave.* Cambridge, Mass.: Harvard University Press, 1949, pp. 13, 22, 47.

[2] Ralph Beals, *Cheran: A Sierra Tarascan Village: Bulletin of the Smithsonian Institution.* Washington, D.C.: pp. 103-4.

[3] See section on Godparents of a Flag.

[4] Maximino Téllez, after a ceremony similar to the one described in chapter 8, raised his dance banner for the first time in Mexico in a dance circle for the members of a newly formed mesa to dance under, in 1883.

[5] Frances Gillmor, *The Dance Dramas of Mexican Villages: Humanities Bulletin No. 5.* University of Arizona, Tucson, Arizona: 1943, p. 5.

THE HILL OF THE BELL

[1] The legend of the creation of the sun and the moon; Mendieta, *Historia Eclesiastica Indiana*, cap. II, p. 79; III p. 80, IV p. 81; Sahagun, Tomo II, pp. 255, 256.

[2] Two years later at the fiesta on New Year's Eve, I was intrigued by the huge ollas (earthen jars) tied on the backs of men. They held 25 litres of holy water that later the jefes poured through a hole in the round depression in the chapel to the ancient altar underneath.

[3] *Papeles de Nueva España, Segunda Serie, Geografía Y Estadistica, Tomo IV (MSS de la Real Academia de la Historia de Madrid Y del Archivo de Indias en Sevilla)* (1579–1582), Madrid, 1905, p. 49.

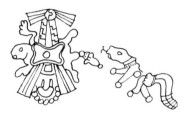

Index